AQA GCSE

FRENCH

Higher

Séverine Capjon
Amandine Moores
Paul Shannon
Consultant: Christophe Fico

OXFORD

OXFORD
UNIVERSITY PRESS

Great Clarendon Street, Oxford, OX2 6DP, United Kingdom

Oxford University Press is a department of the University of Oxford.
It furthers the University's objective of excellence in research, scholarship, and education by publishing worldwide. Oxford is a registered trade mark of Oxford University Press in the UK and in certain other countries.

First published in 2024

British Library Cataloguing in Publication Data
Data available

978-1-38-204578-0

978-1-38-204579-7 (ebook)

10 9 8 7 6 5 4 3 2 1

The manufacturing process conforms to the environmental regulations of the country of origin.

Printed in Great Britain by Bell and Bain Ltd., Glasgow

Acknowledgements

The publisher and authors would like to thank the following for permission to use photographs and other copyright material:

Cover artwork by Sua Balac.

Artwork by Andrew Painter, Gina Stephens, Martyn Cain, Matt Ward, Mo Choy and Sua Balac.

Photos: **p14 (t):** LightField Studios / Shutterstock; **p14 (b), 17 (d), 34, 43 (c), 55 (t), 63 (b):** Monkey Business Images / Shutterstock; **p16 (t):** Alpheton / Shutterstock; **p16 (a-h):** Cosmic_Design / Shutterstock; **p16 (d):** M_Videous / Shutterstock; **p17 (a), 39, 147 (b):** DC Studio / Shutterstock; 17 (b), p18 (l), 108 (m): fizkes / Shutterstock; **p17 (c):** Victor Velter / Shutterstock; **p17 (e), 76 (a), 104:** Drazen Zigic / Shutterstock; **p17 (f):** Odua Images / Shutterstock; **p18 (m):** cheapbooks / Shutterstock; **p18 (r):** PinkCoffee Studio / Shutterstock; **p21 (t):** Cristian Zamfir / Shutterstock; **p21 (b), 60 (m), 64 (r), 86 (c), 108 (t), 132 (r):** Krakenimages.com / Shutterstock; **p22:** WarmWorld / Shutterstock; **p24 (bkg):** Maria Zvonkova / Shutterstock; **p25 (t):** olgsera / Shutterstock; **p25 (m):** Marian Fil / Shutterstock; **p25 (b):** Xavier Lorenzo / Shutterstock; **p26:** Drawlab19 / Shutterstock; **p27 (l):** Sergio Arjona / Shutterstock; **p27 (m):** VN_KK / Shutterstock; **p27 (r):** aire images / Getty; **p28:** silverkblackstoc / Shutterstock; **p28 (bkg), 117 (bkg):** sobakapavlova / Shutterstock; **p30 (t), 80 (m), 124 (t):** Pixel-Shot / Shutterstock; **p30 (b):** Chekyravaa / Shutterstock; **p32 (t):** BalanceFormCreative / Shutterstock; **p32 (m):** tsyhun / Shutterstock; **p32 (b):** Regine Poirier / Shutterstock; **p35 (l):** Philippe Turpin / Getty; **p35 (r):** Lucky Business / Shutterstock; **p36 (a):** Media Lens King / Shutterstock; **p36 (b), 132 (l):** Darren Baker / Shutterstock; **p36 (c):** Bonsales / Shutterstock; **p36 (d):** SpeedKing / Shutterstock; **p38 (l):** Roman Samborskyi / Shutterstock; **p38 (m):** Vadym Pastukh / Shutterstock; **p38 (r), 85:** Frame Stock Footage / Shutterstock; **p40 (l):** Perfect Wave / Shutterstock; **p40 (r):** UlyssePixel / Shutterstock; **p42 (t), 43 (t):** Azat1976 / Shutterstock; **p42 (inset):** Ppictures / Shutterstock; **p42 (b):** Elena Odareeva / Shutterstock; **p43 (m):** francesco de marco / Shutterstock; **p43 (a):** alefbet / Shutterstock; **p43 (b):** Mohamed1637 / Shutterstock; **p43 (c):** Nguyen Quang Ngoc Tonkin / Shutterstock; **p43 (d):** Kanuman / Shutterstock; **p55 (b):** Hadrian / Shutterstock; **p56:** Jose Calsina / Shutterstock; **p58:** Daniel Hoz / Shutterstock; **p59, 65 (t):** BearFotos / Shutterstock; **p60, 66 (b):** Goran Djukanovic / Shutterstock; **p63 (a), 112 (l inset), 155 (b):** Ground Picture / Shutterstock; **p63 (b):** New Africa / Shutterstock; **p63 (c):** Microgen / Shutterstock; **p63 (d):** sirtravelalot / Shutterstock; **p63 (e), 66 (t):** SeventyFour / Shutterstock; **p63 (f), p64 (l):** Jacob Lund / Shutterstock; **p64 (m):** paulaphoto / Shutterstock; **p65 (b):** catwalker / Shutterstock; **p66 (m), 101 (t):** Kiev.Victor / Shutterstock; **p66 (b):** dwphotos / Shutterstock; **p68 (a):** ohrim / Shutterstock; **p68 (b):** SusaImages / Shutterstock; **p68 (c):** dotshock / Shutterstock; **p68 (d):** YKD / Shutterstock; **p69:** Iriskana / Shutterstock; **p70 (t):** Dimitrije Ostojic / Shutterstock; **p70 (bl):** travelview / Shutterstock; **p70 (br):** Radu Razvan / Shutterstock; **p71:** Artur Didyk / Shutterstock; **p72 (l):** VH-studio / Shutterstock; **p72 (r):** jakkapan / Shutterstock; **p74 (tl):** RnDmS / Shutterstock; **p74 (tr):** No sabemos como / Shutterstock; **p74 (m):** Dina Saeed / Shutterstock; **p74 (b):** Mike Flippo / Shutterstock; **p76 (b):** Yapasphoto StefClement / Shutterstock; **p76 (c):** Jerome LABOUYRIE / Shutterstock; **p76 (d):** Nina Mikryukova / Shutterstock; **p77:** Grisha Bruev / Shutterstock; **p78:** taniavolobueva / Shutterstock; **p79:** kitzzeh / Shutterstock; **p80 (l):** BrunoRosa / Shutterstock; **p80 (r):** Tobias Schenk / Shutterstock; **p81:** PA Images / Alamy Stock Photo; **p82:** Matteo Chinellato / Shutterstock; **p83 (l):** Sportimage Ltd / Alamy Stock Photo; **p83 (r):** Abaca Press / Alamy Stock Photo; **p84:** PeopleImages.com - Yuri A / Shutterstock; **p86 (a):** dpa picture alliance / Alamy Stock Photo; **p86 (b):** United Archives / Contributor / Getty; **p86 (d):** Andrea Raffin / Shutterstock; **p86 (e):** AFP / Stringer / Getty; **p88 (t), 89 (t):** vagonik / Shutterstock; **p88 (a):** Ryan Remiorz / The Canadian Press / Alamy Stock Photo; **p88 (b):** Leonardo Cendamo / Contributor / Getty; **p88 (c):** Jean-Marc ZAORSKI / Gamma-Rapho / Getty Images; **p88 (bottom), 89 (b):** Thomas Bethge / Shutterstock; **p89 (a, c):** GL Archive / Alamy Stock Photo; **p89 (b):** Olga Besnard / Shutterstock; **p101 (b):** ELEPHOTOS / Shutterstock; **p103:** Denis Makarenko / Shutterstock; **p105:** Zamrznuti tonovi / Shutterstock; **p106(t):** A_B_C / Shutterstock; **p106, 148:** nickfz / Shutterstock; **p108 (b):** Africa Studio / Shutterstock; **p109:** Samuel Borges Photography / Shutterstock; **p110(a):** Kolpakova Svetlana / Shutterstock; **p110 (b):** andrmoel / Shutterstock; **p110 (c):** Gregory Bergman / Alamy Stock Photo; **p110 (d):** Pierre-Yves Babelon / Shutterstock; **p112 (l):** EiZivile / Shutterstock; **p112 (r inset):** PavelKant / Shutterstock; **p112 (r):** Tang Trung Kien / Shutterstock; **p114 (t):** xbrchx / Shutterstock; **p114 (b):** Sklo Studio / Shutterstock; **p116 (t):** wasiolka / Shutterstock; **p116 (b):** Curioso.Photography / Shutterstock; **p117:** Harmony Video Production / Shutterstock; **p118:** JoeZ / Shutterstock; **p119:** Pressmaster / Shutterstock; **p120:** stockfour / Shutterstock; **p121:** insta_photos Shutterstock; **p122:** Khorzhevska / Shutterstock; **p124 (b):** mimagephotography / Shutterstock; **p125:** Josep Suria / Shutterstock; **p126 (l):** emerald_media / Shutterstock; **p126 (m):** Anna Puzatykh / Shutterstock; **p126 (r):** hrui / Shutterstock; **p127 (t):** xamnesiacx84 / Shutterstock; **p127 (b):** RONEDYA / Shutterstock; **p128 (t):** streetflash / Shutterstock; **p128 (b, bkg):** Wiola Wiaderek / Shutterstock; **p129:** Dmitry Kalinovsky / Shutterstock; **p130 (t):** saranya33 / Shutterstock; **p130 (b):** RogerMechan / Shutterstock; **p131:** Andrew Mayovskyy / Shutterstock; **p133:** S Curtis / Shutterstock; **p134 (t), 135 (t):** Pinkcandy / Shutterstock; **p134 (a):** angelo gilardelli / Shutterstock; **p134 (b):** toicadrian / Shutterstock; **p134 (c):** Lingbeek / Getty; **p134 (d):** romeovip_md / Shutterstock; **p134 (e):** GCRO Images / Shutterstock; **p134 (f):** KKulikov / Shutterstock; **p134 (bottom):** Pajor Pawel / Shutterstock; **p135 (m):** Ivoha / Shutterstock; **p147 (t):** Star Stock / Shutterstock; **p150:** Miljan Zivkovic / Shutterstock; **p151:** CarlosBarquero / Shutterstock; **p155 (t):** gpointstudio / Shutterstock; **p158:** Duet PandG / Shutterstock; **p159:** LeManna / Shutterstock. Backgrounds throughout: Daria Kubrak / Shutterstock, Lenka_X / Shutterstock, Sarunyu_foto / Shutterstock, Xansa / Shutterstock. Icons used throughout: alpha paperart / Shutterstock, Beatriz Gascon J / Shutterstock, Cosmic_Design / Shutterstock.

Every effort has been made to contact copyright holders of material reproduced in this book. Any omissions will be rectified in subsequent printings if notice is given to the publisher.

MIX
Paper | Supporting responsible forestry
FSC® C007785
FSC www.fsc.org

This textbook has been approved by AQA for use with our qualification. This means that we have checked that it broadly covers the specification and we are satisfied with the overall quality. Full details of our approval process can be found on our website.

We approve textbooks because we know how important it is for teachers and students to have the right resources to support their teaching and learning. However, the publisher is ultimately responsible for the editorial control and quality of this book.

Please note that when teaching the AQA GCSE French course, you must refer to AQA's specification as your definitive source of information. While this book has been written to match the specification, it cannot provide complete coverage of every aspect of the course.

A wide range of other useful resources can be found on the relevant subject pages of our website: aqa.org.uk

Contents

Contents

Contents

Introducing AQA GCSE French

Learning vocabulary	Sound–spelling links	Translation skills	Writing	Reading & reading aloud
Dictation	Speaking	Culture	Grammar knowledge	Listening

Understanding how the specification works

The AQA GCSE French specification is divided into three main subject areas, called Themes. This book is divided up in the same way, with colour-coding to help you know where you are.

Theme 1	Theme 2	Theme 3
People and lifestyle	Popular culture	Communication and the world around us

Each Theme is divided into three Topics, making a total of nine Topics to study during the course. The exam is divided up according to the four Language Skills: Listening, Speaking, Reading and Writing. Each one of these has its own separate exam, in the form of an end-of-course paper.

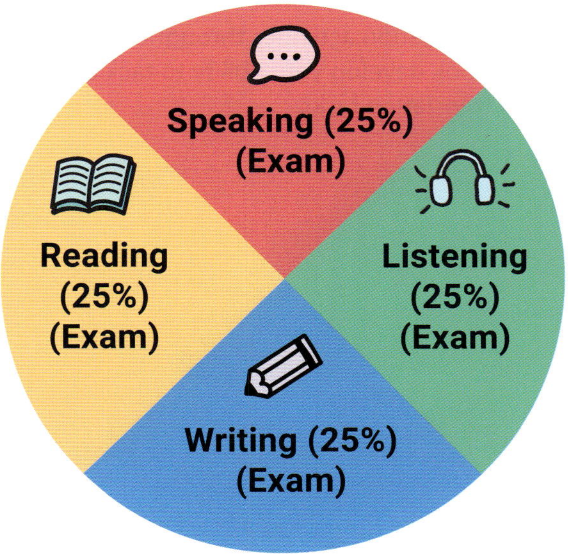

Useful language

The section on pages 10–11 provides useful key vocabulary and phrases which are commonly used in real-life, everyday situations.

Phonics and sound–spelling links

- The section on pages 12–13 groups together all the sounds included in the *Phonétique* boxes and provides tips on how to pronounce widely used words and phrases to speak French confidently and clearly. Your knowledge of how spelling represents sounds will be tested through dictation and a read-aloud task in the exam.
- The *Phonétique* boxes cover all the common sounds in the French language and the sound–spelling links included in the specification, and include pronunciation tips.

Phonétique

Silent final *-e* and final consonants

In French, the final *-e* on a word is not pronounced:

*drôl**e***   *timid**e***   *frèr**e***   *catastroph**e***

Themes and topics

Each Theme is divided into three Topics. Each Theme starts with two introductory double-page spreads introducing key themes, core vocabulary and structures that you may have covered at Key Stage 3. These pages provide an opportunity to recap and practise important language and/or lay the foundations for further learning.

The three Topics are then each covered over four double-page spreads, two at Foundation level and two at Higher level. Each spread introduces specification vocabulary and features a verb focus and a grammar focus. All the key skills required in the specification are also covered, including phonics and cultural knowledge.

Learning vocabulary

Vocabulary support is provided in various ways throughout the book and on Kerboodle:

- Vocabulary lists – the introductory double-page spreads at the start of each Theme include lists of key words and phrases practised in the texts and on the page. Vocabulary from each of the core spreads and the culture pages is listed in the vocabulary pages at the end of each Theme. Items highlighted in grey are words that are useful but do not appear in the specification. It is important that you learn the specification vocabulary.
- Vocabulary tasks – these help to build the vocabulary required in each topic of the specification.
- Interactive activities – the vocabulary builders on Kerboodle provide activities with instant feedback.*
- Glossary – the glossary at the back of the book combines the vocabulary from the Themes' vocabulary pages.

Features

Reading

The Student Book contains plenty of French reading material on the Themes and Topics included within the specification. The activities that follow the reading passages help develop your comprehension skills so that you can access unfamiliar texts in the future.

Listening

Activities with a listening icon next to them help you to improve listening comprehension skills. The audio can be accessed through Kerboodle.

Speaking

The speaking activities are designed to build your confidence in speaking French and to practise using the vocabulary you've learnt in the unit or Theme. There are also practice role plays and photo card activities throughout the book.

Writing

The writing icon indicates an activity that will help you to use the language you've learnt to build sentences and paragraphs of written French.

Translation

Translation activities throughout the book develop your ability to tackle translation tasks.

Language support in speaking and writing

Examples of language to be used or language structure boxes are provided for some speaking and writing tasks. These can be used as models to build your own sentences.

Mon frère Ma sœur Mon cousin	est	plus moins aussi	drôle(s) / sympa(s) timide(s) / strict(e)(s) amusant(e)(s) intelligent(e)(s)	que…
Mes parents	sont			

8 **In pairs, take turns to say what you would do in order to become famous.**

Example: Pour devenir célèbre, je chercherais / je participerais à /

Building grammar knowledge

- Understanding grammar is key to understanding French and building your own phrases. *AQA GCSE French* helps you to consolidate and deepen your grammar knowledge in a logical way with no assumption of prior learning.
- Grammar boxes outline key grammar points, with accompanying activities on the same page to put theory into practice.

Grammaire

Using negative constructions

To make a sentence negative, use *ne … pas* around the verb:

- Additional grammar practice is also provided in two double-page spreads at the end of each Theme.
- Interactive activities on Kerboodle provide further consolidation with instant feedback.*
- There is a grammar section at the back of the Student Book to refer to whenever you need to.

Verbs

Specific emphasis is given to the formation of verbs and tenses, and how they are used.

Les verbes

The present tense of *-re* verbs

To form the present tense of regular *-re* verbs, remove *-re* from the infinitive and add the endings:

Culture

- Culture boxes throughout the book highlight aspects of Francophone culture relevant to each topic.

Culture

In France, students aged 11 to 15 go to *le collège* and at the end, they take exams called *le brevet*, equivalent

- There is a *Culture* double-page spread at the end of each Theme showcasing aspects of Francophone history, literature and contemporary culture.

Language tips

These boxes give extra support and information about what to look out for or how to do a particular activity.

Conseil

Use your knowledge of grammar, especially verbs and tenses, to choose the correct answer. Adverbs of time

Test and revise

There are regular revision and practice opportunities throughout the book in the four test and revise sections (one test per Theme and a cross-Theme test at the end of the book). Each test offers exam-style activities in the four skill areas.

Kerboodle

Kerboodle for *AQA GCSE French* provides resources focused on developing key grammar, vocabulary, phonics and all the language-learning and exam skills required at GCSE. This includes auto-marked interactive activities and tests, worksheets, listening activities with downloadable transcripts, practice questions and assessments, and comprehensive teacher support.

Interactive activities can be completed on tablets or mobile devices.

Kerboodle Books

Kerboodle Books are digital versions of the Student Books, which can be accessed on a range of devices and tablets.

Activities and audio can be launched directly from the page and individual users have their own digital notebook for use within their Kerboodle Book, in which they can use various tools and annotate pages to create their own personalised copy.

*These resources are not part of the AQA approval process.

Useful language

Numbers

French numbers can seem like a challenge, so it's best to revise and learn them in stages.

- Start with the numbers 1–16.

1 *un*	**5** *cinq*	**9** *neuf*	**13** *treize*
2 *deux*	**6** *six*	**10** *dix*	**14** *quatorze*
3 *trois*	**7** *sept*	**11** *onze*	**15** *quinze*
4 *quatre*	**8** *huit*	**12** *douze*	**16** *seize*

- Then you can combine the numbers you know to make others.

17	= 10 + 7	*dix-sept*
18	= 10 + 8	*dix-huit*
19	= 10 + 9	*dix-neuf*

Remember to link the two numbers with a hyphen, when you write them out as words.

- The next stage is to learn the multiples of 10 up to 60, and continue combining numbers as shown.

20	*vingt*
30	*trente*
40	*quarante*
50	*cinquante*
60	*soixante*

21 *vingt et un*, **22** *vingt-deux*, **27** *vingt-sept*, **31** *trente et un*, **35** *trente-cinq*, **49** *quarante-neuf*, **51** *cinquante et un*, **66** *soixante-six*

- The most challenging stage is to learn the numbers above 69. Here, again, it's about combining smaller numbers to make larger ones.

Look at these examples.

70	= 60 + 10	*soixante-dix*
71	= 60 + 11	*soixante et onze*
75	= 60 + 15	*soixante-quinze*
80	= 4 × 20	*quatre-vingts*
81	= 4 × 20 + 1	*quatre-vingt-un*
88	= 4 × 20 + 8	*quatre-vingt-huit*
90	= 4 × 20 + 10	*quatre-vingt-dix*
91	= 4 × 20 + 11	*quatre-vingt-onze*
93	= 4 × 20 + 13	*quatre-vingt-treize*
96	= 4 × 20 + 16	*quatre-vingt-seize*
99	= 4 × 20 + 19	*quatre-vingt-dix-neuf*

(Watch out for the 's' which appears at the end of *quatre-vingt**s*** only.)

- Finally, you need to know *cent* (100) and *mille* (1000).

102 (*cent deux*)

Note *deux-cent**s*** (200) but *deux cent deux* (202).

Numbers are useful to state ages:
J'ai quinze ans. Mon père a cinquante ans.

You also need numbers for prices: 10€ (*dix euros*), 5,50€ (*cinq euros cinquante*), 8,99€ (*huit euros quatre-vingt-dix-neuf*), 100€ (*cent euros*). Notice that French uses a comma, not a full stop, for the decimal point in prices.

Days and dates

- Remember that the days of the week are written with small letters in French.

lundi, mardi, mercredi, jeudi, vendredi, samedi, dimanche

- The same is true of the months.

janvier, février, mars, avril, mai, juin, juillet, août, septembre, octobre, novembre, décembre

- To say the date, simply use *le* + number + month.

le quatorze février, le six mai

Use *le premier* for '1st'.
le premier septembre, le premier juin

Time

There are two ways of telling the time in French: the traditional 12-hour clock method and the 24-hour clock method, which is often used in French, particularly to discuss travel times.

To say what time it is using the traditional 12-hour clock, start with *Il est …*

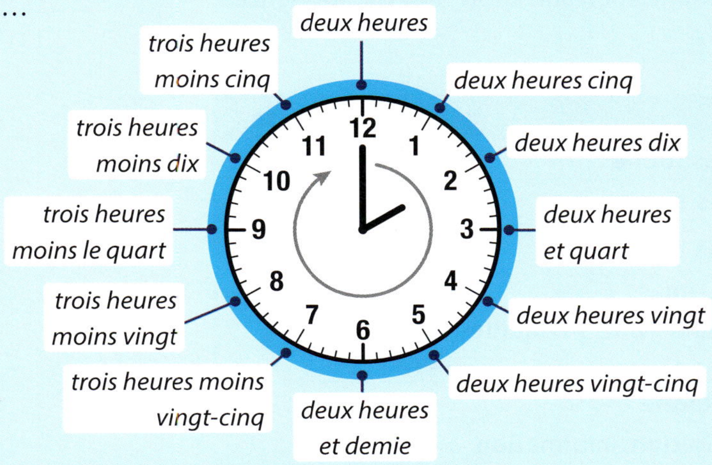

Il est deux heures dix. It's ten past two.

Il est trois heures moins le quart. It's quarter to three.

une heure 1 o'clock, *minuit* midnight, *midi* midday

To say 'half past twelve', use *midi et demi* or *minuit et demi* depending on whether you are referring to midday or midnight.

The 24-hour clock is very straightforward to use, as long as you know the numbers: keep counting from 12 to 24 for the pm times: 11.00, 12.00, 13.00 (1pm), 14.00 (2pm) … 23.00 (11pm).

- For whole hours, simply say the number and *heures*:

  13.00 ⟶ ***treize** heures* (1pm)

- Where minutes are given too, say:

  the first number + *heures* (where the dot appears) + the second number.

  17.27 ⟶ *dix-sept heures vingt-sept*

  21.30 ⟶ *vingt-et-une heures trente*

Interrogatives

Qui?	Who?
Quand?	When?
Comment?	How? / What … like?
Où?	Where?
Pourquoi?	Why?
Combien?	How much? / How many?
Quel …? Quelle …? Quels …? Quelles …?	Which …?
Que …? Qu'est-ce que …?	What …?

Greetings and ages

bonjour!	hello! / good morning!
salut!	hello! / hi!
au revoir!	goodbye!
à tout à l'heure!	see you later!
bonne nuit!	good night!
(comment) ça va?	how are you?
bien, merci	fine, thanks
pas mal	not bad
comme ci comme ça	not too bad
Quel âge as-tu / avez-vous?	How old are you?
J'ai seize ans.	I'm sixteen.
Et toi / vous?	And you?

Conjunctions

et	and
mais	but
ou	or
parce que / qu'	because
où	where
quand	when

Intensifiers

assez	quite
plus	more
très	very
moins	less
trop	too

Adverbs of frequency

jamais	never
rarement	rarely
de temps en temps	from time to time
normalement	normally
parfois / quelquefois	sometimes
souvent	often
toujours	always

Sound–spelling links

The new GCSE exam involves a reading-aloud task and a dictation task to test your knowledge and understanding of sound–symbol correspondences. Learning how spelling represents sounds and using clear pronunciation when speaking French are key skills at GCSE. It is important that you are confident with pronunciation and know how to pronounce words correctly, to help you speak French confidently.

Sound	Example	Page
silent final e	drôl**e**, timid**e**, frèr**e**, catastroph**e**	18
silent final consonant	amusan**t**, bavar**d**, jamai**s**, ennuyeu**x**	18
-aill- / ail	trav**aill**eur, je trav**aill**e, la t**aill**e, trav**ail**	23
-ill- / -ille	ju**ill**et, me**ill**eur, fam**ille**, f**ille**, v**ill**age, m**ill**ion, tranqu**ill**ité, v**ill**e, tranqu**ill**e pare**ill**e, vie**ill**e	23, 133
-gn-	ga**gn**er, espa**gn**ol, monta**gn**e	24, 84
-tion	communica**tion**, organisa**tion**, informa**tion**	35
ç, soft c	**ç**a, **c**'est **c**arrière, **c**onnue, **c**oncert	39
-s-	mai**s**on, plu**s**ieurs, cui**s**ine	39
qu	**qu**elques, musi**qu**e, cha**qu**e	39
th	**th**ème, biblio**th**èque	39
u	j'ai b**u**, j'ai v**u**, t**u** as l**u**	65
ou	n**ou**s, v**ou**s c**ou**rses, p**ou**r, c**ou**ru	65
oi / oy	s**oi**r, m**oi**, hist**oi**re v**oy**ager, env**oy**er, empl**oy**é	65
s-liaison	Nous nou**s** **in**téressons au cinéma.	67
t-liaison	Le cinéma es**t** **ou**vert aujourd'hui.	67
n-liaison	J'aime regarder les films sur mo**n** **o**rdinateur.	67
x-liaison	Il y a deux nouveau**x** **é**crans au cinéma.	67
e	j**e**, l**e**, d**e**	68
eu	d**eu**x, un p**eu**, le j**eu**	68
é (-er, -ez)	all**er**, je suis all**é**, vous all**ez**	69
open eu / œu	l**eur**, plusi**eur**s, c**œur**, s**œur**	73
r	j'ado**r**e, annive**r**sai**r**e, pa**r**ents, décemb**r**e, **r**aison, aut**r**es, ch**r**étien, **r**ecevoi**r**	73
i / y	s**y**stème, ph**y**s**i**que, les P**y**rénées fac**i**le, l**i**sez, **il** **y** aura	81
-ien	b**ien**, v**ien**s, ch**ien**, entret**ien**	81

Sound	Example	Page
j / g	**je**, **j**'ai, je protè**g**e les **g**irafes	84
ch	j'ai de la **ch**ance j'ai **ch**oisi	84
è / ê / ai	tr**è**s, pr**è**s, routi**è**re, ch**è**re f**ê**te, t**ê**te, arr**ê**ter, vous **ê**tes vr**ai**, j'**ai**, j'**ai**m**ai**s, vr**ai**ment	110
a	la c**a**pitale, il y **a**vait, j'h**a**bitais, c**a**n**a**dienne	110
open o	d**o**rmi, l**o**gement, P**o**rtugal	115
au / eau / closed o / ô	**au**jourd'hui, **au**ssi **beau**coup, nouv**eau** vidé**o**, tr**o**p h**ô**tel, dr**ô**le	119
en / an / em / am	pr**en**dre, av**an**t, t**em**ps, ch**am**bre	123
on / om	sal**on**, c**on**tre, c**om**me, t**om**ber	123
ain / in / aim / im	proch**ain**, **in**juste, f**aim**, **im**possible	123
un	l**un**di, empr**un**ter	123
h	**h**ôtel, à l'**h**ôtel **h**istorique, j'**h**abite	131

Phonétique

en / an

Together, these letters make a sound like 'on' in English (but very nasal, high in the nose, and you can't hear the 'n').

Examples: ***en***, *Fr**an**ce*

in

These letters also make a nasal sound, but sound slightly different, more like 'an' in English (as in 'hand').

Examples: *c**in**q*, ***in**juste*

Phonétique

u

The letter 'u' makes a sound a bit like 'oo' in English (but say it with pursed lips, further forward in the mouth).

Examples: *j'ai b**u**, j'ai v**u**, t**u** as l**u***

Phonétique

gn

Together, these letters make a 'nyuh' sound, like in 'onion.'

Examples: *ga**gn**er, espa**gn**ol, monta**gn**e*

Tip box

Intonation

To sound as fluent as possible in French, it is important to think not just about what you say, but also how you say it. You also need to think about 'stress' (where the emphasis is placed within words), 'rhythm' (the beat and flow of the language in sentences) and 'pitch' (varying the tone of your language). Listen to as much authentic French as possible and imitate as best as you can.

Tip box

Reading aloud in French poses challenges when you come across new words, or sometimes words can just come out wrong when you read them out.

- Try to read and understand the sentence before you start.
- Work with a partner and seek their advice once you have finished.
- Practise reading aloud regularly.
- Record yourself and listen to it with a critical ear.

Theme 1
People and lifestyle

Identity and relationships with others

1 **Read the email from Pierre and find the name (in bold) of each person in the photo (a–f).**

papapierre82@monmail.fr

Bonjour! Je m'appelle **Pierre** et j'habite en Suisse avec ma famille. Voici une photo de nous. Je suis à gauche. Je suis le père de deux enfants: un garçon et une fille.

Mon fils s'appelle **Lucas** et il a les cheveux bruns et courts. Sa petite sœur, ma fille, c'est **Alicia**. Elle a les cheveux un peu longs.

Ma femme, leur belle-mère, s'appelle **Nadine** et sur la photo elle porte un t-shirt blanc. La grand-mère de Lucas et Alicia s'appelle **Valérie**. Elle a les cheveux blancs. Leur grand-père, c'est **Antoine**. Il sourit car il est toujours content.

la famille	family
le père	father
le beau-père	stepfather, father-in-law
la mère	mother
la belle-mère	stepmother, mother-in-law
le mari	husband
la femme	wife
le frère	brother
la sœur	sister
l'oncle	uncle
la tante	aunt
le cousin	male cousin
la cousine	female cousin
le fils	son
la fille	daughter
le grand-père	grandfather
la grand-mère	grandmother
mon, ma, mes	my
ton, ta, tes	your
son, sa, ses	his / her
leur, leurs	their

2 **Read the email again and answer the questions.**

a Who is Lucas?

b What is Lucas's hair like? (Give **two** details.)

c What relation is Nadine to Lucas and Alicia?

d Who is Valérie?

e What does Pierre say about Valérie's appearance?

f Why does Antoine smile?

3 **Copy and complete the sentences with the correct word for a member of the family.**

a C'est la fille de mon oncle, c'est ma ___.

b C'est le mari de ma mère, c'est mon ___.

c C'est la femme de mon oncle, c'est ma ___.

d C'est le père de mon cousin, c'est mon ___.

4 **Listen (1–6). Write down each family member Noémie mentions and if her opinion is positive (P), negative (N) or both (P+N).**

je m'entends bien avec	I get on well with
j'adore	I love
j'aime	I like
je n'aime pas	I don't like
content(e)	happy
sympa	nice
gentil(le)	kind
méchant(e)	nasty
strict(e)	strict
sportif / sportive	sporty

Healthy living and lifestyle

1 **Choose the correct word from the box to match the food and drink items (a–j).**

du pain | du fromage | du poisson | de la viande
des frites | des fruits | des légumes | du gâteau
de la glace | du thé | du café | du lait | du vin | de l'eau

2 **Work out the English for the remaining words in the box (activity 1).**

3 **Listen (1–4) and choose *two* correct statements for each person.**

- a I don't do sport.
- b I never ride my bike.
- c I swim three times a week.
- d I love sport.
- e I eat too much meat.
- f I drink lots of water.
- g I eat healthily.
- h I eat lots of fruit and vegetables.

je bois	I drink
je mange	I eat
je fais	I do
la natation	swimming
le vélo	bike, bicycle
sain(e)	healthy
du, de la, des, de l'	some

4 **Read the blog post and answer the questions.**

Thao

Je m'appelle Thao et j'habite au Vietnam. Je suis très actif et j'adore le sport. Je joue au football deux fois par semaine pour l'équipe de ma ville et on gagne souvent des matchs.

Au collège, je fais de la natation car on a une piscine et le samedi, je fais du vélo. C'est très intéressant.

En général, je ne bois pas assez d'eau mais je mange équilibré. Mes parents et moi, on mange du riz, du poisson, un peu de viande et beaucoup de légumes.

Mon ami Dan ne mange jamais de fruits et légumes et en plus il ne fait pas de sport!

actif/active	active
le sport	sport
le football	football
une équipe	a team
la piscine	swimming pool
faire du vélo	to go cycling
le riz	rice

- a How often does Thao play football?
- b What sport does he do at school?
- c What does he do on Saturdays?
- d What is Thao not doing enough of?
- e Name **three** types of food that he eats regularly.
- f What does he say about his friend Dan? Give **two** details.

Education

1 ✏ **Copy and complete the table for yourself, in French.**

Subjects I do this year	Subjects I don't do this year
le français	

2 📖 **Put the sentences (a–h) in the correct order to describe Christelle's school day.**

Christelle

a Après, vers dix heures, j'ai une récréation de 20 minutes.

b L'école commence à huit heures du matin.

c Ensuite, c'est le déjeuner. Je mange et puis je vais à la bibliothèque.

d En premier, j'ai deux heures de maths.

e L'après-midi, je rentre à la maison à cinq heures.

f Après la récréation, j'ai une heure de musique et une heure de français.

g Après le déjeuner, je fais une heure de sciences.

h Mon dernier cours, c'est la géographie.

3 🎧 **Listen (1–8). Write the letter (a–h) of the subject Mathis mentions and whether he has a positive (P) or negative (N) opinion of it.**

4 🎧 **Listen again (1–8). Write in English *two* details for each subject.**

le français	French
l'anglais	English
l'espagnol	Spanish
l'allemand	German
les maths	maths
les sciences	sciences
l'informatique	IT, computer science
la technologie	D&T
la géographie	geography
l'histoire	history
la musique	music
le théâtre	drama

j'ai	I have
je fais	I do
je vais	I go
je suis	I am
je rentre	I return home
le matin	(in) the morning
l'après-midi	(in) the afternoon
la récréation	break
le déjeuner	lunch
la bibliothèque	library
après	after
ensuite	next
puis	then
en premier	first
un, une	a
le, la, les, l'	the

la matière	subject
le prof(esseur)	teacher (m)
la prof(esseure)	teacher (f)
amusant(e)	fun
facile	easy
génial(e)	great
difficile	difficult
ennuyeux / ennuyeuse	boring
nul	rubbish
je déteste	I hate

Work

1 Read the sentences. Choose a job for each person and write the job name in French.

a J'aime travailler avec des enfants dans une école.

b Je travaille dans plusieurs villages. J'apporte les lettres aux personnes.

c Je travaille au théâtre ou dans des studios pour faire des films.

d Je travaille dans un café ou dans un restaurant.

e J'écris mes chansons et je fais des concerts.

f Je fais la sécurité dans les rues.

acteur / actrice

chanteur / chanteuse

policier / policière

professeur(e)

facteur / factrice

serveur / serveuse

2 Listen (1–6) and choose the sector (a–f) each person would like to work in.

a

b

c

d

e

f

travailler	to work
les enfants	children
les chansons	songs
la sécurité	safety, security
les rues	streets
le gouvernement	government
la politique	politics
la construction	construction
l'éducation	education
l'informatique	IT
la mode	fashion

3 Match the statements (1–6) with the hopes for the future (a–f).

1 L'important pour moi, c'est d'avoir un bon salaire.

2 Je veux un travail où je peux voyager.

3 J'espère faire le métier de mes rêves: acteur!

4 Moi, je veux avoir du succès et devenir célèbre.

5 Je veux un travail sûr: je ne veux pas être au chômage.

6 Je veux avoir beaucoup d'indépendance dans mon travail.

a to travel

b to do my dream job

c to have a good salary

d to have a lot of independence

e to become famous

f to have a stable job

au chômage	unemployed
le travail	work
le salaire	salary
espérer	to hope
le succès	success
célèbre	famous
voyager	to travel
le métier	job, occupation
sûr(e)	safe, sure, secure
devenir	to become

1.1F Ma personnalité

OBJECTIVES
- Personality descriptions
- Adjective agreement
- The present tense of regular *-re* verbs
- Phonics: silent final *-e* and final consonants

1 **Read the texts and note down all the adjectives that describe personality.**

Laure

Mes copines me trouvent assez sérieuse car je travaille bien à l'école. Je suis aussi une bonne amie, je pense! C'est vrai, je suis très sympa et amusante. Parfois, je suis embêtante, surtout avec mon petit frère, mais il peut être méchant aussi!

Cédric

Je suis très fier car je suis travailleur et j'aime avoir de bonnes notes. Je suis bavard aussi et jamais timide. Je suis très gentil, surtout avec mes copains. Ma sœur et moi, on est drôles. Elle est toujours heureuse et jamais triste, c'est génial.

Morgane

Mon cousin est drôle et gentil. Il n'est jamais ennuyeux mais il est très paresseux à l'école. C'est une catastrophe. Ses parents, qui sont assez travailleurs, trouvent ça très inquiétant.

2 **Translate the adjectives (activity 1) into English.**

3 **Read the texts again. Copy and complete the statements.**

a Laure's friends find her ___.
b Laure's brother can be ___.
c Cédric is ___ with his friends.
d Cédric's sister is ___ sad.
e Morgane's cousin is lazy at ___.
f Her cousin's parents find this ___.

4 **Copy and complete the sentences, using the French for the adjective given in brackets.**

a Ma sœur est très ___. (*chatty*)
b Mes copains sont toujours ___. (*shy*)
c J'adore mon père mais il est ___. (*lazy*)
d Ma petite sœur est très ___. (*annoying*)
e Ma mère est souvent trop ___. (*serious*)
f Mes profs de sport sont assez ___. (*kind*)

Attention

Remember to make the adjectives agree with the nouns in gender and number.

Grammaire

Adjective agreement

In French, adjectives must agree in gender and number (singular or plural) with the noun. For most adjectives, you add *-e* if the noun is feminine singular, *-s* if the noun is masculine plural, and *-es* if the noun is feminine plural.

Some adjectives follow different patterns:

Masculine		Feminine	
-e	*timid**e***	-e	*timid**e*** (no change)
-x	*sérieu**x***	-se	*sérieu**se***
-f	*neu**f***	-ve	*neu**ve***
-er	*fi**er***	-ère	*fi**ère***

Phonétique

Silent final *-e* and final consonants

In French, the final *-e* on a word is not pronounced:

*drôl**e*** *timid**e*** *frèr**e*** *catastroph**e***

Most final consonants in French are not pronounced.

*amusan**t*** *bavar**d*** *jamai**s*** *ennuyeu**x***

However, the consonants c, r, f and l are often pronounced at the end of a word. Use the English word CaReFuL to help you remember them.

*un par**c*** *fie**r*** *neu**f*** *génia**l***

5 **Read and listen to the dialogue between two spies.**
Listen and write down the words you hear (1–12) to complete the speech bubbles.

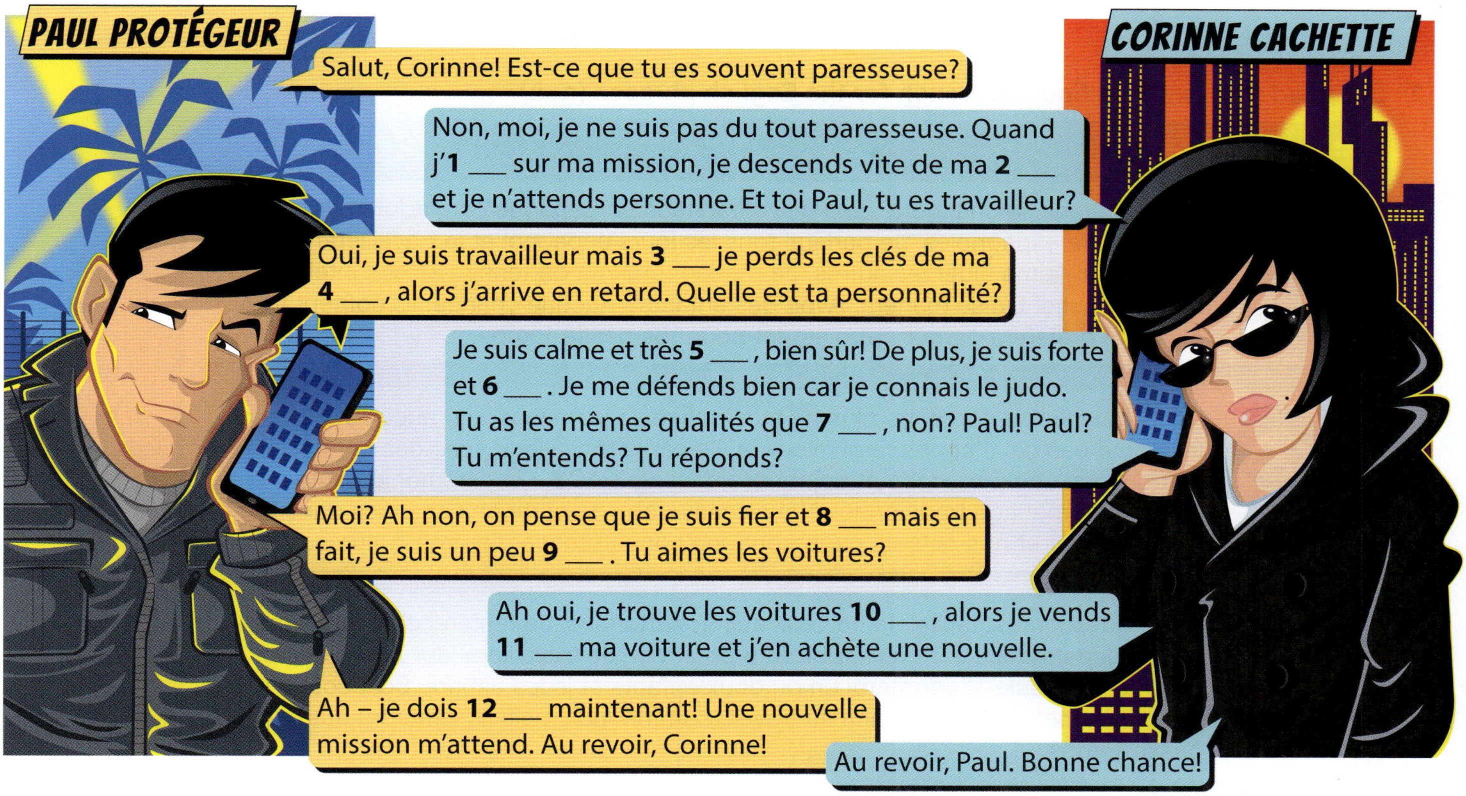

6 **Read the dialogue again and answer the questions.**

a Who sometimes arrives late?
b Who likes cars?
c Who is different from how other people see them?
d Who says they are not lazy?
e Who says they are clever?
f Who says they are shy?

7 **Note down all the regular *-re* verbs in the dialogue.**

8 **Copy and complete the sentences with the present tense of the verb in brackets.**

a J'___ toujours mes frères. (*attendre*)
b Nous ___ les enfants. (*entendre*)
c Mon copain ___ du train. (*descendre*)
d Je ___ souvent mes clés! (*perdre*)
e Tu ne ___ pas au téléphone? (*répondre*)
f Mes parents ___ des vêtements sur Internet. (*vendre*)

9 **Translate the sentences from activity 8 into English.**

Les verbes

The present tense of *-re* verbs

To form the present tense of regular *-re* verbs, remove *-re* from the infinitive and add the endings:

attendre **(to wait)**	
*j'attend**s***	*nous attend**ons***
*tu attend**s***	*vous attend**ez***
il / elle / on attend	*ils / elles attend**ent***

10 **Write a paragraph (50 words) about a famous person. Mention:**

- their name
- positive traits
- negative traits
- what you think of them
- a reason for your opinion.

11 **In pairs, take turns to read out your paragraph from activity 10.**

12 **In pairs, ask and answer the questions.**

- Comment est ta personnalité?
- Et tes amis, ils sont comment?

1.1H Mon futur moi

OBJECTIVES
- Your future plans
- *ne ... aucun(e)*
- The future tense of regular *-er* verbs

1 **Read the texts and find the French for the English phrases (a–h).**

Et à l'avenir?

Adèle

Moi, à l'avenir, je changerai de pays. J'habiterai en Espagne car j'adore la nourriture et la culture espagnoles. Je parlerai tous les jours espagnol et je travaillerai dans un hôpital car j'aime aider les autres. Je rencontrerai ma partenaire idéale: intelligente et travailleuse! On se mariera. Avoir des enfants? Aucune chance, ils coûtent trop cher! On préférera garder notre argent pour nos passe-temps.

Jules

Ah, à l'avenir… J'écouterai plus de musique mais je ne jouerai d'aucun instrument, je n'aime pas ça! J'apprécierai mieux la vie car je travaillerai avec des enfants. Je trouverai une partenaire et on entrera dans un PACS – la cérémonie coûte moins cher qu'un mariage traditionnel. Nous essayerons de partir en vacances dans le monde entier et nos enfants gagneront une connaissance d'autres cultures.

Candice

Cette question est facile! Je ne veux aucun partenaire. Je resterai célibataire car mon indépendance est très importante pour moi. Je travaillerai dur pour acheter ma maison idéale. J'adopterai un ou deux enfants et je les aimerai beaucoup. Ils attacheront de l'importance au travail, comme moi, mais ils aimeront aussi les passe-temps.

a I will speak Spanish every day
b we will get married
c I will appreciate life better
d we will enter a civil partnership
e our children will gain a knowledge of other cultures
f I will stay single
g I will adopt one or two children
h they will also like hobbies

2 **Read the text again and answer the questions.**

a Why does Adèle want to live in Spain? Give **two** details.
b Where will she work and why?
c What will she spend her money on?
d What does Jules say about musical instruments? Give **two** details.
e Why will he choose a civil partnership over marriage?
f What will he do with his partner and children?
g Why will Candice **not** marry?
h Why will she work hard?

3 **Read the texts again. Find *ten* regular verbs in the future tense and translate them into English.**

Example: je changerai – I will change

Culture

The *PACS* (*pacte civil de solidarité*) was introduced in 1999 for both heterosexual and same-sex couples and gave them similar legal and financial advantages to marriage. Same-sex marriage was made legal in France in 2013.

Les verbes

The future tense of regular *-er* verbs

Use the future tense to say what you will do in the future. To form the future tense of regular *-er* verbs, use the stem (the infinitive) and add the endings:

manger **(to eat)**	
*je manger**ai***	*nous manger**ons***
*tu manger**as***	*vous manger**ez***
*il / elle / on manger**a***	*ils / elles manger**ont***

4 Choose the correct option to complete each sentence in the future tense.

a Elle **voyagerai** / **voyagera** à l'étranger.
b Je **commencerai** / **commenceras** mes devoirs.
c Nous **aimerons** / **aimeront** notre maison.
d Il **laveras** / **lavera** sa voiture.
e Je **chercheras** / **chercherai** un(e) partenaire.

5 Listen to Karine (1–3). Copy and complete the sentences.

1 Tomorrow, Karine will go to see her ___.
2 In the future, she will look for ___.
3 Her brother will not ___ in the future.

Grammaire

ne … aucun(e)

The negative expression *ne … aucun(e)* means 'no' or 'not a' or 'not any'. It agrees in gender with the noun it is describing.

*Je **n'**achèterai **aucune** voiture.* I will **not** buy **a** car.

*Je **ne** jouerai d'**aucun** instrument.* I will **not** play **an** instrument.

6 Listen and write down the words you hear to complete the statement.

À l'**1** ___, je **2** ___ me marierai pas mais je **3** ___ en Espagne. Je ne voudrais **4** ___ enfant car ils coûtent trop **5** ___.

7 Copy and complete the sentences with *aucun* or *aucune*.

a Je n'ai ___ chance de gagner la compétition.
b Tu ne trouveras ___ travail.
c Ma mère n'achètera ___ de ces voitures!
d Je n'aime ___ de mes frères.

8 In pairs, take turns to read out one of the texts from activity 1.

9 In pairs, ask and answer the questions.

- Qu'est-ce que tu penses du mariage ou du PACS?
- À l'avenir, tu chercheras quel type de travail?
- Quels sont tes projets?

10 Choose Christophe or Samira (below) and write a paragraph (90 words) about your plans as that person. Mention:

- future jobs
- future relationships
- hopes and dreams.

Christophe
- Calme et sérieux
- Travail facile, le salaire n'est pas important
- Célibataire, aucun enfant
- Faire du jardinage, passer du temps avec les amis, sortir en ville

Samira
- Travailleuse et bavarde
- Bon travail, bon salaire
- Mariage et trois enfants
- Voyager, donner de l'argent à des associations, aider les autres

Je me marierai. Je ne me marierai pas.	
On	se mariera.
	entrera dans un PACS.
Je J'	aiderai / achèterai… rencontrerai / voyagerai / ferai… trouverai / travaillerai… gagnerai beaucoup d'argent.
J'aurai Je voudrais	des enfants / beaucoup d'ami(e)s. un bon travail / une grande maison.

1.2F Les familles de nos jours

OBJECTIVES
- Different types of families
- Comparative adjectives
- The present tense of regular *-ir* verbs
- Phonics: *-aill-* / *-ail* and *-ill-* / *-ille*

1 Read the texts and match them to the pictures.

Comment est ta famille?

Chiara

J'habite avec ma sœur Zara et mes parents à Bruges, en Belgique. Mes grands-parents habitent en Côte d'Ivoire et on va souvent là-bas pour les vacances. À Noël, on se réunit avec mes cousins et on joue à des jeux vidéo – on réussit toujours à gagner car ils sont pires que nous!

Timéo

J'habite à Nice, en France, avec mon père. Le vendredi, quand il finit le travail, on fait les courses: on remplit le frigo pour la semaine. Le dimanche, on adore aller à la plage; c'est aussi amusant que regarder la télé.

Léa

Je suis canadienne et j'habite à Montréal. Mes parents sont séparés. En ce moment je choisis de vivre avec mon père et mon beau-père car ils sont moins stricts que ma mère. J'adore ma demi-sœur et mon demi-frère et on rit tous les jours. On grandit tous ensemble, c'est génial!

Sébastien

Je suis adopté. Je suis né à Calais et maintenant j'habite à Toulouse. Je trouve que Toulouse est une meilleure ville que Calais car la ville est plus intéressante. Je n'ai pas encore de frères et sœurs, mais mes parents attendent un enfant pour le mois de septembre.

1

2

3

4

2 Read the texts again and answer the questions.

a Why do Chiara and her sister always beat their cousins at video games?
b What do Timéo and his dad do after work on Fridays?
c What do they like doing at the weekend?
d Why does Léa prefer living with her dad and stepdad at the moment?
e Why does Sébastien prefer Toulouse to Calais?
f How many brothers and sisters does he have?

3 Translate the sentences into French.

a The beach is as fun as the cinema.
b My dad is less strict than my mum.
c Sport is more interesting than video games.
d Cinema is better than TV.
e My sister is worse than my brother.

Grammaire

Comparative adjectives

Use comparative adjectives to make comparisons:

plus … que	more … than / …er than
moins … que	less … than
aussi … que	as … as

*Angelin est **plus amusant que** Nicole.*
Angelin is **funnier than** Nicole.

*Je suis **moins gentil que** ma sœur.*
I am **less kind than** my sister.

*Elle est **aussi sympa que** moi.* She is **as nice as** me.

Remember to make the adjective agree with the subject of the sentence.

Bon and *mauvais* have irregular comparatives, *meilleur(e)* and *pire*:

*La musique est **meilleure que** la lecture.*
Music is better than reading.

*La télévision est **pire que** la lecture.*
Television is worse than reading.

4 Listen (1–4). Write P for a positive opinion of the person, N for a negative opinion, and P+N if the opinion is both positive and negative.

1 brother	2 grandparents	3 cousin	4 friend

5 Copy and complete the sentences with the present tense of the verb in brackets.

a Il ___ ses devoirs. (*finir*)
b Je ___ toujours les devoirs de maths. (*réussir*)
c Elle ___ son sac de fruits et légumes. (*remplir*)
d Tu ___ quelle émission? (*choisir*)
e Nous ___ notre jeu après le déjeuner. (*finir*)

Les verbes

The present tense of regular *-ir* verbs

To form the present tense of regular *–ir* verbs, remove *-ir* from the infinitive and add the endings:

***finir* (to finish)**	
*je fin**is***	*nous fin**issons***
*tu fin**is***	*vous fin**issez***
*il / elle / on fin**it***	*ils / elles fin**issent***

*Je **choisis** un film.* I choose / am choosing a film.
*Ils **finissent** leurs devoirs.* They finish / are finishing their homework.

6 Look at the picture. In pairs, take turns to ask a question and answer as if this were your family. Use comparative adjectives.

Comment est…?
- ton frère
- ta sœur
- ton cousin
- tes parents

Mon frère Ma sœur Mon cousin	est	plus moins aussi	drôle(s) / sympa(s) timide(s) / strict(e)(s) amusant(e)(s) intelligent(e)(s) gentil(s) / gentille(s) travailleur(s) / travailleuse(s) paresseux / paresseuse(s)	que…
Mes parents	sont			
		pire(s) / meilleur(e)(s)		

7 Use the picture in activity 6 to write a paragraph (90 words) describing your family (using verbs in the present tense). Mention:
- the personality of each person
- who you do / don't get on with
- comparisons between yourself and some of the family members.

Phonétique

-aill- / -ail* and *-ill- / -ille

*trav**aill**eur*	*je trav**aille***	*la t**aille***	*le trav**ail***
*ju**ill**et*	*me**ill**eur*	*la fam**ille***	*la f**ille***

1.2H Mes amis, c'est ma vie!

OBJECTIVES
- Friends and friendship
- Impersonal verbs
- The present participle of regular verbs
- Phonics: soft *g*, hard *g* and *gn*

1 Read the message thread. Then read the statements (a–h) and list them in the correct order to match the conversation.

Amis

Alizée
Salut, Mathis et Emma! On passe la journée ensemble samedi? On fait quoi?

Mathis
On va au parc le matin et à la plage l'après-midi?

Emma
Bonne idée! Mais d'abord, il faut faire les courses. En allant au parc, je vais m'arrêter à la boulangerie pour acheter du pain.

Alizée
Génial, merci. Moi, en passant par le supermarché, j'achèterai des boissons.

Mathis
👍 Très bien! Il manque juste une couverture de pique-nique – j'en ai une!

Emma
Après, il vaut mieux prendre le bus pour aller à la plage. C'est trop loin à pied, non?

Alizée
Oui. En prenant le bus, on gagne du temps et on peut rester plus longtemps dans l'eau.

Mathis
Emma, tu connais le numéro du bus?

Emma
Oui, c'est le 239. En attendant le bus du retour, j'appellerai ma belle-mère car elle préparera le dîner.

Alizée
Il vaut la peine d'être à l'heure – j'adore sa cuisine! 😋

Mathis
Cool! Alors, rendez-vous au parc samedi à neuf heures. À samedi!

une couverture de pique-nique	a picnic blanket

a Emma says she will let her stepmum know when to prepare dinner.
b Alizée says she will buy drinks.
c Mathis says he will bring a picnic blanket.
d Emma says she will buy bread.
e Emma provides the bus route number.
f They agree they should take the bus.
g They decide to go to the park in the morning.
h Mathis suggests a time to meet at the park.

2 In threes, read aloud the message thread in activity 1.

3 Find *four* examples of the present participle in the messages in activity 1. Translate them into English.

Phonétique

Soft *g*, hard *g* and *gn*

g before *e*, *i* or *y* is soft:

*man**g**er* *boulan**g**erie* ***g**entil*

g before *a*, *o*, *u* or a consonant is hard:

***g**âteau* ***g**oût* *lé**g**umes* *rè**g**lement*

gn has a rolled sound:

*ga**gn**er* *espa**gn**ol* *monta**gn**e*

Les verbes

The present participle

When an action happens during, or very quickly after another action by the same person, you can use a present participle for the ongoing action:

*En **allant** au parc, Mathis appelle une copine.* While **walking** to the park, Mathis calls a friend.

*En **arrivant** au parc, il retrouve ses copains.* **Arriving** at the park, he meets his friends.

To form the present participle in French, remove the *-ons* ending from the *nous* form of the present tense, and add *-ant*:

*nous jou**ons*** ⟶ *en jou**ant*** (while playing)

*nous attend**ons*** ⟶ *en attend**ant*** (while waiting)

4 **Copy and combine the pairs of sentences using a present participle.**

Example: Il descend du bus. Il tombe.
→ En descendant du bus, il tombe.

a Il joue bien au foot. Il gagne le match.
b J'arrive au collège. Je vois mes amis.
c Je fais la cuisine. J'écoute de la musique.
d Nous regardons un film. Nous mangeons des glaces.
e Elle achète du pain. Elle rencontre sa cousine.

5 **Listen to three teenagers talking about friendship. Listen and write down the words you hear (1–12) to complete the speech bubbles.**

Je m'entends bien avec mes amies, mais ma copine Émilie n'est pas très **1** ___. Elle n'a jamais le temps d'écouter mes **2** ___! Et quand elle m'écoute, c'est en **3** ___ ou en tchattant sur son portable. Moi, je pense qu'il vaut mieux avoir des amis qui ont du **4** ___ pour nous.

Je suis très proche de mes **5** ___ car je n'aime pas être **6** ___. Mais entre mon ami Thomas et moi, il manque la **7** ___. Thomas ne tient jamais ses promesses. Je crois qu'il vaut mieux avoir un ami sensible **8** ___ nous encourage dans nos décisions.

Entre mon amie Liz et moi, il manque la conversation car elle est très **9** ___ et ne parle pas beaucoup. C'est ennuyeux **10** ___ mais il **11** ___ la peine de rester amis car elle est vraiment sympa et ne ment **12** ___. Le plus important pour moi, c'est d'avoir un ami ou une amie gentil.

6 **Read the texts in activity 5. Copy and complete the table in English.**

	The problem in their friendship (*two* details)	What they say is most important in friendship (*two* details)
Marthe		
Samy		
Omar		

Grammaire

Impersonal verbs

Impersonal verbs don't have forms for all subject pronouns; they are only used with *il* (it) or *cela / ça* (it / that). The equivalent in English often uses 'we' or 'you'.

***Il faut** acheter du pain.*
It's necessary to buy some bread. / **We must** buy some bread.

***Il manque** une couverture de pique-nique.*
We're missing a picnic blanket.

***Il vaut mieux** arriver à l'heure.*
It's better to arrive on time.

***Il vaut la peine** de travailler.*
It's worth working.

7 **Choose one text from activity 5 and translate it into English.**

Attention

When translating, you won't always be able to translate word for word. You may have to change the word order in some phrases, so that your paragraph as a whole makes sense.

8 **Write a paragraph (90 words) about your friendships. Mention:**

- why you get on with your friends
- why friends are important to you
- what problem(s) you may have in friendships.

Example: Je m'entends bien avec …
Je ne m'entends pas avec …
Mes ami(e)s sont important(e)s parce que …
Mon ami(e) est / n'est pas …

2.1F Aïe aïe aïe!

OBJECTIVES
- Health problems and addictions
- Plural nouns
- The near future tense

1 Read the patients' problems (1–3) and match them with the correct response (a–c).

Problèmes

1 J'ai mal à la tête, j'ai mal à la gorge. J'ai aussi mal aux oreilles. Je n'ai pas d'énergie. Je suis très fatigué et je ne mange pas beaucoup. Je suis malade!

2 Allô! C'est pour une urgence! Il y a un accident. Je vois une vieille dame qui a très mal au pied et à la jambe et elle est vraiment inquiète.

3 Aïe aïe aïe, j'ai mal au bras! Je veux jouer au tennis demain mais je ne peux lever le bras gauche et ça me fait vraiment mal.

Réponses

a D'accord, je vais envoyer une ambulance. La dame va aller à l'hôpital et on va tout de suite l'examiner.

b Alors, donnez-moi votre numéro de téléphone. Le médecin va vous appeler et il va peut-être vous donner des médicaments. Il ne faut pas faire d'exercice!

c OK, je vais vous donner un rendez-vous chez le médecin. Il va vous voir cet après-midi… à 16 heures 10, d'accord? Maintenant, vous allez rester au lit. Il faut boire beaucoup d'eau et manger, si vous pouvez.

2 Listen to the phone calls and check your answers.

3 In pairs, read aloud the matching problems and responses.

4 Find in the problems and responses the French for the English phrases (a–h).

- a I have a headache
- b I have earache
- c I'm not eating much
- d I'm ill
- e they will examine her straightaway
- f the doctor is going to call you
- g I'm going to give you an appointment
- h you are going to stay in bed

5 Rewrite the sentences, changing the verb to the near future tense.

- a Je mange des légumes.
- b Il joue au foot.
- c Tu restes au lit?
- d Elle voit ses copains.
- e Je fais de l'exercice.
- f Nous allons au parc.

Les verbes

The near future tense

Use the near future tense to say what you are going to do or will do. You need to use a form of *aller* in the present tense, followed by the main verb in the infinitive:

aller **(to go)**		
je vais	*nous allons*	+ infinitive
tu vas	*vous allez*	
il / elle / on va	*ils / elles vont*	

*Je **vais jouer** au tennis.* I am going to play tennis.

*Vous **allez rester** au lit.* You are going to stay in bed.

6 Read the texts and answer the questions (a–h).

Martin
Posté le 3 octobre

Ma mère a commencé à fumer des cigarettes à l'âge de vingt ans. Elle est souvent malade et le médecin dit que fumer, c'est dangereux. Ça va être difficile d'arrêter car elle a beaucoup de soucis et elle dit que fumer l'aide à rester calme.

Élise
Posté le 27 octobre

Mon ami Thomas prend des drogues. Il dit que ça le relaxe mais je sais que les drogues, ça peut tuer! Je ne suis pas d'accord avec ses choix de vie. Moi, je ne vais jamais prendre de drogues, car je veux rester en bonne santé. Je voudrais vivre très longtemps, alors je vais être active et manger de façon saine: beaucoup de légumes et pas trop de gâteaux!

Karim
Posté le 23 novembre

Ma cousine boit de l'alcool et elle vapote. Elle va faire un effort pour boire moins car elle a peur de tomber malade. Elle va aussi arrêter de vapoter car on ne connaît pas bien les dangers de la e-cigarette.

a What does Martin's mother's doctor say about smoking?
b Why will Martin's mother find it difficult to stop smoking?
c How does smoking cigarettes help her?
d What can drugs do, according to Élise?
e Why will she never take drugs?
f How will Élise try to live a long life? Give **two** details.
g Why is Karim's cousin going to try to drink less alcohol?
h What else will she do and why?

7 Work out the plural form of the nouns.

a une drogue
b un corps
c un accident
d un neveu
e une maladie
f un château

8 Listen and write down the nouns you hear to complete the sentences.

« Je vais boire moins d'**1** ___ et je vais arrêter de fumer car c'est mauvais pour la **2** ___. Ça peut donner des **3** ___. »
« Aïe, j'ai mal au **4** ___ et aux **5** ___! Je vais aller voir un **6** ___. »

9 Translate the sentences into French.

a I have a headache.
b He is going to see the doctor.
c I am going to drink less coffee.
d My sister is going to eat fruit and vegetables.
e I am not going to take drugs.

Grammaire

Plural nouns

Most plural nouns end in *-s*:

un copain → *des copain**s***
une oreille → *des oreille**s***

If the singular noun ends in *-eau*, *-au* or *-eu*, the plural adds an *-x* instead of an *-s*:

*un gât**eau*** → *des gât**eaux***
*un chev**eu*** → *des chev**eux***

If the singular noun already ends in *-s*, *-x* or *-z*, there is no change in the plural:

*un pay**s*** → *des pay**s***
*un choi**x*** → *des choi**x***

2.1H Mes projets « bonne santé »

OBJECTIVES
- Healthy choices
- *avant de* + infinitive
- Two tenses together: present and future

1 Read the blog and find the French for the English words and phrases (a–i).

Accueil | À propos | **Blog** | Nouveau | Intérêts

Le blog de Candice
Ma santé

11h25

Bonjour, tout le monde! Aujourd'hui, je vous parle de mes projets « bonne santé » pour l'année prochaine.

Je mène une vie plutôt saine. Je mange équilibré et je suis végétarienne. **Je ne me sens jamais fatiguée** ou faible car **je gère bien mon temps**. Je fais un peu de sport tous les jours et normalement, **je me couche tôt**.

Alors, mes projets pour l'année prochaine? Avant de passer mes examens, **j'essayerai de me lever plus tôt** car **ça m'aide à me concentrer**. De plus, **je marcherai** régulièrement dans la forêt avec mon chien car j'aime passer du temps dans la nature. **Ça sera amusant, mais ça dépend du temps!** J'adore la natation, alors en été, je nagerai dans la mer mais **je ne risquerai pas de tomber malade**; évidemment, **je porterai un chapeau**.

137

- a healthy
- b balanced
- c weak
- d time
- e early
- f to take my exams
- g the weather
- h swimming
- i to fall ill

2 **Read Candice's blog again and decide whether these activities (a–h) are mentioned in the present (P) or future (F).**

- a eating a balanced diet
- b doing sport
- c going to bed early
- d getting up early
- e walking in the forest
- f enjoying nature
- g swimming in the sea
- h wearing a sunhat

3 **Translate into English the *ten* phrases in bold in the blog.**

Les verbes

Using two tenses together: present and future

We use different tenses together naturally, in speaking and writing. Use present and future tenses to say what you do or are doing now, and what you will do or are going to do in the future.

*Je **mange** des fruits tous les jours mais à l'avenir, je **mangerai** aussi des légumes.*

I **eat** fruit every day but in future I **will eat** / **am going to eat** vegetables too.

4 **Listen (1–4). Copy and complete the table in English.**

	They are going to...	before...
1		
2		
3		
4		

5 **Copy and combine the pairs of phrases, using the future tense and *avant de / d'* + infinitive.**

Example: manger – aller chez le médecin
→Je mangerai avant d'aller chez le médecin.

a trouver une recette saine – faire de la cuisine
b parler au médecin – prendre mon traitement
c nager à la piscine – faire les courses
d préparer le déjeuner – aller en ville
e manger un plat chaud – faire une promenade
f parler au médecin – faire de l'exercice

Grammaire

***avant de* + infinitive**

To say you are going to do something **before** something else, use ***avant de / d'*** + infinitive.

***Avant de** partir, je mangerai des céréales.*
Before leaving, I will eat some cereal.
*Je mangerai des fruits **avant d'**aller courir.*
I'll eat some fruit before going running

6 **Write a paragraph (150 words) about your lifestyle. Mention:**
- what you eat and drink now
- what you do to keep active
- what you will change to improve your health in future.

En ce moment, Actuellement, Maintenant,	j'essaie de manger équilibré je mange / bois beaucoup de... je fais beaucoup de sport je fais de la natation je mène une vie saine	car j'adore les fruits et les légumes. car c'est bon pour la santé. car c'est important pour moi.
À l'avenir, Dans le futur,	je mènerai une vie saine je mangerai équilibré je marcherai plus souvent je nagerai tous les jours	pour rester en bonne santé. parce que c'est bon pour le corps / la santé.
	je ne fumerai pas	car c'est dangereux / c'est un risque.
Avant de Avant d'	faire plus de sport, me coucher ce soir, aller courir, arrêter de (+ *infinitive*),	je (+ *future tense*).

7 **In pairs, take turns to read out your paragraph (activity 6).**

8 **In pairs, ask and answer the questions.**
- Tes amis, ont-ils une vie saine? Pourquoi (pas)?
- Pourquoi certains jeunes fument-ils, à ton avis?
- Comment est-ce que tu te prépareras pour les examens?
- Quels sont tes projets santé avant de devenir adulte?

Culture

Can you guess what the top five most practised sports are in France?

1. Football 2. Tennis 3. Horse-riding
4. Basketball 5. Judo

2.2F Hier, j'ai...

OBJECTIVES
- Recent activities
- Indirect object pronouns
- The perfect tense of regular verbs with *avoir*

1 Read the blog and answer the questions (a–g).

Salut, je m'appelle Corentin et je suis vraiment très sportif. Aujourd'hui, je te parle de mon programme sportif de la semaine dernière.

Lundi, **j'ai joué** une partie de foot. C'est mon sport préféré et je joue pour l'équipe de ma ville, Mougins.

Mardi, **on a participé** à un match et **on a gagné** 3–0. On était super contents car **on a fini** premiers!

Ensuite, mercredi, **j'ai marché** avec mon chien. **J'ai perdu** mon chien dans la forêt et j'ai attendu pendant deux heures! Après, *je lui ai donné un bain* et de la nourriture.

Jeudi, **j'ai essayé** la natation pour la première fois et **j'ai vraiment aimé** ça.

Vendredi soir, j'ai fait une course de 15 kilomètres. Après, **j'ai beaucoup dormi** car j'étais fatigué.

Samedi, **j'ai mangé** au restaurant avec mes parents car c'était mon anniversaire: **ils ont choisi** du poisson avec des légumes mais moi, **j'ai choisi** de la viande et des frites. Et *ils m'ont acheté un nouveau portable* comme cadeau! Génial!

Dimanche, **j'ai fini** mes devoirs et **j'ai regardé** le Tour de France à la télé. Puis **j'ai retrouvé** mon meilleur ami au parc et *je lui ai vendu mon vieux portable!*

Quelle semaine!

a Which team does Corentin play football for?
b What did he do on Tuesday?
c How long did he wait for, when he lost his dog on Wednesday?
d What did he try for the first time on Thursday?
e What did he think of that activity?
f What did his parents choose at the restaurant on Saturday?
g Which **four** things did he do on Sunday?

2 Read the blog again and translate the phrases in bold into English.

3 Listen (1–9) and decide if each sentence is in the present (Pr) or perfect (P) tense.

Les verbes

The perfect tense with *avoir* (regular verbs)

Use the perfect tense to say what you did or have done. To form the perfect tense, use part of the verb *avoir* (to have) + a past participle.

Past participles:

for regular *-er* verbs, replace the *-er* with *-é*:

*jou**er*** → *jou**é***

for regular *-ir* verbs, replace the *-ir* with *-i*:

*chois**ir*** → *chois**i***

for regular *-re* verbs, replace the *-re* with *-u*:

*vend**re*** → *vend**u***

*Nous **avons joué** au foot.* We **played** football.

*J'**ai choisi** des frites.* I **chose** chips.

*Tu **as vendu** ta voiture?* **Have** you **sold** your car?

4 **Copy and complete the sentences, adding the past participle of the verb given in brackets.**

a J'ai ___ beaucoup de fruits. (*manger*)
b Elle a ___ son chien. (*perdre*)
c Nous avons ___ les devoirs. (*finir*)
d Ils ont ___ leur voiture. (*vendre*)
e J'ai ___ de la musique. (*écouter*)
f Elle a ___ pendant huit heures. (*dormir*)
g Il a ___ le film. (*aimer*)

5 **In pairs, take turns to start and finish a sentence describing what Corentin (activity 1) did each day.**

- Alors, lundi, Corentin a…
- … joué au football. Et mardi, il a…
- … gagné un match de foot. Vendredi, il a…

6 **Translate into English the phrases in *italics* in the text in activity 1.**

7 **Copy the sentences, replacing the bold words with an indirect object pronoun in the correct position.**

a Je demande (**à Marie**) de partir.
b Il dit (**à moi**) de manger des fruits.
c Je vends mon vélo (**à toi**).
d Votre frère ressemble (**à vous**).
e Amélie a parlé (**à son frère**).
f Tu as répondu (**à ton professeur**).

Grammaire

Indirect object pronouns

me/m' (before a vowel)	(to) me
te/t' (before a vowel)	(to) you (informal)
lui	(to) him/her/it
vous	(to) you (formal)

Indirect object pronouns replace a noun that would be introduced with the preposition *à* (to). They always go before the verb.

*Je **lui** donne de l'eau.* I give **him** some water./I give some water **to him**.

*Ils **me** donnent un portable.* They are giving **me** a mobile phone.

When the verb is in the perfect tense, the pronoun goes before both parts of the verb:

*Je **lui** ai donné de l'eau.* I gave **him** some water.

*Ils **m'**ont donné un portable.* They gave **me** a mobile phone.

Be careful, because some French verbs need *à* while their English equivalent does not need the word 'to':

*Je **demande à** ma mère.* I ask (to) my mum.

→ *Je **lui** demande.* I ask **her**.

8 **Listen to Khalida (1–5) and decide which activity (a–e) she did on each day of the week.**

a ate out
b tried a new sport
c went shopping
d did schoolwork
e met up with a friend

9 **Copy the storyboard. Think of something you did each day last week. Draw an emoji for each activity and write a caption in the perfect tense for each day.**

Example: Lundi. J'ai joué au foot pour l'équipe de mon école. On a gagné le match. C'était super.

lundi	mardi	mercredi	jeudi	vendredi	samedi	dimanche

2.2H Comment rester en bonne santé?

OBJECTIVES
- The challenges of a healthy lifestyle
- Impersonal expressions
- Irregular present participles

1 Read the article and write down the order in which the points listed (a–h) are made in it.

Aujourd'hui au Québec

Actualités | Économie | **Santé** | Météo | Sport

Santé: une nouvelle étude

Selon une étude récente parmi les jeunes Québécois, il est de plus en plus difficile de rester en bonne santé. Explications de l'expert Marc Talbot…

Aujourd'hui, la plupart des gens sont conscients de l'importance de rester en bonne santé de corps et d'esprit. Le mode de vie occidental inclut certaines pratiques saines et d'autres moins saines. Il est parfois difficile de garder un mode de vie sain et équilibré.

Par exemple, il est facile de dépendre du tabac et beaucoup de personnes continuent de fumer, même en ayant des maladies graves.

Il est important d'être actif tous les jours mais la plupart des gens travaillent dans un bureau, en position assise. En faisant du sport, on peut bénéficier d'une meilleure santé et on peut se faire de nouveaux amis.

Alors, pour essayer de rester en bonne santé, il est nécessaire de prendre de bonnes habitudes. Il est également essentiel de bien conseiller ses amis et sa famille sur une vie saine: en étant ouvert avec eux, on peut les aider à faire de bons choix pour l'avenir.

a It is essential to advise friends and family on healthy living.
b It is sometimes difficult to maintain a healthy lifestyle.
c Most people are aware of the importance of staying healthy.
d It is increasingly difficult to stay healthy.
e It is easy to be dependent on tobacco.
f It is necessary to develop good habits.
g It is important to be active on a daily basis.
h Most people work in an office.

2 Read the article again and answer the questions.

a Who was questioned in the survey?
b What does the text tell us about western life? Give **two** details.
c What do many people do despite serious illness?
d What is the problem for people who work in an office?
e Which **two** benefits of doing sport are mentioned in the text?
f What is the result of being open with family and friends?

Culture

Quebec is a French-speaking province in eastern Canada. It is the only Canadian region where people predominantly speak French. French was recognised as the official language in 1974 and today almost 94% of people living in Quebec speak French.

Québécois (French as spoken in Quebec) has words that are different from French of France and *Québécois*-speakers have a very distinctive accent.

3 Translate the sentences into French.

a It is necessary to do some sport.
b It is possible to see a doctor.
c It is essential to eat vegetables.
d It is difficult to stay healthy.
e It is easy to depend on smoking.
f It is forbidden to drink alcohol here.

4 Find in the article (activity 1) *three* irregular present participles and translate the phrases into English.

5 Copy and complete the sentences with *ayant*, *étant* or *faisant*.

a En ___ du sport, on améliore sa santé.
b En ___ plus sportif, on peut vivre plus longtemps.
c En ___ de bonnes habitudes, on reste en bonne santé.
d En ___ de la natation, on peut se relaxer.

6 Listen (1–4) and choose the statement (a–d) that summarises what each person says.

a It's easy to eat well.
b Doing sport improves energy levels.
c Don't take drugs!
d Always challenge yourself to do more.

7 Listen again (1–4) and note down *three* details for each person.

8 In pairs, read aloud the paragraph beginning *Aujourd'hui...* in the article in activity 1.

9 In pairs, ask and answer the questions.

- As-tu un mode de vie sain? Pourquoi (pas)?
- Que penses-tu du tabac?
- Le sport, c'est important pour toi? Pourquoi (pas)?

10 Write a paragraph (150 words) on healthy living. Mention:

- what you do to stay healthy and the barriers to being healthy
- why leading a healthy lifestyle is important.

Grammaire

Impersonal expressions

Impersonal expressions such as *il est facile de* (it's easy to...) are followed by an **infinitive**.

*Il est facile / difficile de **rester** en bonne santé.*
It is easy / difficult to stay healthy.

*Il est essentiel / possible / nécessaire de **faire** du sport.*
It is essential / possible / necessary to do sport.

*Il est interdit de **fumer**.*
It is forbidden to smoke. / Smoking is forbidden.

Les verbes

Irregular present participles

You have already learnt how to use present participles (see 1.2H). There are three very common irregular present participles that you also need to know, from the verbs *être*, *avoir* and *faire*:

en étant (while / by) being
en ayant (while / by) having
en faisant (while / by) doing

Je fais	du sport / du football. de la natation.		
Je mange Je ne mange pas	beaucoup assez de		fruits / légumes / viande.
Il est C'est	difficile facile important nécessaire	de	manger equilibré. faire du sport / de la méditation. marcher dans la nature. parler avec ses amis / sa famille
Il faut éviter	les drogues le tabac l'alcool	pour	rester en bonne santé. améliorer sa vie. vivre plus longtemps.
C'est	bon mauvais	pour la santé.	

3.1F Lycée et université?

OBJECTIVES
- Studies post-16
- Nouns ending in *-ation*
- Negative constructions
- Phonics: *-tion*

1 Listen to and read Nathan's conversation with his school careers adviser and answer the questions.

Nathan Bonjour, Madame Colas. Je ne sais pas quoi étudier l'année prochaine. Pouvez-vous m'aider?

Mma Colas Oui, bien sûr. Quelle est votre personnalité, Nathan?

Nathan Je suis très patient et j'aime aider les gens. De plus, j'ai une bonne communication. Par contre, je ne suis pas toujours indépendant.

Mma Colas Et vous aimez quelles matières au collège?

Nathan J'adore les sciences. C'est ma passion et j'ai de très bonnes notes. Je n'aime pas l'histoire… je n'écoute jamais en cours d'histoire, c'est trop ennuyeux!

Mma Colas Vous voulez travailler dans un bureau ou dans un autre environnement?

Nathan Je ne veux pas travailler dans un bureau. Je veux aider les gens, je veux un métier dans une organisation publique.

Mma Colas Avez-vous déjà pensé à la médecine? Je pense que c'est une bonne idée pour vous.

Nathan Oui, ça m'intéresse. Qu'est-ce que je dois faire pour devenir médecin?

Mma Colas Alors, il faut continuer à bien travailler en sciences. Après le lycée, il faut aller à l'université pendant plusieurs années. Bonne chance!

Nathan Merci beaucoup. Je ne connais personne qui travaille dans la médecine. Je vais chercher des informations ce soir.

a What is Nathan not sure about for next year?
b What is Nathan's personality like? Give **three** details.
c Which school subject doesn't he like and why?
d Which type of working environment doesn't appeal to him?
e What will he have to do to work in medicine? Give **two** details.
f What is he going to do this evening?

2 Rewrite the sentences in the correct order.

a n' | Il | apprend | ses leçons | jamais | .
b Je | rien | écoute | n' | en classe | .
c M. Marin | personne | aime | n' | .
d pas | as | Tu | n' | de cours de langues | ?
e Elle | veut | pas | ne | à l'université | aller | .

3 Translate into French.

a I do not know what to study next year.
b I don't want to go to university.
c I don't know anyone.
d I am not very organised.
e I never have good grades in science.

Grammaire

Using negative constructions

To make a sentence negative, use *ne … pas* around the verb:

*Je **ne** fais **pas** d'espagnol au collège.*
I **do not** do Spanish at school.

ne is shortened to *n'* in front of a vowel or silent *h*:

*Je **n'**ai **pas** de cours d'anglais aujourd'hui.*
I **don't** have any English lessons today.

These other negative forms follow the same pattern:

*Il **ne** fait **jamais** ses devoirs.* He **never** does his homework.

*Je **ne** comprends **rien**.* I do **not** understand **anything**. / I understand **nothing**.

*Je **ne** vois **personne**.* I do **not** see **anyone**. / I see **no one**.

4 Listen (1–4) and write down the sentences you hear.

5 Turn these verbs into nouns.

a participer
b informer
c situer
d préparer

Phonétique

-tion

*communica**tion*** *organisa**tion*** *informa**tion***

6 In pairs, take turns to read the text aloud.

J'ai une bonne communication et une bonne organisation. À l'avenir, je veux travailler avec des enfants mais je ne veux pas travailler dans une école. Je vais aller au lycée mais je ne veux pas aller à l'université.

7 In pairs, take turns to ask and answer the questions.

- Qu'est-ce-que tu n'aimes pas dans ton collège? Pourquoi pas?
- Dans quel environnement ne veux-tu jamais travailler? Pourquoi?
- Tu veux aller au lycée l'année prochaine? Pourquoi (pas)?
- Tu veux aller à l'université à l'avenir? Pourquoi (pas)?

8 Write a paragraph (90 words) on school and future studies. Describe:

- the subjects you like and dislike, and why
- what you want to do when you leave school
- whether you want to go to university and why (not).

Grammaire

Nouns ending in *-ation*

Some nouns ending in -ation are closely related to an *-er* verb, and their English equivalent also ends in -ation. Simply replace the final *-er* of the verb with *'-ation'*.

Knowing the connection can help you create nouns or understand new ones when you read.

inviter → *invit**ation***

organiser → *organis**ation***

Culture

In France, students aged 11 to 15 go to *le collège* and at the end, they take exams called *le brevet*, equivalent to GCSEs. For the next three school years, they go to *le lycée*, where the final exam is *le baccalauréat* or *le bac*. Many students then choose to go to university, often in or near their home town, and course fees are low.

J'aime Je n'aime pas Ma matière préferée, c'est…	l'histoire. les maths. les sciences.
Je veux Je ne veux pas À l'avenir, je voudrais	aller à l'université. faire un apprentissage de… travailler / voyager. gagner de l'argent. être chanteur / chanteuse. être médecin / professeur(e). être footballeur / footballeuse professionel(le). travailler dans un bureau. travailler avec les enfants. travailler avec les animaux.

3.1H L'école de mes rêves

OBJECTIVES
- Your dream school
- Superlative adjectives
- The conditional of regular *-er* verbs

1 Read about four students' dream schools. Copy and complete the sentences.

Comment serait l'école de tes rêves?

Nina

J'adorerais vraiment porter mes propres vêtements à l'école car je déteste l'uniforme. Mes parents aimeraient m'acheter des vêtements moins chers. **Je commencerais les cours plus tard**, à neuf heures et demie, et j'aimerais avoir Mme Jeauneau comme professeur de français. C'est la prof la plus sympa de l'école.

Nous aimerions avoir plus de choix à la cantine car en ce moment on n'aime pas trop les repas du midi. Nous préférerions une récré plus longue et **on n'étudierait jamais la technologie** – les cours de technologie sont les plus difficiles!

Antoine et Marion

Karine

Mon école est la moins grande de la région, alors nous avons une toute petite bibliothèque. Moi, j'aimerais avoir une grande bibliothèque avec plein de livres en anglais et en espagnol. J'adore les langues. De plus, **j'aimerais construire une salle informatique** seulement pour les leçons de langues.

J'aimerais avoir plus de cours de musique et plus de salles de musique. J'accepterais les portables en cours, donc j'aimerais changer cela dans le règlement scolaire. Par contre, **je n'accepterais jamais le chewing-gum** – j'ai horreur de ça! **J'adorerais avoir une grande piscine** et une grande cour de récréation pour jouer au foot tous les jours avec mes copains. À mon avis, le foot, c'est le plus amusant des sports.

Amadou

a Nina would like to wear ___.
b Nina's parents would like to buy her ___.
c Nina would start her lessons at ___.
d Antoine and Marion would prefer more ___ at the canteen and a longer ___.
e They find technology lessons ___.
f Karine's school is ___ in the area.
g She would like a large library with books in ___ and ___.
h She would build ___.
i Amadou would accept ___ at his dream school.
j Amadou would never accept ___.
k Amadou thinks football is ___ sport.

2 Translate the phrases in bold in activity 1 into English.

3 Listen and read. Answer the questions in English.

Je m'appelle Aida Diouf et j'habite à Dakar, au Sénégal. L'école de mes rêves? J'aimerais l'appeler comme moi: le collège Diouf. J'aimerais avoir seulement 250 élèves et un professeur pour dix élèves. On étudierait toutes les matières mais surtout les sciences car j'aimerais être médecin. On ne porterait pas d'uniforme, c'est tellement nul. On commencerait les leçons à dix heures du matin et on aimerait finir à deux heures de l'après-midi. Parfois, on étudierait d'autres cultures. C'est important pour moi car j'aimerais voyager dans le monde.

a Why would Aida call her ideal school *le collège Diouf*?

b What would the classes be like?

c What would they study? (Give **two** details.)

d What does Aida say about the uniform? (Give **two** details.)

e When would lessons begin and end?

f Why is it important for her to learn about other cultures?

4 Copy and complete the sentences, using the conditional form of the verb in brackets.

a Je ___ avoir de nouveaux professeurs. (*préférer*)

b Elle ___ arriver à dix heures du matin. (*adorer*)

c Dans l'école de mes rêves, on ___ seulement du fast-food. (*manger*)

d Tu ___ faire de la géographie toute la journée? (*aimer*)

e Il ___ plus en cours de musique. (*chanter*)

f Elles ___ plus d'importance aux sciences. (*donner*)

5 In pairs, take turns to read aloud Nina's text (activity 1).

6 In pairs, ask and answer the questions.

- Qu'est-ce que tu aimerais avoir dans l'école de tes rêves?
- Tu étudierais quelles matières?
- Tu aimerais porter un uniforme?
- Tu commencerais les cours à quelle heure?

7 Find *four* phrases containing a superlative adjective in activity 1 and translate them into English.

8 Write a blog post (150 words) about school. Describe:

- the advantages and disadvantages of your current school
- what your dream school would be like.

Les verbes

The conditional of regular *-er* verbs

Use the conditional to describe what **would** happen in the future, or to express a wish.

For *-er* verbs in the conditional, add the imperfect tense ending to the infinitive.

aimer **(to like, to love)**	
*j'aimer**ais***	*nous aimer**ions***
*tu aimer**ais***	*vous aimer**iez***
*il/elle/on aimer**ait***	*ils/elles aimer**aient***

*J'**aimerais** aller au cinéma.*
I **would like** to go to the cinema.

*On **commencerait** les cours à 10 heures.*
We **would start** lessons at 10 o'clock.

Grammaire

Superlative adjectives

For superlatives ('the most…' or 'the least…'), use:

le/la/les plus/moins + adjective

The adjective must agree with the noun it is describing.

*Dans ma famille, mon frère est **le plus** amusant.*
In my family, my brother is **the most** amusing.

The adjectives *bon* and *mauvais* have an irregular superlative:

bon (good) ⟶ *le/la/les/moins meilleur(e)(s)* (the best)

*Cette professeur est **la meilleure**.*

mauvais (bad) ⟶ *le/la/les pire(s)* (the worst)

*Ce professeur est **le pire**.*

3.2F Mon métier créatif

OBJECTIVES
- Jobs in the creative industries
- Indefinite adjectives
- *il y a* and *il y aura*
- Phonics: *c* and *ç*, *s*, *qu* and *th*

1 **Read the texts and answer the questions.**

J'adore mon boulot!

Agnès

J'adore chanter et j'ai commencé à l'âge de cinq ans. **Je chante dans quelques restaurants** et à des mariages. Je voudrais devenir célèbre mais il y a beaucoup d'autres chanteurs, alors c'est très dur de devenir connue! **Tous les chanteurs célèbres** ont de la chance et je rêve de donner un concert. Samedi prochain, il y aura un concours de musique et j'espère gagner.

Thomas

Moi, je suis auteur de livres pour enfants. Ce métier, c'est le meilleur du monde car il y a un grand choix de thèmes: les animaux, les héros, les romans historiques… Et il n'y a pas d'entretien! **Chaque livre est différent** – c'est vraiment passionnant! Demain, dans ma bibliothèque locale, il y aura une soirée où je vais parler de mon dernier livre.

Mehdi

Je suis acteur et mon projet est de faire carrière dans le cinéma. Pour être acteur, je dois avoir confiance en moi car il y a beaucoup de compétition. **Il y a toujours d'autres personnes** qui ont plus d'expérience et **plusieurs fois**, on m'a dit que j'étais nul. En mai, je vais aller au festival du film de Cannes pour voir mes deux acteurs préférés.

a According to Agnès, why is it hard to become famous?

b What does she hope will happen next Saturday?

c According to Thomas, why is being a writer the best job in the world? (Give **two** details.)

d What is he going to do tomorrow evening?

e According to Mehdi, which quality is important for an actor?

f Why is he going to the Cannes film festival in May?

2 **Find *six* phrases containing *il y a* or *il y aura* in activity 1 and translate them into English.**

Les verbes

Il y a* and *il y aura

Il y a means 'there is' or 'there are'.

Il y a *un concert ce soir.* **There is** a concert this evening.

Il y a *beaucoup de concerts.* **There are** lots of concerts.

Il y aura means 'there will be'.

Il y aura *un concert ce soir.*
There will be a concert this evening.

Il y aura *beaucoup de concerts.*
There will be lots of concerts.

Grammaire

Indefinite adjectives

Indefinite adjectives are words like 'other' and 'all' that refer to people or things in a general way. They go before a noun. In French they have to agree with the noun, just like any other adjective.

J'aime les ***autres*** *acteurs.* I like the **other** actors.

J'écris un livre ***chaque*** *année.* I write a book **every** year.

Elle va à ***tous*** *les concerts ici.* She goes to **all** the concerts here.

Singular		Plural		English
Masculine	**Feminine**	**Masculine**	**Feminine**	
autre	*autre*	*autres*	*autres*	other
chaque	*chaque*	–	–	every, each
tout	*toute*	*tous*	*toutes*	all, every
–	–	*plusieurs*	*plusieurs*	several, many
–	–	*quelques*	*quelques*	some, a few

3 **Translate the *five* bold phrases in activity 1 into English.**

4 **Listen (1–5) and answer the questions.**

1 Where did Jonathan listen to Agnès for the first time?
2 Where does Agnès get her inspiration from?
3 Where has she already found success?
4 What happens every Saturday?
5 Why is that good, in his opinion?

5 **Listen (1–4) and write down the sentences you hear.**

6 **In pairs, look at the photo and take turns to ask and answer the questions. Look at the ideas underneath to help you.**

- Parle-moi de la photo.
- Que penses-tu du métier d'influenceur / d'influenceuse?
- Tu voudrais faire quel métier? Pourquoi?

7 **Write *five* sentences to describe the photo.**

Example: Je vois ...
Il est ...
Il a ...
Dans la photo...

Phonétique

c and ç

soft *c*: *ç*, *c + e*, *c + i*
hard *c* : *c + a*, *c + o*, *c + u*

***ç**a*	***c**'est*	
***c**arrière*	***c**onnue*	***c**oncert*

s, qu and th

*mai**s**on*	*plu**s**ieurs*	*cui**s**ine*
***qu**el**qu**es*	*musi**qu**e*	*cha**qu**e*
***th**ème*	*biblio**th**èque*	

3.2H Mon stage en entreprise

OBJECTIVES
- Work experience
- Adverbs of quantity
- *être en train de* and *venir de* + infinitive

1 **Read the blog post and write down the order in which the statements (a–h) are mentioned in the text.**

Rapport de stage

ACCUEIL | À PROPOS | BLOG | NOUVEAU | CONTACT

Salut! Moi, c'est Luc et je viens de faire mon stage en entreprise au Palais-Bourbon – c'est le bâtiment du parlement à Paris. J'ai trop de chance car je veux faire carrière dans la politique. Voici le journal de ma semaine.

Lundi: Aujourd'hui, c'est le jour des visites et le Palais-Bourbon est ouvert aux touristes. Je suis à la réception et je suis en train de donner des informations pour la visite. Il y a beaucoup de touristes britanniques, alors je peux pratiquer mon anglais.

Mardi: Aujourd'hui, il y a une réunion à l'assemblée nationale et j'ai la possibilité d'écouter les discussions entre les députés. Ils sont en train de parler de l'avenir des petites fermes à la campagne. On a vendu certains champs pour construire des maisons.

Mercredi: Ici, au parlement, on vote des lois. Beaucoup de députés sont donc avocats. Aujourd'hui, je suis avec un député qui est aussi avocat et il vient de m'expliquer son rôle au parlement. C'est vraiment intéressant.

Jeudi: Je passe ma journée avec les secrétaires qui travaillent au Palais-Bourbon. Ils répondent au téléphone et envoient des e-mails. Maintenant, je suis en train de photocopier des documents car ils en ont besoin pour leur prochaine réunion.

Vendredi: C'est ma dernière journée ici et quelle journée! Je viens de voir le président et le Premier ministre! Aujourd'hui, ils viennent voir les députés pour parler des grèves récentes en France. C'est vraiment un grand problème.

J'ai passé une excellente semaine ici au Palais-Bourbon. Les députés ont beaucoup de responsabilités et peu de temps libre. Mais j'aime ça car je suis très travailleur! Je veux travailler au gouvernement à l'avenir.

un journal	diary
l'Assemblée nationale	French National assembly
un député	member of parliament (MP)

a The MPs have a lot of responsibility.
b I spend my day with a lawyer.
c I've just done my work experience in the Palais-Bourbon.
d I've just seen the president and the prime minister!
e Tourists can visit the Palais-Bourbon today.
f I'm doing the photocopying.
g They're discussing the fate of small farms.
h Strikes are a big problem at the moment.

2 **Read the blog post again and answer the questions.**

a Why was it fortunate that Luc did his work experience at the Palais-Bourbon?
b On Monday, how was he able to practise his English?
c Why is the National Assembly in conversation with small farms at present?
d On Thursday, why is Luc doing photocopying?
e What will the president and the prime minister talk to MPs about on Friday?
f At the end of the text, what does Luc say about the MPs? (Give **two** details.)

3 Find the *six* examples of *venir de* and *être en train de* in activity 1 and translate them into English.

4 Copy and complete the sentences with the correct form of the verb in brackets.

a Mon frère ___ en train de finir ses devoirs. (*être*)
b Je ___ de finir mon stage en entreprise. (*venir*)
c Elles ___ en train d'envoyer des e-mails. (*être*)
d Il ___ de commencer sa carrière. (*venir*)
e Je ___ en train d'écouter mon professeur. (*être*)
f Nous ___ de faire les courses. (*venir*)

5 Listen (1–5). Choose the correct option to complete each sentence.

1 At the bank, **lots of people want / few people want / no one wants** to get money.
2 In construction, there is **too much / too little / the right amount of** work.
3 There are **lots of / not enough / too many** employees at Isa's workplace.
4 Karim has **more work than before / less work than before / a job in a post office**.
5 According to the survey, more students in **France / England** do work experience.

6 Listen (1–5) and write down the sentences you hear.

7 Write a short blog post to say what you are doing right now in your work experience. Use *être en train de*.

8 In pairs, take turns to read your blog post aloud. Use *venir de* in place of *être en train de*, to answer this question.

Que viens-tu de faire pour ton stage en entreprise?

Culture

The Palais-Bourbon is the meeting place for the National Assembly, the French equivalent of the House of Commons. There, the *députés* (members of parliament), debate, amend and pass laws. Each member of parliament is elected by the French population every five years.

Les verbes

***être en train de* + infinitive, *venir de* + infinitive**

être en train de means 'to be in the middle of' doing something, or doing something right now.

venir de means 'to have just' done something.

Both are followed by another verb in the infinitive:

Je ***suis en train de*** *travailler.*
I am in the middle of working.

Il ***est en train de*** *jouer au foot.*
He is playing football (right now).

Je ***viens de*** *finir mes devoirs.*
I have just finished my homework.

Il ***vient de*** *manger.* He has just eaten.

Grammaire

Adverbs of quantity

These adverbs of quantity are followed by *de* (or *d'* before a vowel or silent *h*):

beaucoup ***de / d'***	a lot of / many
plus ***de / d'***	more (of)
trop ***de / d'***	too much / too many (of)
moins ***de / d'***	less (of)
peu ***de / d'***	little / few (of)

Je fais un stage	à	Londres / Birmingham. la réception / l'accueil.
	chez	Microsoft / mon oncle. un ami de mon père.
Je travaille	dans	une école / un refuge. une entreprise / une usine. un magasin. un restaurant / un hôtel.
	avec	des enfants / animaux.
Je m'occupe d'		enfants / animaux.
En ce moment, je suis en train de		faire des photocopies. prendre des notes. répondre aux e-mails. recevoir les clients. nourrir les animaux. aider / jouer avec les enfants.

Culture

Les sites sacrés dans le monde francophone

1 Read the article and answer the questions.

a Where is Moulay Idriss Zerhoun? Give **two** details.
b In which season do Muslims do this pilgrimage?
c What is this pilgrimage commonly known as? Why?
d Why do people sometimes come back several times?
e What does *Baraka* mean in English? Give **two** details.
f What does Abdel say about his relationship with Allah (God in Islam) after his pilgrimage?

2 Translate the bold phrases in the article into English.

Culture

The *Hajj* is a pilgrimage to Mecca which all Muslims are expected to make at least once during their lifetime if they can afford to. It is one of the Five Pillars of Islam. Mecca is a city situated in Saudi Arabia.

3 In pairs, discuss these questions in English.

- Do you know someone who has taken part in a pilgrimage?
- Would you like to take part in a pilgrimage?
- Can you think of any sacred sites in your country?

Le pèlerinage pour tous

Le Maroc est un pays francophone d'Afrique du Nord. **La population est surtout musulmane.** La ville de Moulay Idriss Zerhoun, située à côté de Fès, est un des sites sacrés du Maroc. Chaque été, **des milliers de musulmans font un pèlerinage** dans cette ville pour voir le tombeau d'Idriss Ier, qui a créé la première dynastie islamique du Maroc.

On l'appelle « le pèlerinage des pauvres » car ce sont souvent **les personnes qui n'ont pas assez d'argent pour faire un pèlerinage à la Mecque** qui viennent ici. Certaines personnes y viennent six fois car elles croient que six pèlerinages à Moulay Idriss Zerhoun vaut la même chose qu'un Hajj (un pèlerinage) à la Mecque.

Pendant ce pèlerinage, **les musulmans peuvent toucher le tombeau d'Idriss Ier** et demander la *Baraka*, qui veut dire la chance et la bénédiction en français.

Abdel raconte: « Pour moi, c'est un voyage spirituel que j'ai déjà fait plusieurs fois dans ma vie. **Je rencontre d'autres personnes et on partage nos histoires**. Je me sens plus proche d'Allah après mon pèlerinage ici. »

sacré	sacred
le pèlerinage	pilgrimage
le tombeau	tomb
la dynastie islamique	Muslim dynasty
la Mecque	Mecca
la bénédiction	blessing

4 Read Aubane's blog post about her pilgrimage to Lourdes, in the French Pyrenees. Did she find the various aspects of her trip (a–e) a positive (P) or negative (N) experience?

Accueil | À propos | Blog | Nouveau | J'aime | 124

Aubane

Moi, c'est Aubane. Je suis française et catholique. Je viens de faire un pèlerinage de quelques jours dans la ville de Lourdes, en France.

J'ai adoré l'ambiance et j'ai parlé avec beaucoup de personnes très intéressantes. Chaque année, des millions de personnes visitent Lourdes. Beaucoup sont handicapées ou très malades. Les pèlerins viennent à Lourdes pour prier, allumer une bougie, aller à la messe et visiter la grotte de Massabielle où il y a la statue de la Vierge Marie.

Moi, j'ai commencé à faire la queue pour toucher la grotte mais il y avait trop de monde, alors je n'ai pas voulu attendre. La messe était très émouvante. Les magasins de Lourdes sont sympas et il y a beaucoup de souvenirs religieux, ce que j'ai apprécié. Par contre, je n'ai pas très bien mangé car la nourriture proposée dans les restaurants était très chère.

un pèlerin	a pilgrim	*émouvant(e)*	moving, emotional
une bougie	a candle	*la grotte*	grotto, cave
la messe	mass (Catholic church service)	*faire la queue*	to queue up

a the people she spoke with
b visiting the grotto
c the mass
d the shops
e the restaurants

Culture

Lourdes, a town in south-western France, is one of the most important Catholic pilgrimage destinations. It is believed that the Virgin Marie appeared to the peasant girl Bernadette Soubirous and others, on several occasions, in the Grotto of Massabielle in Lourdes. Lourdes is also famous for its miraculous healings: many people claim to have been cured by the water that flows in the grotto.

5 Research another pilgrimage site in a francophone country, such as a–d below. Compile some facts:

- some information about the country
- which religion(s) this pilgrimage is for
- a testimony from a pilgrim.

a Les sites sacrés juifs au Maroc

La grotte d'Élie au mont Carmel

b Les sites sacrés musulmans en Algérie

La grande mosquée d'Alger

c Les sites sacrés bouddhistes au Vietnam

La pagode Buu Long à Hô Chi Minh-Ville

d Les sites sacrés catholiques en France

L'abbaye du Mont-Saint-Michel

Grammar practice

The present tense

1 Conjugate the verbs in the present tense.

Je **1** ___ (*s'appeler*) Morgane et j'**2** ___ (*avoir*) 14 ans. J'**3** ___ (*aimer*) jouer au foot et faire du vélo avec mes amis. Le vendredi soir, nous **4** ___ (*sortir*) souvent et nous **5** ___ (*manger*) au restaurant.

Ma sœur **6** ___ (*finir*) toujours ses devoirs avant moi. Mes parents **7** ___ (*penser*) que j'**8** ___ (*utiliser*) trop mon portable. Le soir, après le dîner, ma mère **9** ___ (*prendre*) mon portable, alors mes amis et moi ne **10** ___ (*parler*) pas sur les réseaux sociaux le soir.

2 Copy and complete the sentences with the present tense of the verb in brackets.

a Je ___ travailleur. (*être*)
b Elle ___ quinze ans. (*avoir*)
c Nous ___ en ville. (*aller*)
d Je n'___ pas de sœur. (*avoir*)
e Je ___ attention à ma santé. (*faire*)
f Elle ___ actrice. (*être*)
g Ce soir, ils ___ dans un centre sportif. (*aller*)
h Au collège, nous ___ de l'anglais. (*faire*)

Adjectives

3 Copy the sentences, adding the adjectives in brackets in the correct position, with agreement if needed. Then translate the sentences into English.

a J'ai un chien. (*grand*, *noir*)
b Elle aime les films. (*vieux*, *historique*)
c Ma prof s'appelle madame Howard. (*préféré*)
d Il a un frère. (*petit*, *travailleur*)
e Mon père a trois voitures. (*bleu*)
f Je mange toujours des repas. (*équilibré*)

Grammaire

Most adjectives **follow** the noun they describe, but a few (such as those describing appearance, age, goodness and size) go **before** the noun.

Remember to make the adjective agree with the noun.

The future tense

4 Conjugate the verbs in the future tense.

L'année prochaine, je **1** ___ (*commencer*) dans une nouvelle école au Québec. Ma famille et moi **2** ___ (*habiter*) dans une nouvelle maison à côté de mon collège. Ma sœur **3** ___ (*aimer*) aller à l'école à pied mais moi, je **4** ___ (*préférer*) y aller à vélo. Cet été, on **5** ___ (*rester*) à la maison, car mon frère **6** ___ (*travailler*) dans un café près de chez nous. Ma mère, elle **7** ___ (*chercher*) un nouveau travail à Montréal: elle **8** ___ (*essayer*) d'être cheffe dans un restaurant.

Les verbes

The future tense of regular verbs is formed from the infinitive + endings (which are similar to the present tense of *avoir*).

Comparative adjectives

5 Rewrite the sentences in the correct order. Then translate the sentences into English.

a aussi | que | Le sport | difficile | le travail | est | .

b est | Il | toi | amusant | que | plus | .

c est | meilleure | que | Ma copine | en français | moi | .

d M. Marin | moins | M. Colas | que | strict | est | .

e pire | le foot | Le vélo | que | est | .

6 Write *five* sentences of your own to compare your school subjects.
Example: L'anglais est plus intéressant que l'espagnol.

The near future tense

7 Conjugate the verbs in the near future tense, to make the sentences match the English translation.

a Je ___ voir mes cousins. (*I am going to see my cousins.*)
b Elle ___ étudier les maths. (*She is going to study maths.*)
c ___ -tu faire plus d'exercice? (*Are you going to do more exercise?*)
d Nous ___ ___ ce soir. (*We are going to go out tonight.*)
e Je ___ ___ moins de viande. (*I am going to eat less meat.*)
f Ils ___ ___ en France. (*They are going to work in France.*)

Plural nouns

8 Write the plural form of the nouns.

a un lieu → des ___
b un bras → des ___
c une leçon → des ___
d un château → des ___
e un cheveu → des ___
f un choix → des ___

Present tense and future tense

9 Copy and complete the sentences, putting the verbs in brackets into the present tense or future tense so that they make sense.

a Aujourd'hui, je ___ (*aller*) à l'école mais demain, je ___ (*rester*) à la maison.
b Ce soir, j'___ (*écouter*) de la musique mais maintenant, je ___ (*lire*) un livre.
c En ce moment, mes amis et moi ___ (*faire*) nos devoirs et après, nous ___ (*regarder*) la télé.
d L'année prochaine, mes parents ___ (*acheter*) une nouvelle voiture mais moi, maintenant, je ___ (*vendre*) mon vélo.

Attention

Use the adverbs of time to help you decide which tense to use.

Grammar practice

avant de + infinitive

10 Rewrite the sentences in the correct order.

a mangerai | avant de | des fruits | partir | Je | .

b de la musique | Elle | avant de | écoutera | manger | .

c un film | regarderont | ils | faire du shopping, | Avant de | .

d Avant de | à mon frère | parlerai | je | sortir, | .

e des enfants | Elle | avoir | se mariera | avant d' | .

The perfect tense

11 Translate into French.

a I ate
b she played
c we sold
d they finished
e you changed
f I succeeded
g he lost
h we chose
i she waited

12 Correct the perfect tense error in each sentence and write why it is wrong.

a Je joué au foot hier. (*I played football yesterday.*)
b Elle n'ai pas fini ses devoirs. (*She hasn't finished her homework.*)
c Tu as mange beaucoup de poisson. (*You ate a lot of fish.*)
d J'ai vendé ma voiture. (*I sold my car.*)
e Ils a attendu le train. (*They waited for the train.*)
f Il a travailler dans un restaurant. (*He worked in a restaurant.*)

Indirect object pronouns (singular)

13 Rewrite the sentences, replacing the words in brackets with the correct indirect object pronoun in the correct position: *me*, *te*, *lui*, *vous*.

Example: a Je lui téléphone.

a Je téléphone (**à ma sœur**).
b Il donne le cadeau (**à moi**).
c Je parle (**à toi**).
d J'ai dit (**à mon copain**) qu'il est sympa.
e Nous avons fait un gâteau (**pour vous**).
f J'ai répondu (**à ma mère**).

Impersonal verbs and expressions

14 Copy and complete the sentences, using the impersonal phrase indicated in brackets.

a ___ travailler dur à l'école. (*we must*)
b ___ boire beaucoup d'eau. (*it is better to*)
c ___ faire du sport régulièrement. (*it is worth*)
d Au collège, ___ professeurs. (*we are missing*)
e ___ faire ses devoirs rapidement. (*it is difficult to*)
f ___ arriver en retard au travail. (*it is forbidden to*)

Present participles

15 Copy and combine the pairs of sentences, using a present participle.

Example: Il regarde le match. Il retrouve ses copains. → En regardant le match, il retrouve ses copains.

a Il joue au foot. Il se casse la jambe.
b J'écoute de la musique. Je fais mes devoirs.
c Je suis à l'heure. Je respecte les autres.
d Je bois plus d'eau. Je peux mieux me concentrer.
e J'ai plus de temps. Je peux finir l'exercice.
f On regarde la télé. On parle des émissions.

Les verbes

To form a present participle, remove the *-ons* ending from the *nous* form of the present tense, and add *-ant*.

Three common irregular present participles:

en étant	(while / by) being
en ayant	(while / by) having
en faisant	(while / by) doing

Negative constructions

16 Rewrite the sentences in the correct order. Then translate them into English.

a pas | ne | Je | mange | de poisson | .

b jamais | Mes frères | parlent | ne | à ma sœur | .

c rien | ce soir | ne | Je | fais | .

d n'a | Elle | mangé | pas | de fruits | .

e aucune | chanson | n'aime | Il | .

f Je | personne | connais | ne | au collège | .

Grammaire

Remember that the **negative** sandwiches the verb:

*Je **ne** bois **pas** beaucoup d'eau.*

The conditional

17 Copy and complete the sentences, adding the correct ending to form the verb in the conditional.

a J'adorer___ me marier.

b Nathalie voudr___ manger au restaurant.

c Laura et moi aimer___ aller en ville.

d Tu préférer___ rester chez toi pendant les vacances?

e Mes enfants étudier___ des langues.

f On achèter___ une grande maison.

Les verbes

The conditional is made up of two parts: the stem (for *-er* verbs, it's the same as the infinitive) and an ending (the same as the imperfect tense endings).

Superlative adjectives

18 Choose the correct option to complete each superlative sentence.

a Elle est **le** / **la** / **les** moins sympa.

b Martine et Rosette sont **le** / **la** / **les** plus jolies.

c Ce sont **le** / **la** / **les** moins chers.

d Jean-Paul est **le** / **la** / **les** plus travailleur.

e Cette maison est **le** / **la** / **les** plus grande.

f Ce travail est **le** / **la** / **les** mieux.

être en train de, *venir de* + infinitive

19 Choose the correct option to complete each sentence. Then translate the sentences into English.

a Je **suis en train de** / **viens de** finir mes devoirs. Ils étaient difficiles.

b Il **est en train de** / **vient de** jouer au football. Il s'amuse bien.

c Je **suis en train de** / **viens d'**acheter un nouvel uniforme. Il était très cher.

d Je **suis en train de** / **viens de** manger. C'était bon.

e Mes parents **sont en train de** / **viennent de** préparer le repas. Je vais les aider.

Attention

Je suis en train de…	I am in the middle of (doing something)
Je viens de…	I have just (done something)

Check the tense of the opinion phrase that follows each sentence to help you decide which option is correct.

Higher Vocabulary

Words that are highlighted in grey in this list are words that may be useful, but you won't need to know them for the exam.

Introductory vocabulary

l' ***acteur/actrice (m./f.)*** actor, actress
actif/active active
adorer to love
l' ***allemand (n.) (m.)*** German (language)
aller to go
l' ***ami(e) (m./f.)*** friend
amusant(e) amusing, fun, funny
l' ***anglais (n.) (m.)*** English (language)
anglais(e) (adj.) English
s' ***appeler*** to be called
apporter to bring
après after
l' ***après-midi (m.)*** afternoon
assez quite, enough
au chômage unemployed
autre chose anything else
avoir to have
beaucoup (de) a lot (of)
le ***beau-père*** stepfather, father-in-law
la ***belle-mère*** stepmother, mother-in-law
la ***bibliothèque*** library
bien good, well
blanc (adj.) white
boire to drink
bon(ne) good
bonjour good morning, afternoon
brun(e) brown
ça it, that
le ***café*** coffee, coffee shop
car because
célèbre famous
cependant however
la ***chanson*** song
le/la ***chanteur/chanteuse*** singer
les ***cheveux (m. pl.)*** hair
le ***chômage*** unemployment
cinq five
le ***collège*** (secondary) school
comme such as, like
le ***concert*** concert
la ***construction*** construction
content(e) happy
le ***cours*** lesson
court(e) short
le/la ***cousin(e)*** cousin
dernier/dernière last
détester to hate
deux two
devenir to become
difficile difficult
dix ten
du/de la/des/de l' some
l' ***eau (m.)*** water
l' ***école (f.)*** school
écrire to write
l' ***éducation (f.)*** education
en général in general
en plus in addition
en premier first of all, firstly
l' ***enfant (m.)*** child
ennuyeux/ennuyeuse boring
ensemble together
ensuite then
équilibré(e) balanced
l' ***équipe (f.)*** team
l' ***espagnol (n.) (m.)*** Spanish (language)
espagnol(e) (adj.) Spanish
espérer to hope
être to be
facile easy
le/la ***facteur/factrice*** postman/postwoman
faire to do, make
la ***famille*** family
la ***femme*** woman, wife
la ***fille*** girl, daughter
le ***film*** film
le ***fils*** son
le ***foot(ball)*** football
le ***français (n.)*** French (language)
français(e) (adj.) French
la ***France*** France
le ***frère*** brother
les ***frites (f. pl.)*** chips
le ***fromage*** cheese
le ***fruit*** fruit
gagner to earn, win
le ***gâteau*** cake
gauche left
généralement generally
génial(e) great
la ***géographie*** geography
la ***glace*** ice, ice cream
le ***gouvernement*** government
la ***grand-mère*** grandmother
le ***grand-père*** grandfather
habiter to live
l' ***heure (f.)*** hour, time, o'clock
l' ***histoire (f.)*** history, story
important(e) important
l' ***indépendance (f.)*** independence
l' ***informatique (m.)*** IT, computer science
intéressant(e) interesting
jamais never
je voudrais (vouloir) I would like
jeune young
jouer to play
juillet July
le ***lait*** milk
le/la/l'/les the
la ***leçon*** lesson
le ***légume*** vegetable
la ***lettre*** letter
leur(s) (to) them, their
long(ue) long
la ***maison*** house
manger to eat
(le) ***mardi*** Tuesday
le ***mari*** husband
les ***maths (f. pl.)*** maths
le ***matin*** morning
méchant(e) naughty, nasty
la ***mère*** mother
le ***métier*** job
la ***mode*** fashion
moi me
la ***musique*** music
la ***natation*** swimming
nul(le) rubbish
l' ***oncle (m.)*** uncle
l' ***ordinateur (m.)*** computer
où where
le ***pain*** bread
par contre on the other hand
parce que because
parfois sometimes
passer to spend, to pass
le ***père*** father
la ***personne*** person
le ***petit-déjeuner*** breakfast
la ***photo*** photo
la ***piscine*** swimming pool
plusieurs several
le ***poisson*** fish
le/la ***policier/policière*** policeman/policewoman
la ***politique*** politics
porter to wear
pouvoir to be able to, can
préféré(e) favourite
le ***professeur, prof*** teacher
puis then
la ***récré(ation)*** breaktime
rentrer to go back
le ***restaurant*** restaurant
le ***rêve*** dream
le ***riz*** rice
la ***rue*** street
sain(e) healthy
le ***salaire*** salary
(le) ***samedi*** Saturday
les ***sciences (f. pl.)*** sciences
la ***sécurité*** security
la ***semaine*** week
le/la ***serveur/serveuse*** waiter/waitress
la ***sœur*** sister
sourire to smile
souvent often
le ***sport*** sport
sportif/sportive sporty
strict(e) strict
le ***studio*** studio
le ***succès*** success
la ***Suisse*** Switzerland
super super
sûr(e) safe, sure, secure
sympa nice
la ***technologie*** DT
le ***temps*** time, weather
le ***thé*** tea
le ***théâtre*** drama
toujours always
tous les jours every day
travailler to work
trop de too much, many (of)
trouver to find
le ***tee-shirt*** T-shirt
un peu a little

un(e) a
le *vélo* bike
vers towards
la *viande* meat
le *Vietnam* Vietnam
le *village* village
la *ville* town
le *vin* wine
voici here is
vouloir to want
voyager to travel
vraiment really

1.1F Ma personnalité

acheter to buy
alors so, therefore
arriver to arrive
attendre to wait
au revoir goodbye
aussi also
bavard(e) chatty
bonne chance good luck
calme (adj.) calm, quiet
la *catastrophe* catastrophe
la *clé* key
connaître to know (person, place)
le *copain* friend, boyfriend
la *copine* friend, girlfriend
de plus besides, moreover
descendre to go down, descend, get off
devoir to have to
drôle funny
embêtant(e) annoying
en fait in fact, in reality
en retard late
entendre to hear
fier/fière proud
fort(e) strong
gentil(le) kind
inquiétant(e) worrying
intelligent(e) intelligent
l' *Internet (m.)* internet
le *judo* judo
maintenant now
mais but
même same
la *mission* mission
neuf/neuve new
non no
la *note* grade, result
oui yes
paresseux/paresseuse lazy
partir to leave
passionnant(e) exciting
penser to think
perdre to lose
la *personnalité* personality
personne nobody
la *qualité* quality
quand when
que that
quel(le) which
qui who, which
répondre to answer
salut hi, hello
sérieux/sérieuse serious
son/sa/ses his, her
surtout especially
le *téléphone* phone
timide timid, shy
toi you
ton/ta/tes your
le *train* train
travailleur/travailleuse hard-working
triste sad
trop too much, too many
vendre to sell
vite quick, fast, quickly
la *voiture* car
vrai true, real

1.1H Mon futur moi

à l'avenir in the future
adopter to adopt
aider to help
apprécier to enjoy, appreciate, like
l' *argent (m.)* money
l'/les *association(s) (f.)* associations
aucun(e) no, not one
les *autres (m./f. pl.)* others
aujourd'hui today
l' *avocat(e) (m./f.)* lawyer
le *Canada* Canada
cela it, this, that
célibataire single
certainement certainly
changer to change
cher/chère expensive
chercher to research, to look for
la *compétence* skill
la *connaissance* knowledge
la *course* race
coûter to cost
la *culture* culture
demain tomorrow
développer to develop
donner to give
dur(e) hard
l' *employeur/employeuse (m./f.)* employer
entrer to enter
l' *Espagne (f.)* Spain
essayer to try
excellent(e) excellent
faire du jardinage to garden
le *futur (n.)* future
futur(e) (adj.) future
garder to keep
l' *hôpital (m.)* hospital
idéal(e) ideal
l' *importance (f.)* importance
l' *instrument (m.)* instrument
interculturel(le) intercultural
le *mariage* marriage
se *marier* to marry
la *mer* sea
mieux better
le *monde* people, world
la *Normandie* Normandy
notre/nos our
le *PACS* civil partnership
le *parc* park
le/la *partenaire* partner
partout everywhere
passer du temps to spend time
le *passe-temps* hobby, past time
le *pays* country
le *pilote* pilot
plus more
pourquoi why
préférer to prefer
près (de) near, next to
probablement probably
le *problème* problem
la *question* question
quitter to leave
rencontrer to meet
rester to stay
le *souci* worry
souhaiter to wish
traditionnel(le) traditional
le *type* type
la *vie* life

1.2F Les familles de nos jours

à at, to
adopté(e) adopted
aussi … que as … as
canadien(ne) Canadian
chez moi at my place, at mine
choisir to choose
la *chose* thing
le *cinéma* cinema
comprendre to understand
la *Côte d'Ivoire* Ivory Coast
les *courses (f. pl.)* (grocery) shopping
le *déjeuner* lunch
le *demi-frère* half-brother
la *demi-soeur* half-sister
les *devoirs (m. pl.)* homework
(le) *dimanche* Sunday
écouter to listen (to)
l' *émission (f.)* program
encore again, still
finir to finish
le *frigo* fridge
grandir to grow (up)
le *jeu* game
le *jeu vidéo* video game
là-bas over there
la *lecture* reading
meilleur(e) que better than
moins … que less than
le *mois* month
né(e) born
Noël Christmas
normalement normally
nous we
le/les *parent(s) (m. pl.)* parent(s)
Paris Paris
pire que worse than
la *plage* beach
plus … que more than
pour for
regarder to look, to watch
remplir to fill up
réunir to gather
réussir to succeed
rire to laugh
le *sac* bag
séparé(e) separated
septembre September
la *télé* television
tous all, every

le *travail* work
les *vacances (f. pl.)* holidays
(le) *vendredi* Friday
vivre to live

1.2H Mes amis, c'est ma vie!

à l'heure on time
appeler to call
arrêter to stop
la *boisson* drink
la *boulangerie* bakery
le *bus* bus
la *confiance* trust, confidence
la *conversation* conversation
cool cool
la *couverture* rug, duvet
croire to believe
la *cuisine* cooking, kitchen
d'abord firstly, first of all
la *décision* decision
le *dîner* dinner
encourager to encourage
entre between
gagner du temps to save time
la *gymnastique* gymnastics
l' *idée (f.)* idea
il faut it is necessary to, must
il vaut la peine de it is worth
il vaut mieux it is worth
la *journée* day
juste fair, just, only
longtemps long time
manquer to miss, lack
mentir to lie
la *montagne* mountain
le *numéro* number
patient(e) patient
le *pique-nique* picnic
la *plupart (de)* most (of)
préparer to prepare
proche close
la *promesse* promise
quoi what
rendez-vous rendez-vous, meeting, appointment
le *retour* return
sensible sensitive
seul(e) alone
le *supermarché* supermarket
tenir to hold
voir to see

2.1F Aïe aïe aïe!

à l'âge de at the age of
l' *accident (m.)* accident
l' *alcool (m.)* alcohol
avoir mal to hurt
avoir peur to be scared
la *bouche* mouth
le *bras* arm
le *château* castle
le *choix* choice
la *cigarette* cigarette
commencer to start
le *corps* body
d'accord okay, agreed
la *dame* lady
le *danger* danger
dangereux / dangereuse dangerous
dire say, tell
le *dos* back
la *drogue* drug
l' *effort (m.)* effort
envoyer to send
examiner to examine
l' *exercice (m.)* exercise
la *façon* way
fatigué(e) tired
fumer to smoke
la *gorge* throat
immédiatement immediately
inquiet / inquiète worried
la *jambe* leg
lever to raise
le *lieu* place
le *lit* bed
le *mal* ache
malade ill
mauvais bad
le *médecin* doctor
le *médicament* medication
l' *oreille (f.)* ear
peut-être maybe
le *pied* foot
se *relaxer* to relax
la *santé* health
savoir to know
la *tête* head
tomber to fall
tuer to kill
l' *urgence (f.)* emergency
vapoter to vape

2.1H Mes projets « bonne santé »

actuellement currently
l' *année (f.)* year
avant de before
certain(e)(s) some, certain
le *chapeau* hat
chaud(e) hot, warm
se *concentrer* to concentrate, focus
le *concours* competition
dépendre de to depend on
en ce moment at the moment
enfin finally
évidemment evidently, obviously
faible weak
la *forêt* forest, wood
gérer to organise
l' *été (m.)* summer
se *lever* to get up
marcher to walk
mener to lead
merci thank you
nager to swim
la *nature* nature
obliger to obligate
parler to speak, chat, talk
participer to participate, contribute, take part
passer les examens to take exams
le *plat* dish
prochain(e) next
la *promenade* walk
le *repas* meal
risquer to risk
se *sentir* to feel
le *soleil* sun
le *traitement* treatment

2.2F Hier j'ai…

l' *anniversaire (m.)* birthday
le *bain* bath
le *cadeau* present
le *chien* dog
demander to ask
… fois … time, times
hier yesterday
(le) *jeudi* Thursday
lui (to) him, (to) her
(le) *lundi* Monday
le *match* match
(le) *mercredi* Wednesday
la *nourriture* food
la *nuit* night
le *portable* mobile phone
le / la *premier / première* first
le *programme* schedule
ressembler to look like
le *surf* surf
te / t' (to) you
le *Tour de France* Tour de France
la *partie (de foot)* (football) match, game
vous you (polite, plural)

2.2H Comment rester en bonne santé?

améliorer to improve
assis(e) sat
bénéficier to benefit
le *bureau* office, desk
ça me rend it makes me
conscient(e) conscious
conseiller to advise
continuer to continue
courir to run
de nos jours nowadays
de saison seasonal
le *débat* debate
dépendant dependent, addicted
également equally
l' *esprit (m.)* spirit
essentiel(le) essential
l' *étude (f.)* study
eux them
l' *exemple (m.)* example
l' *expert(e) (m. / f.)* expert
l' *explication (f.)* explanation
facilement easily
frais / fraîche fresh
la *force* strength
les *gens (m. pl.)* people
grave serious
ici here
interdit forbidden
la *majorité* majority
nécessaire necessary
occidental(e) western
ouvert(e) open
parmi among
plutôt rather, quite

la ***position*** position
possible possible
pratique practice
le ***produit*** product, produce
récent(e) recent
sainement healthily
selon according to
le ***tabac*** tobacco
le ***week-end*** weekend

3.1F Lycée et université?

apprendre to learn
bien sûr of course
le ***bureau*** desk, office
la ***classe*** class, classroom
la ***communication*** communication
l' ***environnement (m.)*** environment
étudier to study
indépendant (e) independent
l' ***information (f.)*** information
intéresser to interest
la ***langue*** language
le ***lycée*** school, sixth form
la ***matière*** subject
la ***médecine*** medicine
nouveau/nouvelle new
l' ***organisation (f.)*** organisation
l' ***organisation caritative (f.)*** charity
organisé(e) organised
la ***participation*** contribution
la ***passion*** passion
progresser to progress
la ***situation*** situation
situer to locate
l' ***université (f.)*** university

3.1H L'école de mes rêves

à mon avis in my opinion
accepter to accept, authorise
aimer to like
la ***cantine*** canteen
le ***chewing-gum*** chewing-gum
le ***cyber intimidation*** cyber bullying
l' ***élève (m.)*** pupil
et demie half past
grand(e) big
le ***gymnase*** gymnasium
interdir to forbid, ban
le/la/les meilleur(e)(s) the best
normal(e) normal
pendant during
le/la/les pire(s) the worst
plein (de) lots (of)
plus tard later
la ***région*** region
le ***règlement*** regulation, rule
retourner to go back
tellement so
la ***salle informatique*** IT room
scolaire school
les ***vêtements (m. pl.)*** clothes

3.2F Mon métier créatif

l' ***animal (m.)*** animal
l' ***auteur/autrice (m./f.)*** author
la ***carrière*** career
chanter to sing
chaque each, every
la ***compétition*** competition
connu(e) famous, known
l' ***Europe (f.)*** Europe
l' ***expérience (f.)*** experience
le ***festival*** festival
l' ***heroine (f.)*** (female) hero
l' ***héros (m.)*** (male) hero
historique historic
l' ***influenceur/influenceuse (m./f.)*** influencer
local(e)(s)/locaux local
mai May
montrer to show
le/la ***musicien(enne)*** musician
le ***quartier*** neighbourhood
quelques some, several
le ***roman*** novel
la ***soirée*** evening
le ***thème*** theme

3.2H Mon stage en entreprise

l' ***Angleterre (f.)*** England
l' ***assemblée (f.)*** assembly
avant before
avoir besoin de to need
la ***banque*** bank
le ***bâtiment*** building
la ***brochure*** brochure
la ***campagne*** countryside
le ***champ*** field
le/la ***collègue*** colleague
construire to build
dehors outside
le ***dépliant*** leaflet
le/la ***député(e)*** deputy, MP
la ***discussion*** discussion
le ***document*** document
l' ***enquête (f.)*** survey
l' ***entreprise (f.)*** company
être en train de to be in the middle of
expliquer to explain
la ***feuille*** piece of paper, leaf
froid(e) cold
la ***grève*** strike
il y a there is
le ***journal*** newspaper, diary
la ***loi*** law
le ***magasin*** shop
le ***ministre*** minister
le ***palais*** palace
le ***parlement*** parliament
la ***possibilité*** possibility
le ***poste*** post office
pratiquer to practice
la ***réception*** reception
la ***responsabilité*** responsibility
retirer to withdraw
la ***réunion*** meeting
le ***rôle*** role
le/la ***secrétaire*** secretary
le ***stage (en entreprise)*** work experience
le ***touriste*** tourist
venir de to have just (done something)
la ***visite*** visit
voter to vote

Culture

à côté de near
l' ***abbaye (f.)*** abbey
l' ***Afrique (f.)*** Africa
Allah Allah
allumer to switch on, to light
l' ***ambiance (f.)*** ambiance
l' ***atmosphere (f.)*** atmosphere
autre other
la ***bénédiction*** blessing
la ***bougie*** candle
catholique Catholic
ce que which
ce/cet/cette/ces this, these
la ***chance*** luck, opportunity
la ***dynastie*** dynasty
l' ***émotion (f.)*** emotion
émouvant(e) moving
la ***grotte*** grotto, cave
le ***Hajj*** Hajj
handicapé(e) handicapped
islamique Islamic
le ***jour*** day
le ***magasin*** shop
le ***Maroc*** Morocco
la ***Mecque*** Mecca
la ***messe*** Mass
le ***million*** million
musulman(e) Muslim
le ***nord*** north
la ***pagode*** pagoda
partager to share
pauvre poor
le/la ***pèlerin(e)*** pilgrim
le ***pèlerinage*** pilgrimage
la ***population*** population
prier to pray
proposer to offer, to propose
la ***queue*** queue
raconter to tell, to relay a story
religieux/religieuse religious
sacré(e) sacred
le ***site*** site
six six
le ***souvenir*** souvenir
spirituel(le) spiritual
la ***statue*** statue
le ***tombeau*** tomb
toucher to touch
très very
venir to come
la ***vierge*** virgin
visiter to visit (place)
vouloir dire to mean
le ***voyage*** journey
y there

French is a language with grammatical genders, so some of the words in this list have a masculine and feminine form, which are used for referring to different people. You will not be marked down in the exam for your preferred ways of referring to yourself and others through the use of pronouns, gendered language and grammatical agreements.

Test and revise: Higher Listening

1 You hear this podcast about a school in Burkina Faso.

Choose the correct answer and write the letter.

1 Issa thinks…

A	his class is very quiet.
B	there are too many students in his class.
C	he can concentrate well in his class.

1 mark

2 Issa says that the school day…

A	includes a long break for lunch.
B	is too short.
C	is longer on Saturdays.

1 mark

3 Last year,…

A	Issa didn't do his homework.
B	there was no homework set.
C	there was homework set.

1 mark

4 In the future, Issa wants to work…

A	as an actor.
B	on a farm.
C	with his cousin.

1 mark

Conseil

This task requires you to understand all the details in the audio extract. For the first question, for example, Issa will mention all three options: noise levels, number of students and concentration. You need to listen to the whole audio extract before choosing an answer.

2 You hear some French people talking about their jobs. What is their opinion on the following aspects?

Write **P** for a **positive** opinion
N for a **negative** opinion
P+N for a **positive** and **negative** opinion.

1 Colleagues
2 Salary
3 Working hours
4 The boss

4 marks

Conseil

Before making your final decision, make sure you listen to the whole statement. Listen out for words such as *mais, cependant* and *par contre*, which can introduce a negative opinion even if the sentence started positively.

3 You hear some French students talking about their health.

Complete the sentences in **English**.

1 I like running with… **1 mark**
2 I swim in a pool near… **1 mark**
3 I have made… at the book club. **1 mark**
4 I play football because… **1 mark**

Conseil

This task requires you to listen for specific details and complete sentences in English. Read the sentences carefully and think about language you might hear. For example, in sentence 4, you will need to listen out for a reason, possibly preceded by *car* or *parce que*.

4 **You hear this conversation between Maria and her mother.**

The conversation is about friendship problems.

Answer the questions in **English**.

1 Why did Maria argue with her best friend Elliot? Give **two** reasons. **2 marks**

2 Why couldn't she talk to him at the end of the day? **1 mark**

3 a When **exactly** will Maria talk to him tomorrow morning? **1 mark**

b What will Maria ask him? **1 mark**

Conseil

Read the questions carefully to ensure you provide the necessary information. In this task, question 1 asks you to give **two** reasons and question 3a asks you to be **exact**.

You don't have to write in full sentences, but always check your answers to be sure they make sense.

5 **You hear this news flash on the radio about a minor accident that took place yesterday.**

Choose the **two** correct statements.

Write the **two** correct letters for each section (1–3).

1

A	The accident happened yesterday.
B	The accident happened around 8 p.m.
C	The car tried to avoid a dog that was crossing the road.
D	The car crashed into a wall.

2

A	The man driving the car was Belgian.
B	The man driving the car hurt his arm.
C	The injury is not serious.
D	The man driving the car didn't go to hospital.

3

A	The woman in the car was elderly.
B	The woman in the car wasn't injured.
C	The woman in the car was the driver.
D	The woman in the car was very scared.

6 marks

6 **You listen to two people talking about why they chose to get married.**

Which **two** reasons does each person give?

Write the correct letters for each person (1–2).

A	The wedding did not cost a lot.
B	It is the best symbol of love.
C	They followed their parents' example.
D	It is essential to be married in order to have children.
E	It is a reason to party.
F	It is important in their religion.

4 marks

Dictation A

You will now hear **five** short sentences.

- Listen carefully and, using your knowledge of French sounds, write down in French exactly what you hear for each sentence.
- You will hear each sentence **three** times: the first time as a full sentence, the second time in short sections and the third time again as a full sentence.
- Use your knowledge of French sounds and grammar to make sure that what you have written makes sense. Check carefully that your spelling is accurate.

10 marks

Dictation B

You will now hear **five** more sentences.

Write down in French exactly what you hear for each sentence.

10 marks

Conseil

For this type of task, you could note which statements you think are correct and incorrect, and put a question mark next to the option(s) you're not sure about, the first time you listen. When you listen the second time, make your final decision. If you're still unsure, it is better to guess than to leave a question unanswered.

Test and revise: Higher Speaking

Role play

You are talking to your French friend.

Your teacher will play the part of your friend and will speak first.

You should address your friend as *tu*.

When you see this – ? – you will have to ask a question.

In order to score full marks, you must include at least one verb in your response to each task.

1 Say what you like to eat and drink. (Give **two** details.)

2 Say what you think about healthy eating and why. (Give **one** opinion and **one** reason.)

3 Say what sport you did last week. (Give **one** detail.)

? 4 Ask your friend a question about sport.

5 Say how you relax. (Give **two** details.)

10 marks

Conseil

Remember that you are allowed to take notes for all tasks in the speaking exam. You can refer to these at any point during the test. Use this to help you!

Conseil

For the role play, the most important thing is to convey the message clearly. Make sure you double-check how many pieces of information you are required to give for each point. Keep your sentences short and accurate.

Reading aloud

When your teacher asks you, read aloud the following text **in French**.

Je m'entends bien avec toute ma famille mais surtout avec mon frère.

On joue à des jeux vidéo ensemble et nous faisons beaucoup de sport.

À l'avenir, il voudrait se marier et avoir quatre enfants parce que pour lui il est essentiel d'avoir une grande famille.

Je passerai du temps avec ses enfants.

You will then be asked four questions **in French** that relate to the topic of **Identity and relationships with others**. Make sure you **answer all four questions as fully as you can**.

15 marks

Conseil

For the reading aloud task, you can obtain a maximum of 5 marks for reading the text aloud. When reading aloud, focus carefully on your pronunciation. Try to remember all the French sounds and sound combinations you have learnt.

For the second part of the task, you can obtain a maximum of 10 marks for your responses to the follow-up questions. These need to be communicated clearly and in as much detail as possible. Try to answer all questions and extend your sentences by giving justified opinions, and using a range of tenses and varied intensifiers and adverbs.

Photo card

- During your preparation time, look at the two photos. You may make as many notes as you wish on an Additional Answer Sheet and use these notes during the task.
- Your teacher will ask you to talk about the content of these photos. The recommended time is approximately **one and a half minutes**. You must **say at least one thing about each photo**.
- After you have spoken about the content of the photos, your teacher will then ask you questions related to **any** of the topics within the theme of **People and lifestyle**.

25 marks

Conseil

For the photo card task, you can obtain a maximum of 5 marks for describing the two pictures. You must say at least one thing about each photo. Try to give as much information as possible and use accurate language.

For the follow-up conversation, you can obtain a maximum of 20 marks. Try to develop your answers by giving and justifying opinions using *parce que* or *car,* for example. Aim to use a variety of tenses, adjectives, adverbs, pronouns and intensifiers and to convey your message clearly.

Photo 1

Photo 2

Theme 1 Test and revise: Higher Reading

1 You read a blog post from a French influencer, Ange, who is talking about his family.

Complete these sentences.

Write the letter for the correct option.

Moi, je viens d'une famille nombreuse. Depuis mes dix-huit ans, je n'habite plus avec mes parents. Par contre, mes deux sœurs et mon frère habitent encore chez eux. On a tous grandi ensemble et on s'entend plutôt bien. Cependant, je me dispute parfois avec mon frère.

Ce que je préfère dans ma famille, c'est quand on est tous ensemble pour Noël. L'année dernière, c'était chez mon oncle. On a bien ri et on a appris deux bonnes nouvelles. Ma cousine va avoir un deuxième enfant et une de mes tantes va se marier cet été. C'est trop bien, on va pouvoir faire la fête, ce que j'adore.

1 Ange has not lived with his parents…

A	for 18 years.
B	since he was 18.
C	since his sisters turned 18.

1 mark

2 Ange and his siblings…

A	don't get on at all.
B	never celebrate Christmas together.
C	have grown up together.

1 mark

3 Ange's cousin…

A	is going to have a child.
B	has two children.
C	has just had a child.

1 mark

4 Ange is excited about the summer because…

A	he is going to get married.
B	he will be able to party.
C	he is going to become a father.

1 mark

Conseil

In this task, you need to read the text in detail as the answers are not immediately obvious. For example, in question 1, the options tell you that the key figure is 18, but you need to look at the whole sentence and understand *depuis mes dix-huit ans* to choose the correct answer.

2 You read an article about a singer, Benji. What does the article say about these events?

Write **P** for something that happened **in the past**
N for something that is happening **now**
F for something that will happen **in the future**.

Dans quelques semaines, Benji va donner son premier concert devant des milliers de personnes. À dix-huit ans, il a fait partie d'une émission de télévision française; il n'a pas gagné le concours mais il a adoré participer. Il est maintenant célèbre, surtout parmi les jeunes qui adorent sa musique. Il chante des chansons qui parlent d'amour mais bientôt, il va commencer à chanter sur des thèmes différents. Il adore chanter car c'est le métier de ses rêves.

a His first concert **1 mark**
b Taking part in a TV programme **1 mark**
c Young people loving his music **1 mark**
d Singing about love **1 mark**
e Singing about different themes **1 mark**

Conseil

Use your knowledge of grammar, especially verbs and tenses, to choose the correct answer. Adverbs of time will help you too. For instance, *bientôt* means 'soon' and is therefore referring to the future.

3 **You read this online forum. People are talking about their schools. Who mentions the following aspects (a–e)?**

Write **A** for **Amar**
B for **Bénédicte**
C for **Carine**.

Amar

Je suis assez faible en géographie mais j'aime bien cette matière car le prof m'aide beaucoup. Mon école est grande et je l'aime bien car les bâtiments sont modernes. Je comprends pourquoi il est essentiel de porter un uniforme mais il n'est pas à la mode et l'été on a vraiment trop chaud.

Bénédicte

J'adore aller au collège, même si je n'ai pas toujours de bonnes notes. Moi, je suis forte en langues. Mon uniforme est pratique. Au déjeuner, on a une récréation et j'aime parler et passer du temps avec mes amies car cette année elles ne sont pas dans la même classe que moi, ce qui est un peu dommage.

Carine

Je n'aime pas trop ma nouvelle école. Les salles de classe sont petites et je ne me suis pas encore faite de nouveaux amis, alors je passe les récréations toute seule. Cependant, il n'y a pas trop de devoirs, ce que j'apprécie, et les profs sont plutôt jeunes, travailleurs et intéressants. Je ne m'inquiète pas pour mes notes car elles sont bonnes.

a Enjoying time with friends

b Disliking the uniform

c Having good grades

d Liking the school buildings

e Having hard-working teachers

5 marks

Conseil

In this task, ensure that you check all three texts when answering each question. For example, friends are mentioned in both Bénédicte's and Carine's texts, so you need to read the relevant sentences in detail before choosing an answer.

4 **Translate these sentences into English.**

a En allant en ville, je rencontre ma sœur.

b Cette année, mon frère n'apprend aucune l angue au collège.

c Quand je serai adulte, je travaillerai comme avocat.

d Hier, elle a essayé la natation et ça l'a fatiguée.

e Mes parents vont se disputer à cause de mes notes.

10 marks

5 **Translate these sentences into English.**

a Il vaut mieux arriver à l'heure au collège.

b Avant de finir ses études, il commencera son travail.

c Ils ne s'entendent jamais avec ces deux cousins qui sont embêtants.

d Mes parents m'ont acheté de jolis vêtements pour le mariage de mon oncle.

e Je ne vais plus manger de viande car je suis devenue végétarienne.

10 marks

Conseil

When translating into English, you must give the meaning of the whole sentence without necessarily translating word for word. Identify the verb and tense the sentence is in before you start. When you have finished, make sure you haven't forgotten to translate any words, and proofread your English translation to check for accuracy. If there is a word that you don't know at all, it is better to include a similar word (e.g. a noun, adjective or adverb) than to leave a gap in your translation

Test and revise: Higher Writing

1 Translate the following sentences into French.

a I must do a lot of sport to stay healthy.

b There isn't enough homework in Year 10.

c Next year, my friend will work harder at school.

d My sister and I saw the best film last Sunday.

e Before going out, I am going to prepare lunch.

10 marks

Conseil

For this task, you need to convey your message clearly. Check the tense required and conjugate your verbs correctly. If you don't know the exact word, use a synonym (a word with a similar meaning). Check you have translated all the words.

Either question 2.1 or question 2.2

2.1 You are emailing your Belgian friend about yourself, your family and friends.

Write approximately **90** words in **French**.

You must write something about each bullet point.

Describe:

- the type of person you are
- what you did with your friends recently
- your future relationships.

15 marks

Conseil

For this task, you must write something about all the bullet points but there is no need to cover them equally. Your message must be conveyed clearly and you must use varied vocabulary and grammar. Make sure you make accurate references to all three time frames. Try to include opinions and justify them using *parce que* or *car*.

2.2 You are emailing your Swiss friend about school and jobs.

Write approximately **90** words in **French**.

You must write something about each bullet point.

Describe:

- the advantages and disadvantages of your school
- what you did recently at school
- what you plan to do once you leave school.

15 marks

Either question 3.1 or question 3.2

3.1 You are writing a post for your blog. Your post is about being a teenager.

Write approximately **150** words in **French**.

You must write something about both bullet points.

Describe:

- the advantages and disadvantages of being a teenager
- your future lifestyle.

25 marks

3.2 You are writing a post for your blog. Your post is about jobs and work experience.

Write approximately **150** words in **French**.

You must write something about both bullet points.

Describe:

- the advantages and disadvantages of your dream job.
- what you did recently in your work experience.

25 marks

Conseil

For this task, you must write something about both bullet points but there is no need to cover them equally. You need to communicate your message clearly and develop your ideas as much as possible. You should aim to use complex language, including a variety of vocabulary and grammatical structures. Varied and complex language can mean using different ways of expressing opinions, various persons of verbs, intensifiers, adjectives, a range of tenses, negatives, pronouns and conjunctions.

Theme 2
Popular culture

Free-time activities

1 **Match the sentence halves.**

1 Tu écoutes	a son roman préféré.
2 Nous jouons	b au théâtre.
3 Vous allez	c aux cartes.
4 Je fais	d la radio.
5 Elle lit	e du camping.

le camping	camping
les cartes	cards
la radio	radio
le roman	novel
le théâtre	theatre

2 **Read the blog post and answer the questions.**

Zoé

Le soir, j'aime beaucoup jouer à des jeux vidéo. C'est passionnant. Le week-end, je vais parfois au cinéma avec mes copines, mais je préfère aller au théâtre car c'est plus intéressant. Mon frère aime lire après le dîner, mais son activité préférée, c'est la danse. Il fait ça le mercredi.

posté le 26 septembre à 12:43

a When does Zoé play video games?
b What does she think of playing video games?
c What does Zoé sometimes do at the weekend, and who with?
d What does Zoé prefer doing, and why?
e When does Zoé's brother read?
f What is his favourite activity?
g When does he do that activity?

le soir	(in the) evening
le week-end	weekend
le dîner	dinner
le jeu vidéo	video game
le cinéma	cinema
la danse	dance
passionnant	exciting

3 **Listen (1–6) and choose the correct picture (a–f).**

a

b

c

d

e

f

détester	to hate
préférer	to prefer
le livre	book
autre chose	something else
ennuyeux	boring
tous les jours	every day

4 **Listen again (1–6) and decide whether each person's opinion is positive (P) or negative (N).**

Sport and leisure

1 **Choose the correct word from the box to match the places (a–j).**

a

b

c

d

e

f

g

h

i

j

le café
le centre sportif
la chambre
le cinéma
le jardin
la montagne
le parc
la piscine
la plage
le stade

2 **Read the email. Copy and complete the sentences (a–f).**

Mon frère et moi, nous aimons être actifs. Nous allons au centre sportif trois fois par semaine. Pendant les vacances, nous allons à la campagne. Nous faisons du vélo sur les petites routes. Ce n'est pas dangereux. Parfois mon frère va à la montagne et il court. Ça, c'est très dur! Moi, j'aime mieux courir dans le parc car je trouve ça plus facile.

Mustapha

la campagne	countryside
la fois	time
la route	road
les vacances	holidays
aimer mieux	to prefer
courir	to run
faire du vélo	to go cycling
actif	active
dur	hard
facile	easy

a Mustapha and his brother enjoy being…
b They go to the… three times a week.
c In the holidays they go to…
d They cycle on… because it's…
e Sometimes Mustapha's brother runs in…
f Mustapha prefers… because it's…

3 **Listen and write down the order in which the activities (a–f) are mentioned.**

a football | b running | c cycling
d games | e swimming | f watching TV

le chien	dog
une équipe	team
la famille	family
la sœur	sister
sportif/sportive	sporty

4 **Listen again and write down who they do each activity with.**

Customs, festivals and celebrations

1 Match the sentences (1–6) to the celebrations (a–f).

1 Demain, c'est l'anniversaire de ma mère. On va au restaurant.
2 Le jour de l'An, nous invitons des amis chez nous.
3 C'est la fin du Ramadan. Après une visite à la mosquée, on célèbre ça à la maison.
4 À Noël, on fait la fête avec la famille et on donne des cadeaux à tout le monde.
5 Quand on aime quelqu'un, le 14 février, c'est un jour important.
6 Aujourd'hui, c'est la fête des Mères, alors j'achète des fleurs.

a Valentine's Day | b Mother's Day | c a birthday
d New Year's Day | e Christmas | f Eid

le cadeau	present
la fin	end
les fleurs	flowers
la mosquée	mosque
à la maison	at home
célébrer	to celebrate
faire la fête	to party
inviter	to invite

2 Match the sentence halves.

1 Cet été, je vais à	a des billets en ligne.
2 D'abord, je réserve	b notre groupe préféré.
3 Les billets coûtent	c un festival.
4 Le festival commence	d beau.
5 Nous allons voir	e le 4 août.
6 Il va faire	f cher.

le billet	ticket
le groupe	band
coûter	to cost
réserver	to book
il fait beau	the weather is fine
cher	expensive
en ligne	online

3 Read the comments. Copy and complete the sentences (a–f).

C'est bien d'envoyer des cartes pour le jour de l'An.

En France, le 26 décembre n'est pas un jour férié.

À Hanouka, chaque famille a ses propres traditions.

Certaines personnes se marient à l'église.

Souvent, on mange un gâteau à une fête d'anniversaire.

Le dimanche de Pâques, on peut se lever tard.

a At New Year, it's good to…
b 26 December is not…
c At Hanukkah, each family…
d Some people get married…
e At a birthday party, people often…
f On Easter Sunday, you can…

la fête	party
Pâques	Easter
envoyer	to send
certains	some
chaque	each
propre	own
tard	late

4 Listen to find out about the *fête nationale*. Write down the order in which the different aspects (a–f) are mentioned.

a dancing
b procession
c music
d cafés
e lots of people
f fireworks

le défilé	procession
le feu d'artifice	firework display
les gens	people
la rue	street
minuit	midnight
écouter	to listen
voir	to see
partout	everywhere

Celebrity culture

1 Listen (1–6) and choose the correct profession (a–f) for each person.

a

b

c

d

e

f

2 Listen again (1–6) and write down *one* further detail for each person.

un acteur	actor
une chanteuse	female singer
un chef de cuisine	head chef
un écrivain	writer
une femme politique	female politician
une championne de natation	swimming champion

3 Read the advice and choose the correct tip (a–e) that each celebrity gives.

Clément
À mon avis, les réseaux sociaux sont importants. On doit utiliser ces sites et il ne faut pas être timide.

Maéva
Il y a beaucoup de chanteurs et de chanteuses. Ce n'est pas un métier facile et il faut travailler dur.

Éva
Si vous voulez devenir influenceur, partagez vos idées avec des amis. Connaissez-vous déjà des personnes qui écrivent un blog?

Raphaël
Essayez de vivre une vie normale. On peut être célèbre et avoir un partenaire et une famille en même temps.

Adam
Si vous voulez voyager, acceptez cette proposition. Partez, visitez le monde et rencontrez plus de personnes intéressantes!

a Share your ideas!
b Work hard!
c Travel!
d Use social media!
e Live a normal life!

la recette	recipe
devenir	to become
espérer	to hope
s'intéresser à	to be interested in
à l'étranger	abroad
francophone	French-language / from the French-speaking world

4 Read the advice again (activity 3). Copy and complete the sentences.

a Clément says you mustn't…
b Maéva thinks that singing isn't…
c Éva asks if you know anyone who…
d Raphaël says that you can be famous and…
e Adam believes that you will meet…

le concours	competition
un métier	career, job
la vie	life
connaître	to know
partager	to share
rencontrer	to meet
vivre	to live
il faut	it is necessary to
il ne faut pas	you must not
timide	shy
quelqu'un	someone
en même temps	at the same time
déjà	already

4.1F Le week-end dernier

OBJECTIVES
- Leisure activities in the past
- Emphatic pronouns (*moi, toi*)
- The perfect tense: irregular past participles
- Phonics: *u* and *ou*, *oi* and *oy*

1 **Read the texts and decide which activity (a–f) each person did.**

Qu'est-ce que tu as fait le week-end dernier?

Nina

J'ai passé le week-end à Genève chez une copine. Elle a visité toute la ville avec moi. On a fait beaucoup de promenades et on a pris le bus pour faire la visite de la ville. Nous avons vu des sites comme l'église Saint-Pierre et le jardin des Alpes. C'était génial! J'ai reçu un petit cadeau de ma copine – elle est très gentille.

Henri

Samedi, j'ai fait les courses, comme toujours! J'ai vu mon meilleur copain et nous avons écrit un blog ensemble. Le soir, j'ai téléchargé un film amusant et mon beau-père a regardé ce film avec moi – nous avons beaucoup ri. Dimanche, j'ai vu mes grands-parents. J'ai mis mon pantalon noir préféré. On a joué à un jeu de société et on a bu du thé. J'ai beaucoup aimé!

Yasmine

Samedi matin, j'étais fatiguée. J'ai lu mon livre préféré, *Le Petit Prince*. L'après-midi, mon frère et moi, nous avons fait des gâteaux. Mon frère n'a pas eu de chance – il a trop mangé de gâteau et il a été malade! Dimanche, j'ai eu plus d'énergie et j'ai couru sur la plage près de chez moi. J'ai adoré.

un jeu de société **a board game**

a met up with family
b did some sport
c went sightseeing
d went online
e made cakes with a family member
f took public transport

2 **Read the texts again and answer the questions.**

a Who was Nina in Geneva with?
b What did that person give Nina?
c What did Henri do with his friend?
d What did Henri do with his stepdad?
e What did Yasmine do on Saturday morning?
f Where was the beach that Yasmine went to?

3 **Find *eight* irregular past participles in the text (activity 1) and work out their infinitive.**

Les verbes

The perfect tense: irregular past participles

Many common verbs have an irregular past participle in the perfect tense. These include:

Infinitive	Perfect tense	English
avoir	*j'ai eu*	I had
être	*j'ai été*	I was
faire	*j'ai fait*	I did / have done
mettre	*j'ai mis*	I put / have put
prendre	*j'ai pris*	I took / have taken
courir	*j'ai couru*	I ran / have run
lire	*j'ai lu*	I read / have read
rire	*j'ai ri*	I laughed / have laughed
voir	*j'ai vu*	I saw / have seen
recevoir	*j'ai reçu*	I received / have received
boire	*j'ai bu*	I drank / have drunk
écrire	*j'ai écrit*	I wrote / have written

4 Copy and complete the email with the correct past participles.

valerie@monmail.fr

Dimanche dernier, j'ai **1** ___ (*mettre*) mon pantalon préféré et j'ai **2** ___ (*lire*) un livre. Ensuite, j'ai **3** ___ (*faire*) une partie de Mille Bornes avec ma famille et j'ai **4** ___ (*avoir*) de la chance – j'ai gagné!

L'après-midi, j'ai **5** ___ (*prendre*) le bus pour aller en ville. J'ai **6** ___ (*voir*) mes copains et nous avons **7** ___ (*boire*) un café. Nous avons **8** ___ (*écrire*) des e-mails à nos amis à Londres et nous avons **9** ___ (*recevoir*) des réponses amusantes. On a beaucoup **10** ___ (*rire*)!

Phonétique

u* and *ou*, *oi* and *oy

j'ai ***bu***	*j'ai* ***vu***	*tu as* ***lu***
*n**ou**s*	*v**ou**s*	
*c**ou**rses*	*p**ou**r*	*c**ou**r**u***
*s**oi**r*	*m**oi***	*hist**oi**re*
*v**oy**ager*	*env**oy**er*	*empl**oy**é*

Mille Bornes '1000 milestones', a classic French card game

5 Listen to Hugo and Alice and decide which activities (a–h) each person mentions.

- **a** watching a film
- **b** drinking coffee
- **c** reading
- **d** writing a letter
- **e** shopping
- **f** going running
- **g** going into town
- **h** doing homework

6 Listen (1–4) and write down the sentences you hear.

7 In pairs, take turns to read aloud one of the texts from activity 1: Nina, Henri or Yasmine.

8 In pairs, ask and answer the questions.

- Tu es allé(e) où le week-end dernier?
- Qui était avec toi?
- Qu'est-ce que tu as fait?
- Qu'est-ce que tu as vu?

9 Write a paragraph (50 words) to describe what you did last weekend. Mention:

- where you went
- who was with you
- what you saw
- what you did
- your opinion.

Grammaire

Emphatic pronouns (*moi*, *toi*)

We use the pronouns *moi* and *toi* after a preposition or for emphasis:

Amélie a fait les courses ***avec moi****.* Amélie went shopping **with me**.
J'ai un cadeau ***pour toi****.* I have a present **for you**.
Ils ont bu un café ***sans moi****.* They drank a coffee **without me**.
J'ai lu la recette ***chez toi****.* I read the recipe **at your house**.

Culture

Le Petit Prince was written and illustrated by Antoine de Saint-Exupéry. Since publication in 1943, it has sold over 140 million copies worldwide. It has been translated into more than 500 different languages and dialects, and has even appeared on stamps!

4.1H Télé, cinéma, musique!

OBJECTIVES
- TV, cinema and music
- Reflexive pronouns in the correct position
- Reflexive verbs in the present tense (plural forms)
- Phonics: liaison

1 **Read the texts and find the French for the English phrases (a–g).**

Qu'est-ce que tu aimes comme films?
comme émissions de télé? comme musique?

J'adore le cinéma africain! Récemment, j'ai vu le film camerounais *Sango Malo*. Je recommande ce film. J'utilise mon portable pour regarder la télé. Chez nous, nous nous couchons tard quand nous regardons notre émission préférée. Comme musique, j'écoute de la musique rap. Mon frère préfère la musique pop, donc nous nous disputons souvent à la maison. C'est embêtant. **Jade**

J'aime regarder des films d'action avec mon père. Nous nous entendons bien, papa et moi. Récemment, nous avons regardé *Le Journal d'un pêcheur* pour la deuxième fois. À la télé, nous adorons les comédies et nous nous intéressons aux actualités. Mon genre de musique préféré, c'est le rock. J'écoute de la musique quand je me lève tôt. En ce moment, j'apprends à jouer du piano, mais c'est dur! Je ne vais jamais à des concerts parce que les billets coûtent trop cher. **Raphaël**

Ma sœur et moi, nous nous ressemblons beaucoup. Nous aimons le cinéma francophone et nous regardons les mêmes émissions à la télé. Nous nous relaxons souvent devant le petit écran. Nos séries préférées s'appellent *Dix pour cent* et *Osmosis*. Nous apprécions aussi la musique. L'année dernière, nous avons vu notre chanteur préféré en concert. **Farah**

les actualités	current affairs

a we go to bed late
b we argue
c we get on well
d we are interested in current affairs
e we are similar to each other
f we often relax
g our favourite programmes are called…

2 **Read the texts again and answer the questions.**

a What does Jade recommend?
b How does Jade watch TV?
c What annoys Jade?
d What has Raphaël done recently for the second time?
e What does Raphaël find hard?
f What does Raphaël find expensive?
g Who does Farah watch TV with?
h Who did Farah see last year?

3 **Translate the sentences into French.**

a I watch my favourite programme on my phone.
b We sometimes argue when I go to bed late.
c I'm interested in music and I play the piano.
d My sister likes watching action films with me.

4 **Copy and complete the sentences with the correct form of the reflexive verb.**

a Nous ___ vers dix heures. (*se coucher*)
b Ton frère et toi, vous ___ bien? (*s'entendre*)
c Elles ___ à la plage. (*se relaxer*)
d Nous ___ à Noël. (*s'écrire*)
e Mes amis ___ si le cinéma est ouvert. (*se demander*)
f Vous ___ toujours! (*se disputer*)
g Nous ___ facilement au centre commercial. (*se perdre*)

5 **Translate the completed sentences from activity 4 into English.**

6 **Listen (1–5) and write down the sentences you hear.**

7 **In pairs, take turns to read aloud a text from activity 1.**

8 **In pairs, ask and answer the questions.**

- Ton frère / Ta sœur et toi, vous vous entendez bien?
- Vous vous intéressez à quoi?
- Vous vous relaxez comment?
- Vous trouvez ça comment?

9 **Write a paragraph in French (90 words) about how you and your friends spend your free time.**

Attention

In activity 9, include some reflexive verbs in the *nous* form and see if you can use the *ils / elles* form too.

Culture

Africa has a thriving French-language film industry, which is highly regarded worldwide. FESPACO (*Festival Panafricain de Cinéma et de Télévision de Ouagadougou*), the main African film festival, is held every two years in Ouagadougou, the capital of Burkina Faso.

Les verbes

Reflexive verbs

Some verbs are used with reflexive pronouns (*me*, *te*, *se*, *nous*, *vous*, *se*) placed immediately before the verb:

se relaxer **(to relax)**	
*je **me** relaxe*	*nous **nous** relaxons*
*tu **te** relaxes*	*vous **vous** relaxez*
*il / elle / on **se** relaxe*	*ils / elles **se** relaxent*

Some of these verbs describe something that you do to yourself:

*Je **me demande** si le magasin est ouvert.*
I **ask myself** / ***wonder*** if the shop is open.

The reflexive pronoun sometimes carries the meaning of 'each other':

*Nous **nous entendons** bien.*
We get on well **with each other**.

Some reflexive verbs carry a meaning that is neither 'to yourself' nor 'each other':

*Le week-end, nous **nous relaxons**.*
We **relax** at the weekend.

Phonétique

Liaison

Sometimes the normally silent last consonant of a word is pronounced when the next word begins with a vowel. This is called a liaison.

The rules for liaison are complex and it is best to listen out for examples. With reflexive verbs, the final -*s* on *nous* and *vous* forms a liaison with a vowel afterwards, but the -*ons* and -*ez* endings do not.

*Nous nou**s*** (liaison) ***in**téressons* (no liaison) *au cinéma.*

*Le cinéma es**t*** (liaison) ***ou**vert* (no liaison) *aujourd'hui.*

*J'aime regarder des films sur mo**n*** (liaison) ***o**rdinateur.*

*Il y a deux nouveau**x*** (liaison) ***é**crans au cinéma.*

4.2F En voyage!

OBJECTIVES
- Leisure activities around the world
- *en* and *à* with places
- The perfect tense with *être*
- Phonics: *e* and *eu*; *-e*, *-er* and *-ez*

1 **Read the texts. Copy and complete the sentences (a–h).**

Accueil | À propos | Blog | Derniers articles | Intérêts

L'année dernière, je suis partie au Maroc avec ma famille. Nous sommes arrivés à Tanger après un long voyage en bateau. À Tanger, j'ai fait du surf – c'était super! Pendant les vacances, nous avons aussi pris le bus. **Nous sommes descendus du bus à Fez**, une ville historique. À Fez, nous sommes allés à un concert de musique traditionnelle. **Anna**

Moi, **je suis née à La Réunion**. L'automne dernier, je suis retournée là-bas. **Je suis allée voir ma cousine** et nous sommes parties à la montagne ensemble. Nous avons vu le « Grand Raid de La Réunion » – c'est un ultra-marathon de 162 kilomètres, un vrai défi! **Le soir, nous sommes retournées à Saint-Louis** où habite ma cousine. **Lucie**

Pendant les vacances, je suis parti au Canada. **Ma sœur est venue avec moi**. Nous sommes restés trois semaines à Montréal. Ma sœur a joué au hockey sur glace, un sport très populaire au Canada. **Elle est tombée** mais ce n'était pas grave. Après, ma sœur et moi, nous sommes allés voir un match de foot. **Thomas**

L'année dernière, j'ai passé mes vacances en France. **Je suis resté une semaine** à Avignon pendant le célèbre Festival d'Avignon, et mon frère a joué dans une pièce de théâtre. La ville était pleine de vie! Après le festival, **nous sommes rentrés chez nous ensemble**. **Max**

a Anna and her family went to Morocco by ___.
b They went to Fez by ___.
c Lucie went to La Réunion last ___.
d Her cousin lives in ___.
e Thomas went to Montréal with ___.
f He saw a ___ with his sister.
g Max visited Avignon during the ___.
h His brother took part in a ___.

2 **Translate the phrases in bold in activity 1 into English.**

3 **In the texts in activity 1, find and list all the verbs in the perfect tense with *être*.**

Phonétique

e* and *eu

je *le* *de* *deux* *un peu* *le jeu*

Les verbes

The perfect tense with *être*

14 common verbs use *être* instead of *avoir* in the perfect tense. You can learn them in pairs of opposites:

aller (to go)	*venir* (to come)
arriver (to arrive)	*partir* (to leave)
entrer (to go in)	*sortir* (to go out)
monter (to go up)	*descendre* (to go down)
tomber (to fall)	*retourner* (to go back)
rester (to stay)	*rentrer* (to come back / to return home)
naître (to be born)	*mourir* (to die)

With these verbs, the past participle agrees with the subject: add *-e* for the feminine form and *-s* for plural.

arriver **(to arrive)**	
je suis arrivé(e)	*nous sommes arrivé(e)s*
tu es arrivé(e)	*vous êtes arrivé(e)(s)*
il est arrivé	*ils sont arrivés*
elle est arrivée	*elles sont arrivées*
on est arrivé(e)(s)	

4 Copy and complete the sentences with the perfect tense of the verb in brackets.

a Mon frère ___ aux États-Unis. (*aller*)
b Ta sœur ___ à quelle heure? (*arriver*)
c Nous ___ deux semaines au bord de la mer. (*rester*)
d Ils ___ à la maison. (*rentrer*)
e Ma mère ___ au concert avec nous. (*venir*)
f Charlotte et Mélanie ___ à midi. (*partir*)

5 In pairs, read aloud one of the texts in activity 1.

6 In pairs, ask and answer the questions.

- L'année dernière, tu es allé(e) où en vacances?
- Qu'est-ce que tu as fait là-bas?
- Les vacances, c'était comment?

7 Listen (1–4) and answer the questions.

a Which new activity did Victor try in Marseille?
b What did he think of it? Give **two** details.
c How long did Aurélie stay in Dakar?
d Which sport is popular there?
e What did Nader think of the journey to La Réunion?
f What did he think of the holiday in general?
g Where did Jasmine spend her holiday?
h What did she do with her friend?

8 Listen (1–4) and write down the sentences you hear.

9 Write a paragraph (50 words) about what you did on a recent holiday. Use the details on the profile card. Mention:

- where you went
- who you went with
- where and how long you stayed
- what you did
- your opinion of the holiday.

Grammaire

en, au, aux, à **with countries and towns**

To say 'in' or 'to' a feminine name of a country, use *en*:
Elle habite ***en*** *Suisse. Il va* ***en*** *Suisse.*

To say 'in' or 'to' a masculine name of a country, use *au*:
Je travaille ***au*** *Maroc. Nous partons* ***au*** *Maroc.*

To say 'in' or 'to' a plural name of a country, use *aux*:
Vous habitez ***aux*** *États-Unis?*

To say 'in' or 'to' a town or island, use *à*:
Ils travaillent ***à*** *Paris. Je vais* ***à*** *La Réunion.*

Phonétique

-é, -er, -ez

*je suis all**é***   *all**er***   *vous all**ez***

- France
- with family
- in Paris, for five days
- visited historic sites, went to a football match
- great!

4.2H Le sport, c'est ma passion!

OBJECTIVES
- Extreme sports
- Agreement with preceding direct object pronouns
- Modal verbs in the perfect tense

1 Read the texts and find the French for the English phrases (a–f).

Mon sport préféré

J'adore tous les sports, mais j'aime surtout être active en plein air. J'ai souvent fait du kayak avec mes copines. Je trouve cela amusant, mais c'est assez difficile quand il y a des courants. Une fois, je suis tombée du kayak et une copine a dû entrer dans l'eau pour me sauver! Puis notre prof de kayak a dû nous sauver toutes les deux! Récemment, un de mes cousins a essayé le canyoning au Maroc. Ce sport a l'air très dangereux et il n'est pas pour moi. Je pense qu'il vaut mieux regarder les autres qui ont plus de courage.

À Montréal où j'habite, on peut faire du zorbing. Qu'est-ce que c'est? Alors, on entre dans une énorme boule en plastique et on descend une pente. C'est fou, non? Dès que j'ai vu ce sport, j'ai voulu l'essayer. C'est assez facile et si on tombe sur l'herbe, on ne risque pas de se blesser. Il y a aussi le « bubble foot », une sorte de football où on joue dans ces boules. Vous cherchez une activité un peu différente? Je peux vous aider à en trouver une!

Tout le monde connaît le Tour de France, la plus célèbre course de vélo du monde. Mais à mon avis, il vaut mieux venir ici dans les îles Caraïbes pour découvrir le Tour de Guadeloupe. Il y a beaucoup de concurrents – l'année dernière, des centaines de cyclistes ont participé aux dix étapes du Tour. Ils ont dû faire une distance de plus de 1 200km, avec des ascensions étonnantes. C'est un vrai défi pour les cyclistes et c'est aussi un événement passionnant pour les gens qui les regardent. J'ai pu prendre de belles photos.

en plein air	outdoors
le courant	current
la boule	ball, bubble
la pente	slope
l'ascension	climb, ascent

a I especially like to be active
b a friend had to go into the water
c this sport looks very dangerous
d you go down a slope
e I wanted to try it
f I was able to take some nice photos.

Attention

Impersonal verbs

Il vaut mieux + infinitive	It is better to…
Cela vaut la peine de + infinitive	It is worth…

2 Read the texts again and answer the questions.

a Why did Magali's friend go into the water?
b What did their kayaking teacher have to do?
c Who tried canyoning in Morocco?
d What does Louis say about falling onto the grass?
e How does Louis describe bubble football? Give **two** details.
f What does Sandrine say about the *Tour de France*? Give **two** details.
g Apart from the distance, what makes the *Tour de Guadeloupe* challenging? Give **two** details.

3 Rewrite the sentences in the correct order.

a vous / vois / Je / à la piscine / .

b tous les jours / lit / Elle / les / .

c aide à / Ma mère / nos devoirs / nous / faire / .

d ai / à l'école / les / vus / Je / .

e regardés / Karim / faire du kayak / a / nous / .

4 Translate the sentences from activity 3 into English.

5 Copy and complete the sentences, using the perfect tense of the verb in brackets.

a Nous ___ faire du zorbing. (*vouloir*)

b Tu ___ entrer dans l'eau? (*devoir*)

c Il ___ rester à la maison. (*pouvoir*)

d J'___ prendre des photos. (*vouloir*)

e Ils ___ participer à dix étapes. (*devoir*)

6 Listen (1–3) and choose the correct option to complete each sentence.

a Élodie wanted to become a professional ice hockey player when she was **10 / 12 / 13**.

b Now Élodie thinks it's better to **play for pleasure / watch others play / play other sports**.

c Lucas discovered swimming when he **moved to a different town / made new friends / went to a new school**.

d Lucas's friends prefer **team / winter / dangerous** sports.

e Camille does karate **every day / twice a week / every other week**.

f Camille **still wants to try / has tried / wanted to try** canyoning.

7 Listen (1–5) and write down the sentences you hear.

8 Write an email (150 words) to a friend. Describe:

- an activity you have tried and your opinion of it
- why your friend should try this activity.

Grammaire

Preceding direct object pronouns

Direct object pronouns (*nous*, *vous*, *les*) replace nouns and help avoid repetition. In French, they always go **before** the verb, unlike in English where they go **after**.

Je regarde les matchs de foot. Je ***les*** *regarde le week-end.*

I watch football matches. I watch **them** at the weekend.

Notre prof ***nous*** *voit en ville.* Our teacher sees **us** in town.

In the perfect tense, the direct object pronoun goes before both parts of the verb. The past participle adds *-e* and / or *-s* to agree with the pronoun:

Les filles ont fait du kayak et nous ***les*** *avons regardé****es****.*

The girls went kayaking and we watched them.

Les verbes

Modal verbs in the perfect tense

The past participles of the modal verbs *devoir*, *pouvoir* and *vouloir* are *dû*, *pu* and *voulu*.

As in the present tense, these verbs are followed by a verb in the infinitive.

Elle ***a dû*** *s'entraîner dur.* She **had** to train hard.

*Enfin, j'****ai pu*** *rester sur mes skis.* At last I **was able to** / I **could** stay on my skis.

Hier, nous ***avons voulu*** *essayer un nouveau sport.* Yesterday we **wanted** to try a new sport.

9 In pairs, take turns to describe the photo, and ask and answer the questions.

- Parle-moi de la photo.
- Quels sports as-tu déjà essayés?
- Tu les trouves comment?
- Tu aimes faire des sports dangereux? Pourquoi (pas)?

5.1F Bon anniversaire!

OBJECTIVES
- Birthdays and other personal special days
- Direct object pronouns: *me, te, vous, le, la*
- The present tense of common irregular verbs
- Phonics: *-eur* / *-œur* and *r*

1 **Match the dates (1–8) to the special days (a–h).**

1 le 25 décembre
2 le 14 juillet
3 le 14 février
4 le 1er janvier
5 le 1er mai
6 un jour entre le 22 mars et le 25 avril
7 un jour en mars ou avril
8 pendant trois jours, en septembre ou octobre

a C'est la fête du Travail en France.
b C'est Noël.
c C'est la Saint-Valentin, la fête des amoureux.
d C'est l'Aïd-el-Fitr.
e C'est Pâques.
f C'est la fête nationale en France.
g C'est le Rosh Hashanah.
h C'est le jour de l'An.

2 **Read the text and choose the *five* correct statements.**

L'anniversaire de mon frère

Mathilde

Aujourd'hui, c'est l'anniversaire de Xavier, mon petit frère. Cette année, il a onze ans. C'est un bon âge, je crois. Xavier reçoit toujours beaucoup de cadeaux et il court dans le salon où il ouvre les paquets. Il rit quand il voit ma carte d'anniversaire car je le connais bien et j'écris toujours un message amusant.

Le cadeau préféré de Xavier, c'est un billet pour un match de foot. Il adore le Paris Saint-Germain et normalement il suit les matchs en ligne. Moi aussi, je suis fan de foot et je vais aller au match avec lui.

Le soir de son anniversaire, il invite plusieurs amis à la maison. On mange un gâteau délicieux – c'est notre père qui le prépare – et on boit du cola. On joue à des jeux et on écoute de la musique. On ne se couche pas tôt!

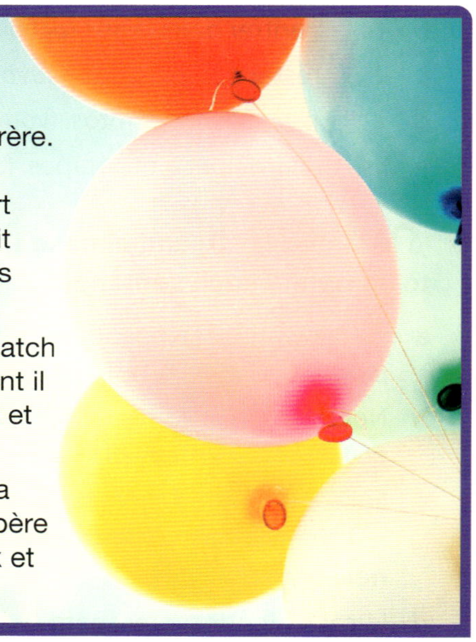

a Mathilde is older than Xavier.
b Xavier opens his presents in the kitchen.
c Mathilde always writes a funny message on Xavier's birthday card.
d Xavier's favourite present is a football shirt.
e Mathilde likes football too.
f Xavier's friends come over in the evening.
g Mathilde baked her brother's birthday cake.
h They go to bed late.

3 **Find in the text (activity 2) examples of the *ten* irregular verbs given in *Les verbes*. List them and translate them into English.**

Example: je crois – I believe

4 **Choose the correct option to complete each sentence.**

a Ma sœur **reçoit** / **reçois** / **recevoir** beaucoup de cadeaux.
b Tu **courir** / **cours** / **court** très vite!
c J'ai soif, alors je **boit** / **boire** / **bois** de l'eau.
d Tu **connais** / **connaître** / **connaît** la Saint-Valentin?
e J'**écris** / **écrit** / **écrire** une carte d'anniversaire pour ma copine.
f On **rire** / **ris** / **rit** souvent pendant le spectacle.

Les verbes

Irregular verbs in the present tense

These verbs are irregular and you will need to learn them:

	voir **(to see)**	***boire*** **(to drink)**	***croire*** **(to believe)**	***écrire*** **(to write)**	***rire*** **(to laugh)**
je/j'	*vois*	*bois*	*crois*	*écris*	*ris*
tu	*vois*	*bois*	*crois*	*écris*	*ris*
il/elle/on	*voit*	*boit*	*croit*	*écrit*	*rit*

	courir **(to run)**	***connaître*** **(to know)**	***recevoir*** **(to receive)**	***suivre*** **(to follow)**	***ouvrir*** **(to open)**
je/j'	*cours*	*connais*	*reçois*	*suis*	*ouvre*
tu	*cours*	*connais*	*reçois*	*suis*	*ouvres*
il/elle/on	*court*	*connaît*	*reçoit*	*suit*	*ouvre*

5 **Listen (1–4) and decide if each person has a positive (P), negative (N) or positive and negative (P+N) opinion of Christmas.**

6 **Listen again and answer the questions.**

1 What does Morgane's little sister enjoy?
2 Why is Christmas a double celebration for Tanguy?
3 Name **two** types of presents that Chloé says children ask for.
4 What does Vincent do instead of celebrating Christmas? Give **two** details.

7 **Listen (1–4) and write down the sentences you hear.**

8 **Copy and complete the sentences with the correct pronoun.**

a Je ___ connais. (*her*)
b Il ___ aide. (*me*)
c Tu ___ vois. (*him*)
d Je ___ suis. (*you, formal*)
e Elle ___ invite. (*you, informal*)

9 **In pairs, complete the role play. Take turns to ask and answer the questions. Answer in full sentences.**

You are talking to your French friend about special days.

1 *Que penses-tu de Noël?*
Give **one** opinion of Christmas.
2 *Tu aimes quelle fête?*
Say what your favourite festival is. (Give **one** detail.)
3 *Le jour de ton anniversaire, tu aimes faire quoi?*
Say what you like to do on your birthday. (Give **one** detail.)
4 *Tu aimes passer les occasions spéciales avec qui?*
Say who you like spending special days with. (Give **one** detail.)
5 Ask your friend a question about their birthday.

Phonétique

-eur* / *-œur* and *r

These words have an open *-eu* sound:

*l**eur**   plusi**eur**s   c**œur**   s**œur***

Roll the 'r' a little in these words:

*j'ado**r**e   annive**r**saire   pa**r**ents   décemb**r**e*
r**aison   aut**r**es   ch**r**étien   **r**ecevoi**r

Grammaire

Direct object pronouns: *me, te, vous, le, la*

Direct object pronouns (*me, te, vous, le, la*) replace nouns and help avoid repetition. In French, they always go before the verb, unlike in English where they go after.

*Tu **me** crois.* You believe **me**.
*Je **te** suis.* I follow **you** (informal).
*Elle **vous** invite.* She invites **you** (polite).
*Ils **le** mangent.* They eat **it** (masculine).
*Nous **la** prenons.* We take **it** (feminine).

The pronouns *me*, *te*, *le* and *la* are shortened before a vowel:

*Il **t'**aide.* He helps you.

10 **Write *five* sentences in French to describe how someone you know (it could be a friend or family member) spends a special day.**

5.1H Je faisais la fête comme ça

OBJECTIVES
- Describing popular customs in the past
- *y* and *en*
- The imperfect tense

1 Read the texts. Copy and complete the statements (a–e).

Jérôme

Je suis né en Suisse. Dans mon village, situé près de Fribourg, la fête du Mardi gras était très traditionnelle. Cette fête existe depuis presque soixante ans et je m'en souviens bien. Le mardi après-midi, des groupes d'enfants défilaient dans les rues et chantaient. Les adultes apprenaient les chansons aux plus petits.

Luc

Au temps de mon enfance, nous n'avions pas de télévision. La vie était simple, mais elle était vraiment agréable. Quand il y avait un jour férié, nous invitions souvent des voisins chez nous et nous jouions aux cartes. Nous nous entendions bien. À Pâques, nous visitions Paris parce que ma tante y habitait. Elle était catholique et nous allions toujours à la messe. Après, nous faisions une promenade au bord de la Seine – même s'il faisait mauvais!

Imane

Moi, j'ai grandi au Maroc. Nous y célébrions toutes les fêtes musulmanes car ma famille était musulmane. Des fêtes, il y en a beaucoup, mais j'aimais surtout l'Aïd al-Fitr qui marque la fin de Ramadan. Après la prière du matin, nous prenions un petit-déjeuner festif et nous offrions des cadeaux à la famille et aux amis. Mes cousins nous appelaient car ils habitaient loin de chez nous. Le soir, mes parents préparaient des gâteaux traditionnaux et nous en mangions ensemble.

défiler	to parade, to process
la messe	(Catholic) mass
la prière	prayer

a In Jérôme's village, children ___ and ___ in the streets.
b The ___ taught the traditional songs to the children.
c Imane's favourite festival was ___.
d Imane's cousins lived ___.
e Imane's family ate ___ together.

2 Translate Luc's text into English.

Culture

Mardi gras is equivalent to Shrove Tuesday or Pancake Day but is a much bigger event in those countries where it is celebrated. It is a popular festival in many parts of Europe and in American states that had a strong historical French influence. New Orleans – *la Nouvelle-Orléans* – is the classic example.

3 Copy and complete the sentences, using the imperfect tense of the verb in brackets.

a Il ___ bien au foot. (*jouer*)
b J'___ content. (*être*)
c Tu ___ les traditions? (*aimer*)
d Vous ___ des gâteaux? (*manger*)
e Nous ___ du bruit dans les rues. (*faire*)
f Mes parents ___ des amis à la maison. (*inviter*)

4 Listen to Anaïs and Max talking about how they used to spend special days (1–6). Answer the questions in English.

1 In which month did Anaïs's favourite special day take place?
2 What did Anaïs like seeing on that occasion? Give **two** details.
3 What did Anaïs's brother do in the carnival? Give **two** details.
4 What was Max's favourite day?
5 Where did Max and his family go on that day?
6 Name **two** activities Max and the others did during the daytime.

5 Find the French for the English phrases, in the activity 1 texts.

a I remember it well.
b My aunt used to live there.
c we used to celebrate all the Muslim festivals there
d We used to eat some together.

6 Listen (1–5) and write down the sentences you hear.

7 In groups, carry out a survey of students' favourite days of the year. Record the results and present them to the class.

– Quel est ton jour préféré?
– Comment as-tu passé cette journée-là l'année dernière?
– Tu as passé la journée avec qui?

Les verbes

The imperfect tense

To form the imperfect tense, take the *nous* form of the present tense, remove the final *-ons* and add these endings:

chanter **(to sing)**	
*je chant**ais***	*nous chant**ions***
*tu chant**ais***	*vous chant**iez***
*il / elle / on chant**ait***	*ils / elles chant**aient***

Verbs ending in *-ger* and *-cer* are slightly different, and être has the imperfect stem *ét-*:

manger **(to eat)**	***commencer*** **(to start)**	***être*** **(to be)**
je mangeais	*je commençais*	*j'étais*
tu mangeais	*tu commençais*	*tu étais*
il / elle / on mangeait	*il / elle / on commençait*	*il / elle / on était*
nous mangions	*nous commencions*	*nous étions*
vous mangiez	*vous commenciez*	*vous étiez*
ils / elles mangeaient	*ils / elles commençaient*	*ils / elles étaient*

Grammaire

The pronouns *y* and *en*

The pronoun *y* replaces *à* + noun. It often means 'to it', 'at it' or 'there'.

*Je vais **à la rivière**. J'**y** vais maintenant.*

The pronoun *en* replaces *de* + noun. It often means 'of it', 'of them' or 'some'.

*Nous mangeons **de la viande**. Nous **en** mangeons tous les jours.*

8 Write an email (90 words) to your Belgian friend about your favourite special day. Describe:

- your favourite special day and how you spend it
- what you used to do on that day when you were younger
- what you will do on the next public holiday.

Example: Mon jour préféré, c'est…
Ce jour-là, je…
Quand j'avais… ans, je faisais / j'allais…
Au prochain jour férié, je ferai / j'irai…

5.2F Les fêtes dans le passé et à l'avenir

OBJECTIVES
- Past and future festivals
- Definite and indefinite articles
- Two tenses together: past and near future

1 Read the texts and find the French for the English phrases (a–h).

Jaël

Ma famille est juive et chaque année, nous célébrons Hanouka, la fête des Lumières. C'est une fête qui dure huit jours. L'année dernière, elle a commencé le jeudi 7 décembre. Nous sommes restés à la maison et nous avons fait la fête avec nos voisins. Cette année, nous allons passer Hanouka chez mes cousins qui habitent à la campagne.

Inaya

Ici au Cameroun, nous avons beaucoup de festivals. L'année dernière, le pays a connu son premier festival Diaspora Kitchen, un festival de cuisine. Pendant deux jours, plus de vingt chefs camerounais et américains ont partagé des recettes traditionnelles et familiales. J'espère que ce festival va se passer tous les ans parce que **je vais étudier la cuisine** pour devenir chef.

Sacha

En France, le 14 juillet, c'est la fête nationale. On célèbre la fin de la monarchie française en 1789. **L'année dernière, je suis allé à Paris** et j'ai vu le grand défilé. **Il y avait des gens partout**. Cette année, je vais rester dans ma ville. Il y aura un feu d'artifice et **je vais faire la fête avec mes copains.**

Hugo

J'habite en France, à 20 km de la Suisse. En décembre dernier, j'ai passé une journée en Suisse pour voir la fête de l'Escalade. **On a écouté des chansons traditionnels.** Les habitants ont servi de la soupe aux légumes et du vin chaud – et c'était gratuit! En décembre prochain, nous allons retourner à cette fête. Nous allons manger dans un café au marché.

le vin chaud mulled wine

a a festival that lasts eight days
b we celebrated with our neighbours
c traditional and family recipes
d I'm going to stay in my town
e there will be a firework display
f the local people served vegetable soup
g it was free
h we are going to return to this festival

2 Copy and complete the sentences.

a Last year Hanukkah ___ on 7 December.
b Jael's cousins live ___.
c More than 20 ___ took part in the *Diaspora Kitchen* festival.
d Inaya hopes that the festival will take place ___.
e Sacha saw the big ___ for the *fête nationale* in Paris.
f Next year Sacha will celebrate with ___.
g At the last *Escalade* festival Hugo listened to ___.
h Next December Hugo and his family will eat at ___.

3 Listen (1–4). For each person, write down:

- whether they are talking about the past or the future
- one further detail.

4 Choose the correct options to complete each sentence.

a Hier, nous **sommes restés** / **allons rester** à la maison, mais demain, nous **avons passé** / **allons passer** la journée en ville.

b L'année dernière, **j'ai vu** / **je vais voir** le grand défilé militaire à Paris et **je suis retourné** / **je vais y retourner** l'été prochain.

c Cette année, ma famille **a fait** / **va faire** la fête mais l'année dernière, nous **étions** / **allons être** malades.

d Demain, on **a chanté** / **va chanter** dans la rue. Hier, on **a écouté** / **va écouter** les autres groupes.

Attention

When choosing a tense, look for adverbs of time to give you clues.
Hier and *l'année dernière* refer to the past.
Demain and *l'année prochaine* refer to the future.
Aujourd'hui and *cette année* could refer to past, present or future.

5 Translate the bold phrases in the texts (activity 1) into English.

6 In pairs, prepare a presentation about a recent visit to the *Festival Terre et Nature* and your plans to go there together again next year.

7 Write a description (90 words) of a festival or special day. Describe:

- your favourite festival or special day
- what you did on that day last year
- how you are planning to celebrate that day next year.

Les verbes

Two tenses together: past and near future

In your writing and speaking, you will often need to use different tenses in the same sentence or paragraph. This also sounds natural and adds more interest.

*Hier, **nous avons pris** le train, mais demain **nous allons prendre** la voiture.* (perfect + near future)

*Quand **j'étais** petite, **je partais** en vacances avec ma famille. L'année prochaine, **je vais partir** avec des copines.* (imperfect + near future)

Grammaire

Definite and indefinite articles

The definite article (*le, la, l', les*) and the indefinite article (*un, une, des*) are sometimes used in French when they are not needed in English:

*J'aime **les** films.* I like films. (literally: I like **the** films.)

***L'**année dernière, elle est restée à **la** maison.* Last year, she stayed at home. (literally: **The** last year… at **the** house.)

Mon jour / festival préféré, c'est…
Normalement, je vais… / je reste…
Je passe la journée avec…
Je mange… / Nous mangeons…
Je bois… / Nous buvons…
J'aime ce jour parce que…
L'année dernière, j'ai passé / nous sommes allé(e)s…
L'année prochaine, je vais aller / on va passer…

5.2H On y va, au festival?

OBJECTIVES
- Planning a trip to a festival
- Relative clauses with *que, qui, quand* and *où*
- The future tense of *être, avoir, aller* and *faire*
- Revising superlative adjectives

1 Read the text and find the French for the English phrases (a–e).

Le festival de Cannes

Au mois de mai, comme tous les ans, la ville de Cannes va recevoir des milliers de professionnels du cinéma. Le festival de Cannes est **un des événements les plus importants du monde du cinéma**. Pendant douze jours, un public invité aura l'occasion de juger une sélection de vingt et un films. On montrera des films dramatiques, des comédies, des documentaires et des films d'animation. Tout cela fera un spectacle unique.

Le moment le plus important du festival sera la cérémonie des prix, où le célèbre tapis rouge attend les gagnants de la Palme d'or et d'autres prix comme le Grand Prix et le Prix du jury. **La Palme d'or est la plus haute distinction**, qui ira au meilleur film. **On donnera le Grand Prix au film le plus original** et le Prix du jury ira au film d'un jeune réalisateur talentueux. Il y aura également des prix pour **la meilleure actrice et le meilleur acteur**.

Quand on pense au festival de Cannes, **on pense aux plus grandes stars de l'écran avec leurs plus beaux vêtements**. Mais c'est aussi un lieu où les journalistes se rencontrent pour découvrir la créativité, l'innovation et l'expression artistique. L'accès au festival est réservé aux professionnels, mais chaque soir on propose un film que tout le monde peut apprécier. On appelle cela le Cinéma de la Plage, car cela se passe dehors, sur une plage!

juger	to judge
le tapis	carpet
le gagnant	winner
le réalisateur	film director
talentueux	talented

a an invited audience will have the opportunity
b they will show drama films
c all that will make a unique show
d which will go to the best film
e there will also be prizes for

2 Copy and complete the sentences.

a The Cannes festival takes place every year in the month of ___.
b The judging takes place over a period of ___ days.
c The *Grand Prix* is awarded to the most ___ film.
d The festival is an opportunity for ___ to meet.
e Open-air screenings are accessible to ___.

3 Translate the ***six*** bold phrases in the text into English.

Grammaire

Revising superlative adjectives

Use the definite article followed by *plus*:

***le plus grand** festival* the biggest festival

*les films **les plus intéressants*** the most interesting films

Remember two irregular forms:

*la **meilleure** actrice* the best actress

*le **pire** film* the worst film

Culture

The Cannes film festival is one of Europe's three biggest film festivals, alongside those in Venice and Berlin. Among the long list of prizes and distinctions awarded each year is the Palm Dog Award – for the best canine performance on the big screen!

4 Copy and complete the sentences, using the future tense of the verb in brackets.

a Cette année, j'___ au festival de Cannes. (*aller*)
b Il y ___ beaucoup de gens dans les rues. (*avoir*)
c Tu ___ la fête avec ta famille? (*faire*)
d Je ___ contente de voir les artistes. (*être*)
e Tu ___ l'occasion de participer aux jeux. (*avoir*)
f Mon frère ___ au cinéma avec ses copains. (*aller*)

5 In pairs, read the completed sentences (activity 4) aloud.

6 Listen (1–5) and write down the sentences you hear.

7 Translate the sentences (activity 6) into English.

8 Listen to Aurélie and Florien talking about music festivals in Belgium (1–8). Answer the questions in English.

1 In which month did Aurélie go to the Ronquières festival last year?
2 How much did a three-day ticket cost her?
3 What does Aurélie think of the cost?
4 Why isn't she going back to Ronquières this year?
5 Why does Florien like the programme for *Francofolies*? (Give **two** details.)
6 Why is Aurélie attracted to the *Ardentes* festival? (Give **two** details.)
7 Why is going there by bus a good option?
8 In order to go to the *Ardentes* festival, what must they do and why?

9 Translate into French.

a We will go to the festival by bus.
b It's a festival that takes place every year.
c There will be lots of pop music that I love.
d Last week I went to the cinema where I saw a film.
e Next year I will celebrate with friends.

10 In pairs, take turns to describe the photo, and then ask and answer the questions.

- À l'avenir, tu veux voir un film dehors? Pourquoi?
- Est-ce que tu es déjà allé(e) à un festival?
- Qu'est-ce que tu penses des festivals de musique?

Les verbes

Irregular verbs in the future tense

In the future tense, the **endings** are the same for regular and irregular verbs, but the stem of each verb needs to be learnt separately. Here are four common irregular verbs:

être	*avoir*	*aller*	*faire*
*je ser**ai***	*j'aur**ai***	*j'ir**ai***	*je fer**ai***
*tu ser**as***	*tu aur**as***	*tu ir**as***	*tu fer**as***
*il / elle ser**a***	*il / elle aur**a***	*il / elle ir**a***	*il / elle fer**a***

Grammaire

Relative clauses with *qui, que, quand* and *où*

These question words can also be used in relative clauses.

qui is used to refer to the subject of the sentence and is usually followed by a verb.

que is used to refer to the object of a sentence and is usually followed by a noun or pronoun.

*C'est un festival **qui** se passe à Genève.* It's a festival **which** happens in Geneva.

*Voici le chanteur **que** tu connais.* Here is the singer **that / whom** you know.

*On entend la musique officielle **quand** le festival commence.* We hear the official music **when** the festival starts.

*On voit la salle **où** les acteurs reçoivent leur prix.* We see the room **where** the actors receive their prizes.

6.1F Vous voulez être célèbre?

OBJECTIVES
- Tips on becoming famous
- Infinitives used as nouns
- The imperative (*tu* and *vous* forms)
- Phonics: *i*, *y* and *-ien*

1 **Read the advice given by three successful people. Decide who says each statement below (a–h).**

Maël

Suivez mon exemple! Si vous êtes sportif comme moi, **jouez bien et participez à des concours** aussi souvent que possible. Il ne faut pas être timide! Perdre un match, ce n'est pas la fin du monde. Il y aura toujours une autre occasion. **Écoutez vos amis** et votre famille quand ils veulent vous aider.

Céleste

Si vous avez une compétence, développez-la! **Montrez aux autres que vous pouvez faire quelque chose de spécial.** Pour moi, c'était la musique. Chanter, c'est ma vie! Je suis handicapée. Mon quotidien est parfois difficile, mais je veux vraiment suivre ma passion. Être handicapé n'est pas une raison pour éviter de faire quelque chose.

Amir

J'ai eu de la chance et je suis devenu célèbre à l'âge de vingt ans. J'ai eu l'occasion de voyager partout dans le monde et j'ai gagné beaucoup d'argent. Mais **faites attention**! Les célébrités ne sont pas toujours heureuses. On peut être célèbre mais seul. Parfois, je voudrais vivre une vie calme avec ma famille, sans paparazzi.

a Losing a match is not the end of the world.
b Being disabled is no reason for avoiding doing something.
c Singing is my life.
d I had the opportunity to travel throughout the world.
e Famous people are not always happy.
f My daily life is sometimes difficult, but I really want to follow my passion.

2 **Translate the bold sentences in the texts into English.**

3 **Copy and complete the instructions with the *vous*-form imperative of the verb in brackets.**

a ___ l'écran. (*regarder*)
b ___ la musique. (*écouter*)
c ___ du vélo. (*faire*)
d ___ les paroles. (*lire*)
e ___ ici. (*attendre*)
f ___ un blog. (*écrire*)

4 **In pairs, take turns to choose a text from activity 1 and read it aloud.**

Les verbes

The imperative

The imperative is used to give someone advice or instructions.

For most verbs, the *vous*-form imperative is the same as the normal *vous* form of the present tense, but without the pronoun.

Venez ici! Come here!

Dormez bien. Sleep well.

Faites du sport. Do some sport.

The *tu*-form imperative is usually the same as the *tu*-form of the present tense but without the pronoun. For *-er* verbs and *aller*, drop the final *-s*.

Viens ici! Come here!

Regarde! Look!

Va dans la cuisine. Go into the kitchen.

5 Listen to the advice (1–6). Copy and complete the table.

	Instruction	Reason
1		

6 Find *three* examples of an infinitive used as a noun in activity 1.

Example: Perdre un match, ce n'est pas la fin du monde.

7 Translate the sentences into English.

a Arrêter de fumer est une bonne décision.
b Lire me relaxe.
c Faire du yoga est une activité saine.
d Chanter me fait oublier mes problèmes.
e Vouloir, c'est la clé du succès!
f Organiser un voyage, c'est difficile.

8 Listen (1–4) and write down the sentences you hear.

9 In pairs, complete the role play. Take turns to ask and answer the questions. Answer in full sentences.

You are talking to your Belgian friend about celebrities.

1	*Qui est ta célébrité préférée et pourquoi?*
	Name a celebrity you like and give **one** reason for liking them.
2	Ask your friend whether she / he has a favourite celebrity.
	Name your favourite celebrity.
3	*Quelle sorte de musique aimes-tu?*
	Say what kind of music you like. (Give **one** detail.)
4	*Comment écoutes-tu de la musique?*
	Say how you listen to music. (Give **one** detail.)
5	*Que penses-tu des réseaux sociaux?*
	Say what you think of social media. (Give **one** detail.)

10 You are helping to write an article about becoming famous. Write *five* sentences giving advice, using the *vous*-form of the imperative.

Example: Écoutez votre famille!
Partagez vos idées avec…

Les verbes

Infinitives used as nouns

French infinitives can be used as nouns, often at the beginning of a sentence.
In English, they correspond to present participles ending in '-ing'.

Faire des photos *est simple.*
Taking photos is simple.

Apprendre à lire *est important.*
Learning to read is important.

Phonétique

i, y* and *-ien

*fac**i**le*	*l**i**sez*	*i**l y** aura*	
*s**y**stème*	*ph**y**sique*	*les P**y**rénées*	
*b**ien***	*v**ien**s*	*ch**ien***	*entret**ien***

Attention

In the role play, keep your responses short and simple. Use language that you know and are sure of.

Make sure you use a verb in each response.

Culture

Assia El Hannouni is a French Paralympian who is almost blind. Her main event is the 800m sprint, which she runs against athletes both with and without disabilities. She has won several gold medals at the Paralympics and in 2007, she established a new world record in her disability category for the women's 800m sprint.

6.1H Tu ferais quoi pour être célèbre?

OBJECTIVES
- How and why people might become famous
- Emphatic pronouns: *lui, elle, nous, vous, eux, elles*
- The conditional of *avoir, être, faire* and *aller*

1 **Read what these young people say they would do to become famous. Find the French for the English phrases (a–h).**

La célébrité pour vous?

Cela ne m'intéresserait pas d'être une « célébrité de 15 minutes ». Je préférerais devenir une célébrité pour toute la vie. Mais cela demanderait du temps et des efforts. D'abord, **je ferais du travail bénévole**, peut-être dans un refuge pour animaux. Après, je créerais un blog. Il serait important d'être créatif et de créer quelque chose de différent car il y a un très grand nombre d'influenceurs dans le monde. **Lou**

Pour devenir célèbre, j'étudierais les célébrités qui existent déjà. Comme ça**, j'aurais une idée** des choses à éviter et des choses à faire. Ma spécialité, c'est la cuisine. **Il serait intéressant** de savoir comment les chefs célèbres ont développé leur carrière. Je m'intéresserais aussi aux problèmes qu'ils ont rencontrés. **Souleymane**

Moi, je chercherais d'autres personnes dans ma ville avec le même centre d'intérêt que moi, pour la mode. **J'irais voir** un créateur de mode à son travail et je lui demanderais des conseils. Je lui montrerais mes idées et il me donnerait son opinion. L'idéal serait de devenir ami avec un créateur bien connu, mais **je ne pense pas que ce serait facile**. Je ferais aussi des recherches sur Internet pour étudier l'histoire de la mode. **Juliette**

Nager est ma passion. En ce moment, je fais rapidement des progrès. Pour devenir célèbre, je travaillerais encore plus dur et je participerais à plus de concours. J'irais même à l'étranger. Une fois célèbre, **je ferais toujours de mon mieux**. Je respecterais mes fans et je les remercierais pour leur soutien. Avec l'argent que je gagnerais, j'aiderais ma famille. **Édouard**

le créateur de mode fashion designer

a it would not interest me
b I would prefer to become
c that would demand time
d I would study celebrities who already exist
e with the same interests as me
f to become friends with
g once I'm famous
h I would thank them for their support

2 **Decide which person in activity 1 says each statement (a–h).**

I would…

a like to be a lifelong celebrity
b ask him for advice
c have an idea of things to avoid
d go abroad
e do some research online
f be interested in the problems they had
g always do my best
h do some voluntary work

3 Translate the bold phrases in activity 1 into English.

4 Copy and complete the sentences with the conditional form of the verb in brackets.

a Je ___ seule chez moi. (*être*)
b Qu'est-ce que tu ___ pour nous? (*faire*)
c Elle ___ à la piscine avec eux. (*aller*)
d Tu ___ la même carrière que lui. (*avoir*)
e Le travail ___ difficile sans elle. (*être*)
f Je ___ un effort pour vous! (*faire*)

5 Translate into French.

a I would meet a lot of celebrities.
b Voluntary work would be interesting.
c I would create a blog about cooking.
d She would work in a team.
e My family would help me.

6 Translate the sentences in activity 4 into English.

7 Listen to Chloé and Gabriel talking about their role models, Sandie Toletti and Akamz. Answer the questions in English.

a When did Sandie start playing football?
b When did she start her international career?
c Which **two** things about Sandie does Chloé find inspiring?
d What was Akamz famous for, at the age of 17?
e Which **two** things are we told about Akamz's personality?
f Who does Akamz sometimes dance with? (Give **two** details.)

8 In pairs, take turns to say what you would do in order to become famous.

Example: Pour devenir célèbre,
je chercherais / je participerais à / il serait important de…

Les verbes

The conditional of *avoir, être, faire* and *aller*

The conditional is used to say what someone **would** do or what **would** happen in the future. It also expresses a wish (I would like…).

For -*er* verbs, the stem is the same as the infinitive and the **endings** are the same as for the imperfect tense.

*j'aimer**ais***	*nous aimer**ions***
*tu aimer**ais***	*vous aimer**iez***
*il / elle / on aimer**ait***	*ils / elles aimer**aient***

*Je **chercherais** du travail.* I **would look** for work.
*Il **aimerait** apprendre à nager.* He **would like** to learn to swim.

The conditional forms of *avoir, être, faire, aller* have an irregular stem plus the same endings as above.

avoir **(to have)**	***être*** **(to be)**	***faire*** **(to do)**	***aller*** **(to go)**
*j'aur**ais***	*je ser**ais***	*je fer**ais***	*j'ir**ais***
*tu aur**ais***	*tu ser**ais***	*tu fer**ais***	*tu ir**ais***
*il / elle / on aur**ait***	*il / elle / on ser**ait***	*il / elle / on fer**ait***	*il / elle / on ir**ait***

Grammaire

Emphatic pronouns

The emphatic pronouns *moi, toi, lui, elle, nous, vous, eux* and *elles* are used after prepositions and after the conjunction *que*.

*Viens avec **moi**!*	Come with **me**!
*C'est pour **toi**.*	It's for **you** (*familiar singular*).
*On y va sans **lui** / **elle**.*	We'll go without **him** / **her**.
*Il habite chez **nous**.*	He lives at **our** house.
*Je suis moins patient que **vous**.*	I'm less patient than **you** (*formal / pl.*).
*Nous travaillons avec **eux**.*	We work with **them** (*male or mixed*).
*C'était une surprise pour **elles**.*	It was a surprise for **them** (*female*).

Mon modèle: Sandie Toletti

Mon modèle: Akamz

mon modèle my role model

6.2F La vie de célébrité

OBJECTIVES
- Pros and cons of being famous
- Possessive adjectives
- The present tense of *avoir, être, faire* and *aller*
- Phonics: *j, g, ch,* and *gn*

1 **Match the interview questions (1–6) to the responses (a–f).**

Interview avec une célébrité

1. Que faites-vous comme travail?
2. Voyagez-vous beaucoup?
3. Quelle personnalité avez-vous?
4. Est-ce que l'argent est important pour vous?
5. Êtes-vous prête à partager votre vie personnelle avec le public?
6. Que faites-vous pour rester en bonne santé?

a Quand je ne travaille pas, je vais souvent à la salle de sport. Je fais aussi de la natation. J'ai de la chance car j'ai ma propre piscine.

b Je suis positive et souvent heureuse. Je ne suis jamais paresseuse.

c Oui, il faut accepter cela si on est célèbre. J'ai choisi cette carrière. Mais j'essaye de protéger mon mari et mes enfants.

d Oui, je vais souvent à l'étranger. Cet été, mon groupe et moi allons au Canada pour participer à un spectacle.

e Je suis danseuse et chanteuse. Je fais surtout du hip-hop, mais j'aime d'autres styles comme le jazz.

f Oui et non. La vie est plus facile quand on est riche, mais certaines célébrités riches sont tristes malgré leur succès.

2 **In pairs, read the interview aloud.**

3 **Listen (1–4) and write down the sentences you hear.**

Phonétique

j, g, ch* and *gn

__j__e protè__g__e les __g__irafes

__j__'ai de la __ch__ance *__j__'ai __ch__oisi*

ga__gn__er *espa__gn__ol* *monta__gn__e*

4 **Copy and complete the sentences using the present tense of the verb in brackets.**

a Elle ___ en Suisse. (*aller*)

b Vous ___ beaucoup de chance. (*avoir*)

c Nous ne ___ pas paresseux. (*être*)

d Qu'est-ce que tu ___ pour rester en bonne santé? (*faire*)

e Ma famille ___ beaucoup d'influence sur moi. (*avoir*)

f Il ___ de belles chansons. (*faire*)

5 **Translate the sentences (activity 4) into English.**

Les verbes

The present tense of *avoir*, être, *faire* and *aller*

These very common verbs are irregular in the present tense:

	avoir **(to have)**	***être*** **(to be)**	***faire*** **(to do)**	***aller*** **(to go)**
je/j'	*ai*	*suis*	*fais*	*vais*
tu	*as*	*es*	*fais*	*vas*
il/elle/on	*a*	*est*	*fait*	*va*
nous	*avons*	*sommes*	*faisons*	*allons*
vous	*avez*	*êtes*	*faites*	*allez*
ils/elles	*ont*	*sont*	*font*	*vont*

6 Read about one actor's lifestyle and answer the questions (a–f) in English.

La vie d'un acteur sénégalais

Ousmane est acteur. Il est fier de son métier et de son succès. Mais comment est sa vie quotidienne? Comment voit-il ses fans? Ousmane répond à nos questions.

« Ma vie quotidienne n'est pas complètement différente de votre vie quotidienne! Le matin, je me lève, je prends le petit-déjeuner, je travaille pendant la journée, je rentre à la maison, je mange, je me relaxe et je me couche. Mais mon travail est extraordinaire! J'ai la chance de découvrir des endroits fantastiques et de rencontrer des gens passionnants. Mes collègues sont super et ils m'encouragent beaucoup quand je suis fatigué. C'est bien d'avoir un grand nombre de fans et je reçois souvent des messages. »

Ousmane a aussi une vie de famille. Sa partenaire est également bien connue: elle est journaliste et a son propre site. Le couple vit à Dakar, la capitale du Sénégal, avec ses deux enfants. Pour Ousmane, sa famille est aussi importante que sa carrière. Par exemple, il aime passer du temps avec ses parents et son oncle qui habitent près de la plage.

a How does Ousmane compare his daily life with that of others?
b What does he say he is lucky to do? (Give **two** details.)
c How do Ousmane's colleagues support him?
d What does Ousmane say about his fans? (Give **two** details.)
e What do we learn about his partner? (Give **three** details.)
f How does Ousmane view his family compared with his career?

7 Translate the sentences into French.

a I am proud of my job.
b Her life is interesting.
c Your (*familiar*) colleagues are great.
d We have our own website.
e She lives with her two children.

8 Listen to an extract from a podcast about the YouTube star, Michou. Copy and complete the sentences.

a Michou was born in ___.
b Michou has more than ___ followers.
c Michou doesn't always find his YouTube work ___.
d Having a large number of fans is sometimes ___.
e Michou likes sharing ___ with other young people.
f Michou hopes to have a long ___.

9 In pairs, take turns to ask and answer the questions.

- Quels sont les avantages d'être célèbre?
- Quels sont les inconvénients d'être célèbre?

Example:
On peut voyager / faire / rencontrer…
On doit travailler / avoir…
C'est dur / difficile / embêtant…

10 Write a paragraph describing the pros and cons of being a celebrity.

Grammaire

Possessive adjectives

In French, the words for 'my', 'your', 'his', etc. agree with the noun that follows.

	masculine singular*	feminine singular	plural
my	*mon*	*ma*	*mes*
your (familiar, singular)	*ton*	*ta*	*tes*
his / her	*son*	*sa*	*ses*
our	*notre*	*notre*	*nos*
your (formal, plural)	*votre*	*votre*	*vos*
their	*leur*	*leur*	*leurs*

* and feminine singular before a vowel or silent 'h' (*mon amie*)

*Elle adore **son** métier.* She loves **her** job. (*métier* is masculine singular)

***Notre** vie est facile.* **Our** life is easy. (*vie* is feminine singular)

*Je rencontre **mes** fans.* I meet **my** fans. (*fans* is plural)

6.2H Des francophones célèbres

OBJECTIVES
- French-speaking celebrities
- *il y a* and *depuis*
- The perfect tense of reflexive verbs

1 **Match the texts about five francophone celebrities (1–5) to their photos (a–e).**

1 Hasna Benhassi est une athlète marocaine. Elle est née le 1er juin 1978 à Marrakech. **Elle s'est spécialisée dans les courses de 800 m et de 1 500 m**. Elle a participé trois fois aux Jeux olympiques d'été où elle a gagné des médailles d'argent et de bronze. **Hasna s'est mariée à un autre athlète marocain**, Mouhssin Chehibi, et ils ont une fille.

2 Le Corbusier était un architecte d'importance mondiale. Il est né en Suisse en 1887 mais il s'est installé en France où il a travaillé jusqu'à sa mort en 1965. **Pendant sa longue carrière, il s'est intéressé à la simplicité des formes** et à la création du bonheur. Le Corbusier est largement considéré comme « le père de l'architecture moderne ».

3 Née en 1968, Céline Dion est une chanteuse canadienne. **Elle s'est mise à chanter dans les années 1980**. Sa carrière s'est ensuite développée rapidement et Céline Dion s'est imposée comme une des grandes voix de la musique pop dans les années 1990. Elle a appris l'anglais comme deuxième langue mais elle n'a jamais arrêté de chanter en français.

4 Léopold Senghor avait beaucoup de talents: il était poète, écrivain et premier président de la République du Sénégal de 1960 à 1980. Dans son rôle politique, il est devenu le symbole de la coopération entre la France et ses anciennes colonies en Afrique. Il s'est montré capable d'apporter le changement.

5 L'actrice Isabelle Adjani est née en 1955. Son père venait d'Algérie et sa mère était d'origine allemande. **Elle s'est inspirée de plusieurs actrices et acteurs américains** et elle a joué dans plus de trente films. En 1997, à cause de la pression des médias et de ses fans, Isabelle Adjani s'est décidée à quitter Paris. Elle s'est ensuite installée à Genève, en Suisse, et revient souvent en France.

a

b

c

d

e

se spécialiser	to specialise
s'installer	to settle
s'imposer	to get established, to make a name for oneself
la pression	pressure

2 **Read the texts again. Copy and complete the sentences.**

a Hasna Benhassi has won ___ and ___ medals at the Olympics.

b Le Corbusier worked in ___ until his death.

c Céline Dion started singing in ___.

d She speaks ___ and ___.

e Léopold Senghor encouraged ___ between France and Africa.

f Isabelle Adjani was inspired by American ___.

g She left France in 1997 to live in ___.

3 **In pairs, take turns to choose a text and read it aloud.**

4 **Translate the bold phrases in the texts in activity 1.**

5 **Copy and complete the sentences using the perfect tense of the verb in brackets.**

a Il ___ en 2004. (*se marier*)
b Tu (*masc. subject*) ___ à partir? (*se décider*)
c Elle ___ de cette chanteuse. (*s'inspirer*)
d Je (*masc. subject*) ___ à ses vidéos. (*s'intéresser*)
e Je (*fem. subject*) ___ à danser il y a cinq ans. (*se mettre*)

6 **Listen to extracts from six interviews (1–6). Answer the questions in English.**

1 When did the journalist write her first article?
2 For how long has the fashion designer had his own label?
3 When did the actress obtain her Canadian nationality?
4 For how long has the influencer had his blog?
5 Since when has the politician been interested in political issues?
6 When did the guitarist give his first concert?

7 **Listen again (1–6) and write down in English *one* further detail that each person mentions.**

8 **Choose the correct option to complete each sentence: *depuis* or *il y a*.**

a Elle a gagné son premier prix ___ trois semaines.
b J'ai rencontré ce chanteur ___ un an.
c Il habite au Sénégal ___ vingt ans.
d Nous avons lancé notre marque de vêtements ___ deux jours.
e Je m'intéresse à la danse ___ mon enfance.
f Il joue pour l'équipe nationale ___ 2020.

9 **Translate the completed sentences (activity 8) into English.**

10 **In pairs, take turns to ask and answer the questions.**

- Tu voudrais être célèbre? Pourquoi (pas)?
- Parle-moi d'une personne célèbre que tu as vue – à la télé ou en réalité.
- Qu'est-ce que tu sais au sujet de cette personne?
- Quelle célébrité voudrais-tu rencontrer à l'avenir? Pourquoi?

11 **Research a celebrity and write an article (150 words) about them. Describe:**

- how your chosen celebrity became famous and what they have achieved
- what they plan to do in the future.

Les verbes

The perfect tense of reflexive verbs

Reflexive verbs take *être* in the perfect tense. This means that the past participle agrees with the subject: if the subject is feminine, the past participle adds an *-e*.

*je me suis reposé(**e**)*
*tu t'es reposé(**e**)*
il s'est reposé
*elle s'est reposé**e***

Grammaire

il y a **(ago) and *depuis* (since)**

Besides meaning 'there is / there are', *il y a* also means 'ago' when followed by a time phrase.

*Elle s'est mariée **il y a** cinq ans.*

She got married five years **ago**.

*Ils sont partis **il y a** dix minutes.*

They left 10 minutes **ago**.

depuis means 'since' or 'for'. In French it is normally used with a present tense verb, unlike English, where the past tense is used.

*Elle **joue** pour cette équipe **depuis** 2020.*

She **has been playing** for this team **since** 2020.

*Il **apprend** le français **depuis** quatre ans.*

He **has been learning** French **for** four years.

Culture

Des écrivains francophones

1 Read the text and answer the questions.

La littérature francophone

Ce ne sont pas seulement les Français qui écrivent en langue française. Voici quelques exemples d'écrivains qui vivent dans d'autres pays francophones.

Roch Carrier, Canada

Roch Carrier est né au Québec en 1937. Il a écrit environ cinquante romans, contes, collections de poèmes et pièces de théâtre. Il a gagné le prix littéraire du Québec en 1964. Quatre ans plus tard, son livre *La guerre, yes sir!* – un roman qui décrit la situation des Québécois pendant la Deuxième Guerre mondiale – a confirmé sa réputation dans son pays et à l'étranger. Il a aussi écrit des histoires pour enfants. On a traduit plusieurs de ses livres en anglais.

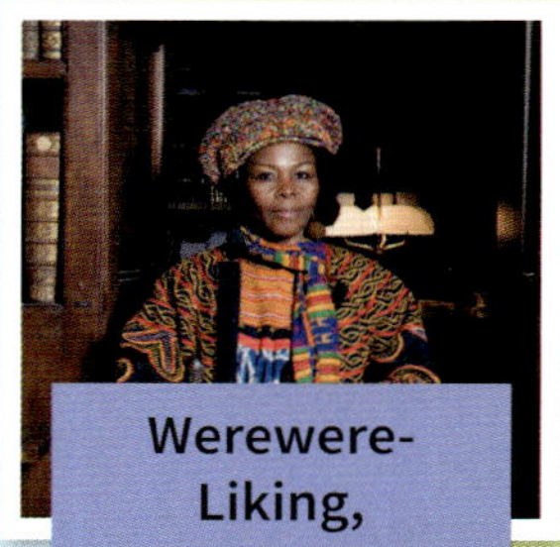

Werewere-Liking, Cameroun et Côte d'Ivoire

Werewere-Liking est une artiste d'origine camerounaise qui vit en Côte d'Ivoire depuis 1978. Elle a recherché les traditions orales de son peuple d'origine, les Bassa. Son travail est divers: elle est non seulement écrivaine mais aussi chanteuse, danseuse, actrice et peintre. En 1985, elle a fondé le groupe de théâtre Ki-Yi Mbock qui aide des jeunes défavorisés à se lancer dans une carrière artistique.

Kettly Mars, Haïti

Kettly Mars est née en 1958 à Port-au-Prince en Haïti. Sa carrière a commencé dans les années 1990 avec des poèmes. Ensuite, elle a écrit des nouvelles et des romans. Elle s'est inspirée de différents thèmes comme l'amour, la nature et les objets quotidiens. Dans ses livres, elle parle aussi des droits des femmes. Elle a été membre du jury du prix littéraire Henri Deschamps en Haïti et elle a elle-même obtenu plusieurs prix littéraires.

Who...

a researched the traditions of their culture?
b started with poetry?
c produced roughly 50 literary works?
d wrote children's stories?
e wrote about women's rights?
f acts as well?

2 Read the text again. Copy and complete the sentences.

a Roch Carrier wrote *La guerre, yes sir!* four years after…
b The novel *La guerre, yes sir!* is set during…
c In 1978, Werewere-Liking…
d Werewere-Liking founded a theatre group to help…
e Three themes that have inspired Kettly Mars are…
f Kettly Mars has won…

le conte	tale
la guerre	war
le peuple	people
le / la peintre	painter
fonder	to found
défavorisé	disadvantaged
la nouvelle	short story
littéraire	literary
le chef-d'œuvre	masterpiece
le dessin	drawing

3 **In pairs, each choose one of the writers from activity 1. Find out *four* additional pieces of information about them and present the information to your partner in French. You may find these headings helpful:**

- ville de naissance
- école et université
- famille
- prix
- causes défendues.

Culture

Arguably the most famous of all French-language writers is Victor Hugo (1802–1885), best known for his novels *Notre-Dame de Paris* and *Les Misérables*. He produced a large number of works during a 60-year career, including poetry collections, plays and some 4,000 drawings. He was also active in politics, expressing controversial views which ultimately led to his exile.

4 **Read about the writer Guillaume Musso and decide what the figures (a–h) refer to.**

Guillaume Musso

Né en 1974 à Antibes sur la côte méditerranéenne, Guillaume Musso est l'auteur français le plus vendu actuellement. Il occupe cette première place depuis 2011. Il a commencé à écrire à l'âge de 19 ans et a publié son premier roman, *Skidamarink*, en 2001. Ce roman commence par le vol de la *Joconde* au musée du Louvre à Paris.

En 1999, Guillaume Musso a eu un grave accident de voiture. En 2004, il a écrit le roman *Et après*, l'histoire d'un enfant revenu de la mort. On a vendu deux millions d'exemplaires de ce roman, on l'a adapté au cinéma et on l'a traduit en plus de 20 langues.

publier	to publish
la Joconde	*Mona Lisa*
l'exemplaire	copy (of book)

a 1974
b 2011
c 19
d 2001
e 1999
f 2004
g 2 million
h more than 20

5 **Research another contemporary French-speaking writer (a–d) and compile a fact file in English. Include:**

- year and country of birth
- year of first publication
- type of writing
- prizes and distinctions
- other work (e.g. film, art)
- current country of residence.

a Leïla Slimani
b Édouard Louis
c Yasmina Reza
d Olivier Norek

Culture

Often regarded as the most famous painting in the world, Leonardo da Vinci's portrait *La Joconde*, known in English as the *Mona Lisa*, is the most popular attraction for visitors to the Louvre art museum in Paris.

Grammar practice

The perfect tense

1 Copy and complete the sentences with the perfect tense of the verb in brackets. Then translate the sentences into English.

a Tu ___ le train ce matin? (*prendre*)
b Elle ___ à cinq heures. (*arriver*)
c J'étais fatiguée quand je ___ du bus. (*descendre*)
d Nous ___ des billets pour le concert. (*réserver*)
e Mes parents ___ il y a quelques minutes. (*sortir*)
f Vous ___ bien ___ au festival? (*dormir*)

Les verbes

Most verbs use *avoir* as their auxiliary verb in the perfect tense. Some use *être*, particularly those describing movement, such as *aller*, *partir* and *retourner*. Remember that the past participle of verbs that take *être* needs to agree with the subject.

The present tense of reflexive verbs

2 Copy and complete the sentences with the correct present tense form of the reflexive verb in brackets. Then translate the sentences into English.

a En général, je ___ à dix heures. (*se coucher*)
b Nous ___ bien avec nos voisins. (*s'entendre*)
c Le week-end, tu ___ à la maison. (*se relaxer*)
d Vous ___ toujours dans ce centre commercial. (*se perdre*)
e Mon frère ___ avec un de ses copains. (*se disputer*)
f Mes cousines ___ Jade et Camille. (*s'appeler*)

Prepositions

3 Choose the correct preposition to complete each sentence.

a Vous allez **au** / **en** / **à** Maroc (*m*)?
b Je pars **à** / **au** / **en** Suisse (*f*).
c On va **à** / **en** / **au** Paris.
d Tu pars **au** / **aux** / **en** États-Unis?
e Elles vont **en** / **au** / **à** Canada (*m*).
f Nous passons les vacances **au** / **en** / **aux** Antilles.

Grammaire

To say 'to' or 'in' a place, use *à* with a town or city, *au* with a masculine country name, *aux* with a plural country name and *en* with a feminine country name.

The perfect tense of modal verbs

4 Copy and complete the sentences with the correct perfect tense form of the verb. Then translate the sentences into English.

a Nous ___ attendre plus de trois heures. (*devoir*)
b Hier, j'___ voir le défilé en ville. (*vouloir*)
c Ils ___ gagner beaucoup d'argent. (*pouvoir*)
d Vous ___ participer au concours? (*vouloir*)
e Ma mère ___ rentrer à la maison. (*devoir*)
f Tu ___ suivre le match aujourd'hui? (*pouvoir*)

Direct object pronouns

5 Rewrite the sentences in the correct order. Then translate them into English.

a avons | ce matin | Nous | les | vus | .

b à rester | vous | Cette activité | en bonne santé | aide | .

c je | ai essayé | un sport intéressant | C'est | et | l' | hier | .

d ses films | trouve | je | J'aime | car | les | amusants | .

e apprend | en sécurité | nous | à jouer | Notre prof | .

f et | souvent | J'aime | mon oncle | le | je | vois | .

Grammaire

Direct object pronouns, *me*, *te*, *le*, *la*, *nous*, *vous* and *les*, go before the verb.

The present tense of common irregular verbs

6 Choose the correct form of the verb in each sentence.

a Tu **bois** / **boit** / **boire** de l'eau?
b Je **courir** / **court** / **cours** dans le parc.
c Mon frère **ris** / **rit** / **rire** tout le temps.
d Je **connais** / **connaître** / **connaît** très bien mon voisin.
e Tu **recevoir** / **reçois** / **reçoit** souvent des cadeaux?
f Mon chien **voir** / **vois** / **voit** quelque chose.

The imperfect tense

7 Copy and complete the sentences with the correct imperfect tense form of the verbs in brackets.

a Quand j'___ petite, ma famille n'___ pas de télévision. (*être*, *avoir*)
b Notre vie ___ simple et nous ne ___ pas beaucoup. (*être*, *sortir*)
c Parfois, nous ___ une promenade, même s'il ___ mauvais. (*faire*, *faire*)
d Nous ___ bien et tout le monde ___ . (*s'entendre*, *rire*)
e À l'école, j'___ des chansons et je ___ beaucoup de bruit! (*apprendre*, *faire*)
f À Noël, nous ___des cadeaux à nos amis et nous ___ à l'église. (*offrir*, *aller*)

Les verbes

For all verbs except *être*, the imperfect tense stem is the *nous* form of the present tense without the *-ons* ending. The stem of *être* is *ét-*.

Pronouns *y* and *en*

8 Choose *y* or *en* to complete each sentence correctly.

a Tu connais la ville de Tours? Nous **y** / **en** allons chaque année.
b Tu as combien de frères et sœurs? Moi, j'**y** / **en** ai trois.
c Tu aimes le poisson? Nous **y** / **en** mangeons deux fois par semaine.
d Mon oncle habite à Montréal et moi aussi, j'**y** / **en** habitais quand j'étais petit.
e Nous avions un appartement à Paris parce que ma mère **y** / **en** travaillait.
f Ces gâteaux sont excellents. J'**y** / **en** prends deux.

Grammar practice

The future tense

9 **Copy and complete the sentences with the future tense of the verb in brackets.**

a S'il fait beau, je ___ du vélo. (*faire*)
b Tu ___ quinze ans la semaine prochaine? (*avoir*)
c On ___ au festival ensemble. (*aller*)
d Je ___ fatiguée après le concert. (être)
e Le prix ___ au meilleur film. (*aller*)
f Il y ___ des personnes célèbres dans la rue. (*avoir*)

Les verbes

The future tense consists of the future stem, plus the endings (which match the present tense of *avoir*). Learn the stem of useful irregular verbs: *aller* – ***ir***-, *avoir* – ***aur***-, *être* – ***ser***-, *faire* – ***fer***-.
For regular -*er* verbs, the stem is simply the infinitive.

Relative clauses with *que*, *qui*, *quand*, *où*

10 **Choose the correct word to complete each sentence.**

a Je mange **quand** / **où** / **qui** j'ai faim.
b C'est le festival **que** / **qui** / **où** tu connais.
c Je ne sais pas **que** / **quand** / **où** le festival commence.
d Voici le restaurant **que** / **quand** / **où** nous allons manger.
e C'est le film **que** / **qui** / **où** a gagné le meilleur prix.
f C'est la pièce de théâtre **que** / **qui** / **quand** nous allons voir.

The imperative

11 **Copy and complete the sentences with the correct form of the imperative.**

a ___ le défilé, Théo! (*regarder*)
b Tu as faim? ___ ton repas! (*finir*)
c S'il vous plaît, ___ devant la porte, madame. (*attendre*)
d ___ les paroles de la chanson, Amir! (*écouter*)
e ___ son exemple si vous voulez réussir. (*suivre*)
f ___ votre nom ici, s'il vous plaît. (*écrire*)

Grammaire

Remember that we use the *tu* form when talking to a family member or friend, but the *vous* form when talking to two or more people, or to someone we are not on familiar terms with.

The conditional

12 **Copy and complete the sentences with the correct form of the conditional.**

Dans un monde idéal, …

a il n'y ___ pas de pauvreté. (*avoir*)
b on ___ heureux. (*être*)
c ma famille ___ souvent en vacances. (*aller*)
d on ___ beaucoup de temps libre ensemble. (*avoir*)
e je ___ toujours de mon mieux. (*faire*)
f il ___ beau tous les jours. (*faire*)

Les verbes

The conditional is used to say what someone **would** do or what **would** happen in the future. Learn the stem of useful irregular verbs: *aller* – ***ir***-, *avoir* – ***aur***-, *être* – ***ser***-, *faire* – ***fer***-.
For regular -*er* verbs, the stem is simply the infinitive. The endings match the imperfect tense endings.

Emphatic pronouns

13 Copy and complete the sentences with the correct preposition and emphatic pronoun.

a J'ai choisi quelque chose ___. (*for you (polite form)*)

b C'est difficile ___. (*without you (familiar, singular)*)

c Tu veux jouer aux cartes ___? (*with us*)

d Vous venez ___? (*to my home*)

e Je vais arriver ___. (*before them (m)*)

f Tu as déjà joué ___? (*against him*)

Possessive adjectives

14 Choose the correct form of the possessive adjective to complete each sentence. Then translate the sentences into English.

a Je passe beaucoup de temps avec **mon / ma / mes** famille (*f*).

b Elle a célébré **son / sa / ses** succès (*m*).

c Tu t'entends bien avec **ton / ta / tes** collègues?

d Il a choisi **son / sa / ses** carrière (*f*) quand il était petit.

e Nous n'avons pas **notre / nos** propre piscine (*f*).

f Ils partagent **leur / leurs** vie (*f*) avec le public.

Grammaire

Possessive adjectives need to agree with the noun that follows.

The perfect tense of reflexive verbs

15 Copy and complete the sentences with the correct form of the perfect tense. Then translate the sentences into English.

a Il ___ l'année dernière. (*se marier*)

b Après le match, j'étais fatigué et je ___. (*se reposer*)

c Ma carrière ___ rapidement. (*se développer*)

d Je suis devenue chanteuse et je ___ de la musique africaine. (*s'inspirer*)

e Isabelle, pourquoi est-ce que tu ___ à partir? (*se décider*)

f Marc ___ à danser à l'âge de quinze ans. (*se mettre*)

Les verbes

All reflexive verbs are conjugated with *être* in the perfect tense. The past participle usually agrees with the subject, just as with other verbs that take *être*.

il y a and *depuis*

16 Choose *il y a* or *depuis* to complete each sentence. Then translate the sentences into English.

a Elle joue pour sa ville **il y a / depuis** deux ans.

b Nous apprenons l'espagnol **il y a / depuis** six mois.

c J'ai rencontré le chanteur **il y a / depuis** trois semaines.

d Ils travaillent dans le commerce **il y a / depuis** l'année dernière.

e L'équipe a joué ici **il y a / depuis** quelques jours.

f L'actrice a quitté son pays de naissance **il y a / depuis** dix ans.

Grammaire

Il y a means 'ago' and is usually used with a verb in the perfect tense.

Depuis means 'since' or 'for' and is usually used with the present tense in French, whereas the past tense is often used in English.

Higher Vocabulary

Words that are highlighted in grey in this list are words that may be useful, but you won't need to know them for the exam.

Introductory vocabulary

accepter to accept
acheter to buy
l' *activité (f.)* activity
adorer to love
aimer to like
aimer mieux to prefer
aller to go
l' *ami(e) (m./f.)* friend
l' *an (m.)* year
l' *anniversaire (m.)* birthday
août August
après after
attendre to wait
aujourd'hui today
autre (adj.) other
l' *avis (m.)* opinion
avoir to have
beaucoup a lot
le *billet* ticket
le *blog* blog
boire to drink
bon(ne) good
ça that
le *cadeau* present
le *café* coffee, coffee shop
la *campagne* countryside
le *camping* campsite
car because
la *carte* card
célèbre famous
célébrer to celebrate
le *centre* centre
certain(e)(s) some, certain
la *chambre* bedroom
chanter to sing
le/la *chanteur/chanteuse* singer
chaque each, every
le/la *chef (de cuisine)* chef
cher/chère expensive
chez nous at/to our place
le *chien* dog
la *chose* thing
le *cinéma* cinema
commencer to start
le *concours* competition
connaître to know (person, place)
le *copain* friend, boyfriend
la *copine* friend, girlfriend
courir to run
coûter to cost
créatif/créative creative
d'abord firstly, first of all
dangereux/dangereuse dangerous
la *danse* dancing
le/la *danseur/danseuse* dancer
décembre December
le *défilé* parade
déjà already
demain tomorrow
détester to hate
devenir to become
devoir to have to
(le) *dimanche* Sunday
le *dîner* dinner
donner to give
dur(e) hard
écouter to listen (to)
écrire to write
l' *écrivain(e) (m./f.)* writer
l' *église (f.)* church
en ligne online
ennuyeux/ennuyeuse boring
entendre to hear
envoyer to send
l' *équipe (f.)* team
espérer to hope
essayer to try
l' *été (m.)* summer
à l'étranger abroad
être to be
facile easy
faire to do, make
faire beau to be nice (weather)
la *famille* family
il faut it is necessary
la *femme politique* politician (female)
le *festival* festival
la *fête* party, celebration
le *feu d'artifice* firework displays
le *film* film
la *fin* end
la *fleur* flower
la *fois* time, occasion
le *foot(ball)* football
français(e) French
francophone French-language
le *frère* brother
le *gâteau* cake
les *gens (m. pl.)* people
grand(e) big
le *groupe* band
l' *hiver (m.)* winter
l' *homme politique (m.)* politician (male)
l' *idée (f.)* idea
important important
intéressant(e) interesting
s' *intéresser à* to be interested in
inviter to invite
le *jardin* garden
le *jeu* game
jeune (adj.) young
jouer to play
le *jour* day
le *jour de l'An* New Year's Day
le *jour férié* public holiday
la *lecture* reading
se *lever* to get up
lire to read
le *livre* book
mais but
la *maison* house
manger to eat
marcher to walk
se *marier* to get married
le *match* match
même same
(le) *mercredi* Wednesday
la *mère* mother
le *métier* job
minuit midnight
la *mode* fashion
moi me
la *montagne* mountain(s)
la *mosquée* mosque
la *musique* music
la *natation* swimming
national(e)(s)/nationaux national
Noël Christmas
l' *offre (f.)* offer
ouvert(e) open
Pâques Easter
le *parc* park
parfois sometimes
partager to share
le/la *partenaire* partner
partout everywhere
passionnant(e) exciting
pendant during
la *personne* person
petit(e) small
la *piscine* swimming pool
la *place* place, square, spot
la *plage* beach
plus more
possible possible
poster to post
pourquoi why
pouvoir to be able to, can
préféré(e) favourite
préférer to prefer
la *proposition* proposition
quand when
quelqu'un somebody, someone
la *radio* radio
la *recette* recipe
regarder to watch
rencontrer to meet
le *réseau* network
les *réseaux sociaux (m. pl.)* social media
réserver to book
le *roman* novel
la *route* road
la *rue* street
la *semaine* week
si if
social social
le *site web* website
la *sœur* sister
le *soir* evening
souvent often
sportif/sportive sports, sporty
le *stade* stadium
la *star* star, celebrity
tard late
la *télé(vision)* television
télécharger to download
le *temps* time, weather
le *théâtre* theatre
timide shy

tous les jours every day
tout le monde everyone
la *tradition* tradition
travailler to work
trouver to find
utiliser to use
les *vacances (f. pl.)* holidays
le *vélo* bike
la *vidéo* video
la *visite* visit
vivre to live
voir to see
vouloir to want
voyager to travel
le *week-end* weekend

4.1F Le week-end dernier

les *Alpes (f. pl.)* Alps
amusant(e) amusing, fun, funny
l' *après-midi (m.)* afternoon
le *beau-père* stepfather, father-in-law
britannique British
le *bus* bus
cela that
la *chance* luck, opportunity
les *courses (f. pl.)* (grocery) shopping
dernier / dernière last
les *devoirs (m. pl.)* homework
l' *e-mail (m.)* e-mail
l' *énergie (f.)* energy
ensuite then
gentil(le) kind
les *grands-parents (m. pl.)* grandparents
le *jeu de société* board game
malade ill, sick
le *matin* morning
meilleur(e) best, better
mettre to put (on)
le *pantalon* trousers
la *partie* part, round of (game)
le *portable* mobile phone
prendre to take
la *promenade* walk, stroll
puis then
quelque some
recevoir to receive
la *réponse* answer
rire to laugh
(le) *samedi* Saturday

sans without
le *site* (tourist) site
le *SMS* text message
le *thé* tea
toujours always
trop too
venir to come
la *ville* town, city
visiter to visit (place)

4.1H Télé, cinéma, musique!

l' *action (f.)* action
les *actualités (f. pl.)* current affairs
africain(e) African
s' *appeler* to be called
apprécier to enjoy, appreciate, like
apprendre to learn, to teach
aussi also
bien well, good
camerounais(e) Cameroonian
ce / cet / cette / ces this
le *centre commercial* shopping centre
la *comédie* comedy
le *concert* concert
se *demander* to wonder
se *disputer* to argue
l' *écran (m.)* screen
embêtant(e) annoying
faire mauvais to be bad (weather)
le *genre* kind, type
jamais never
le *moment* moment
noir(e) (adj.) black
le *papa* dad
le *pêcheur* fisherman
le *piano* piano
le *rap* rap
recommander to recommend
se *relaxer* to relax
se *ressembler* to look alike
la *série* (TV) series
tôt early
vers at about (time)

4.2F En voyage!

l' *année (f.)* year
arriver to arrive
l' *automne (m.)* autumn
le *bateau* boat
le *bord* edge
le *Canada* Canada
la *capitale* capital city
cependant however
comment how
le *défi* challenge
descendre to get off, go down
difficile difficult
ensemble together
entrer dans to go into
les *États-Unis (m. pl.)* United States
grave serious
habiter to live
haut high
l' *heure (f.)* hour, time, o'clock
historique historic
le *hockey sur glace* ice hockey
l' *île (f.)* island
le *kilomètre* kilometre
là-bas over there
le *Maroc* Morocco
la *mer* sea
le *midi* midday
le *mois* month
monter to go up
mourir to die
naître to be born
partir to leave
passer to spend (time)
le *pays* country
la *pièce (de théâtre)* play (theatre)
populaire popular
les *Pyrénées (f. pl.)* Pyrenees
rentrer to go home
rester to stay
retourner to return
la *Réunion* Reunion (island)
la *salle* room
le *Sénégal* Senegal
le *sport* sport
la *Suisse* Switzerland
le *surf* surfing
tomber to fall
traditionnel(le) traditional

l' *ultra-marathon (m.)* ultramarathon
le *voyage* journey
vrai(e) true, real

4.2H Le sport, c'est ma passion!

aider to help
l' *ascension (f.)* climb
avoir l'air to seem, look
beau / bel / belle beautiful, nice
se *blesser* to get hurt
la *boule* ball, bubble
le *canyoning* gorge walking
la *centaine* about a hundred
chercher to research, to look for
chez to the place of, at the place of, at, with
le *club* club
le *concurrent* competitor
conseiller to advise
le *cœur* heart
le *courage* courage
courant current
la *course* race
le / la *cycliste* cyclist
découvrir to discover, find out
dès que as soon as
différent(e) different
la *distance* distance
l' *eau (m.)* water
enfin finally
énorme enormous
entrer to enter
s' *entraîner* to train
l' *étape (f.)* stage
étonnant astonishing
l' *événement (m.)* event
éviter (de) to avoid
fou / folle mad
la *Guadeloupe* Guadeloupe
l' *herbe (f.)* grass
les *les îles Caraïbes (f. pl.)* Caribbean islands
il vaut la peine it is worth
il vaut mieux it is better to
il y a there is / are
le *kayak* kayaking
maintenant now
moderne modern
le *monde* people, world

la ***montée*** climb
le ***moyen*** means
nouveau/nouvelle (adj.) new
où where
participer (à) to participate, take part (in)
la ***passion*** passion
penser to think
la ***pente*** slope
la ***photo*** photo
le ***plaisir*** pleasure
le ***plastique*** plastic
le ***plein air*** open air
près de near
le ***prix*** prize, price
profiter de to make the most of, enjoy
progresser to make progress
le ***risque*** risk
risquer to risk
sauver to rescue
seul(e) alone
le ***ski*** ski
tous/toutes les deux both
vraiment really

5.1F Bon anniversaire!

Aïd-el-Fitr Eid al-Fitr
l' ***amoureux/amoureuse (m./f.)*** lover
assez (de) enough, quite
les ***autres (m./f. pl.)*** others
avril April
la ***célébration*** celebration
la ***chaussure*** shoe
chrétien(ne) (adj.) Christian
le ***cola*** coke
la ***collecte*** collection
commercial commercial
content(e) pleased, happy
croire to believe
délicieux/délicieuse delicious
dîner (v.) to have dinner
divorcé(e) divorced
donc so
double double
entre between
le ***fan*** fan
février February
janvier January
juillet July
mai May
mars March
le ***message*** message
moins less
musulman(e) (adj.) Muslim
l' ***occasion (f.)*** occasion, chance, opportunity
octobre October
ouvrir to open
le ***paquet*** parcel
plusieurs several
préparer to prepare
la ***raison*** reason
rarement rarely
le ***salon*** lounge
septembre September
spécial(e) special
suivre to follow
le ***travail*** work
triste sad
les ***vêtements (m. pl.)*** clothes

5.1H Je faisais la fête comme ça

adulte adult
agréable pleasant
s' ***amuser*** to have fun
appeler to call
le ***bruit*** noise
le ***car*** bus, coach
le ***carnaval*** carnival
catholique Catholic
défiler to parade
depuis since
l' ***enfance (f.)*** childhood
l' ***enfant (m.)*** child
l' ***Europe (f.)*** Europe
festif/festive festive
la ***forêt*** forest, wood
grandir to grow up
la ***journée*** day
jusque until
loin far
long(ue) long
Mardi gras Shrove Tuesday
marquer to mark, score
même si even if
la ***messe*** mass
offrir to offer, give
par contre on the other hand
le ***petit-déjeuner*** breakfast
(un) peu (a) little
presque nearly
la ***prière*** prayer
prochain(e) next
relaxant(e) relaxing
la ***Seine*** River Seine
simple simple
situé(e) situated
se ***souvenir de*** to remember
soixante sixty
la ***tante*** aunt
le/ ***voisin(e)*** neighbour

5.2F Les fêtes dans le passé et à l'avenir

américain(e) (adj.) American
l' ***avenir (m.)*** future
le ***Cameroun*** Cameroon
la ***chanson*** song
la ***date*** date
l' ***escalade (f.)*** climbing
étudier to study
extraordinaire extraordinary
familial(e) (adj.) family
le ***goût*** taste
Hanouka Hanukkah
l' ***histoire (f.)*** history, story
juif/juive (adj.) Jewish
les ***légumes (m. pl.)*** vegetables
la ***lumière*** light
le ***marché*** market
militaire military
la ***monarchie*** monarchy
la ***nature*** nature
le ***passé*** past
la ***rencontre*** meeting
la ***sandwicherie*** sandwich bar
la ***soupe*** soup
le ***spectacle*** show
la ***Terre*** Earth
le ***vin chaud*** mulled wine

5.2H On y va, au festival?

l' ***accès (m.)*** access
l' ***animation (f.)*** animation
artistique artistic
la ***cérémonie*** ceremony
chaud(e) hot
connu(e) known, famous
la ***créativité*** creativity
dehors outside
dire to say
la ***distinction*** distinction
le ***documentaire*** documentary
dramatique dramatic
également as well
l' ***expression (f.)*** expression
facile easy
le/la ***gagnant(e)*** winner
l' ***innovation (f.)*** innovation
le/la ***journaliste*** journalist
juger to judge
le ***jury*** jury
le ***lieu*** place
le ***millier*** about a thousand
original(e) original
officiel(le) official
professionnel(le) professional
proposer to offer
le ***public*** audience
réservé reserved
la ***sélection*** selection
talentueux/talentueuse talented
le ***tapis*** carpet
unique unique

6.1F Tu ferais quoi pour être célèbre?

accessible accessible
l' ***argent (m.)*** money
le ***basket*** basketball
calme (adj.) calm, quiet
la ***célébrité*** celebrity
classique (adj.) classical
la ***compétence*** skill
l' ***exemple (m.)*** example
faire attention to be careful
le/la ***footballeur/footballeuse*** footballer
handicapé(e) (adj.) disabled
l' ***influenceur/influenceuse (m./f.)*** influencer
le/la ***joueur/joueuse*** player
organiser to organise
oublier to forget
les ***paroles (f. pl.)*** words, lyrics
réussir to succeed
sourire to smile
le ***yoga*** yoga

6.1H Qu'est-ce que je ferais pour être célèbre?

l' *animal (m.)* animal
bénévole (adj.) voluntary
le/la *bénévole (n.)* volunteer
le *conseil* advice
le/la *créateur/créatrice* creator, designer
créer to create
demander to ask
développer to develop
l' *effort (m.)* effort
exister to exist
faire de son mieux to do your best
inspirer to inspire
l' *intérêt (m.)* interest
la *minute* minute
le *modèle* role model
nager to swim
le *nombre* number
l' *opinion (f.)* opinion
passionné(e) passionate
patient(e) (adj.) patient
la *personnalité* personality
plutôt rather
le *progrès* progress
rapidement quickly
le *refuge* shelter
remercier to thank
ressembler to resemble
respecter to respect
sérieux/sérieuse serious
le *soutien* support
la *spécialité* speciality
une fois once

6.2F La vie de célébrité

l' *Amérique (f.)* America
l' *avantage (m.)* advantage
complètement completely
le *couple* couple
devant in front of
espagnol(e) (adj.) Spanish
fantastique fantastic
gagner to win
la *girafe* giraffe
le *hip-hop* hip-hop
l' *influence (f.)* influence
le *jazz* jazz
malgré despite
le *mari* husband
la *nuit* night
l' *oncle (m.)* uncle
par by
paresseux/paresseuse lazy
passionant(e) exciting
personnel personal
positif/positive positive
prêt(e) ready
le *problème* problem
propre own
protéger to protect
quotidien(ne) daily
répondre to answer
riche rich

6.2H Des francophones célèbres

l' *Algérie (f.)* Algeria
améliorer to improve
ancien(ne) ancient
apporter to bring
l' *architecte (m.)* architect
l' *architecture (f.)* architecture
arrêter to stop
l' *article (m.)* article
avant before
le *bonheur* happiness
le *bronze* bronze
canadien(ne) Canadian
capable capable
à cause de because of
le *changement* change
le/la *citoyen(ne)* citizen
la *colonie* colony
considérer to consider
la *coopération* cooperation
le *début* beginning
se *décider* to make up one's mind
établir to be established
la *forme* shape
Genève Geneva
s' *imposer* to get established
s' *installer* to settle
le *journal* newspaper, diary
jusque until
lancer to launch
largement widely
la *marque* brand
les *médias (m. pl.)* media
se *mettre à* to begin to
montrer to show oneself
la *mort* death
la *nationalité* nationality
obtenir to obtain
olympique Olympic
le/la *poète* poet
politique (adj.) political
le *président* president
la *presse* press
la *pression* pressure
la *qualité* quality
la *question* question
régulièrement regularly
reposer to rest
la *République* Republic
le *rêve* dream
revenir to come back
seulement only
la *simplicité* simplicity
se *spécialiser* to specialise
au sujet de about
super great
la *voix* voice

Culture

l' *amitié (f.)* friendship
l' *accident (m.)* accident
actuellement currently
adapter to adapt
l' *amour (m.)* love
l' *anglais (m.)* English (language)
l' *auteur (m.)* author (male)
l' *autrice (f.)* author (female)
avoir lieu to take place
le *but* goal
combiner to combine
confirmer to confirm
le *conflit* conflict
le *conte* tale
la *côte* coast
la *culture* culture
culturel(le) cultural
décrire to describe
défavorisé(e) disadvantaged
démocratique democratic
le *dessin* drawing
divers varied
le *droit* right
l' *éducation (f.)* education
elle-même herself
en plus in addition
environ roughly
l' *établissement (m.)* establishment
excellent excellent
exemplaire copy
la *femme* woman, wife
fonder to found
la *guerre* war
l' *image (f.)* image, picture
la *Joconde* Mona Lisa
la *langue* language
littéraire literary
la *littérature* literature
marocain(e) Moroccan
méditerranéen Mediterranean
mondial(e) world(wide)
le *musée* museum
la *naissance* birth
la *nouvelle* short story
l' *objet (m.)* object, subject
oral(e) oral
l' *origine (f.)* origin
le/la *participant(e)* participant
le/la *peintre* painter
le *peuple* people
le *poème* poem
présent present
promouvoir to promote
publier to publish
le *Québec* Quebec
le/la *Québécois(e)* person from Quebec
le/la *réalisateur/réalisatrice* film director
rechercher to research
réunir to reunite
soutenir to support
le *texte* text
toucher to touch
traduire to translate
l' *université (f.)* university
vendre to sell
la *voiture* car
le *vol* theft

Test and revise: Higher Listening

1 You hear some well-known Belgian people talking about fame. What is their opinion on the following aspects?

Write **P** for a **positive** opinion
N for a **negative** opinion
P+N for a **positive** and **negative** opinion.

1 The press
2 Family life
3 Wealth
4 Travel

4 marks

Conseil

In this type of task, listen out for positive and negative opinions. Linking words and phrases, such as *mais* and *d'un autre côté*, can indicate a contrast of opinions, but listen carefully to the whole extract to be sure.

2 You hear this podcast about a Canadian festival.

Choose the correct answer and write the letter.

1 This year's festival began on…

A	3 June.
B	8 June.
C	11 June.

1 mark

2 The number of participants was…

A	smaller than last year.
B	the same as last year.
C	greater than last year.

1 mark

3 On the last day there was…

A	singing.
B	dancing.
C	singing and dancing.

1 mark

4 The organisers were pleased with…

A	the quality of the shows.
B	the involvement of young people.
C	people's behaviour.

1 mark

3 You hear some French students talking about their free time.

Complete the sentences in **English**.

1 My club meets on Wednesdays to… **1 mark**
2 Swimming is a good pastime when… **1 mark**
3 I like to be… as often as possible. **1 mark**
4 In the holidays, I am going to read the novel that… **1 mark**

Conseil

Before listening, try to anticipate the French words you are likely to hear, based on the English words in the sentences. Sometimes you will hear an exact translation, such as *mercredi* for 'Wednesday', but sometimes synonyms or different wordings will be used.

4 You hear this conversation between two school friends, Emma and Valentin.

The conversation is about influencers.

Answer the questions in **English**.

1 Why does Emma want to become an influencer? Give **two** reasons. **2 marks**
2 What has put Valentin off the idea of trying to become an influencer? **1 mark**
3 What **two** disadvantages of being an influencer does Valentin mention? **2 marks**

Conseil

Sometimes the recording will include phrases or sentences that are not directly tested, but which provide the context. Focus on the questions and make sure your answers contain the required information.

Conseil

In this type of task, don't be tempted to choose an answer based on just a single word. Often, one of the incorrect answer options refers to something mentioned in the recording but which conveys a different meaning.

5 You hear this news item on the radio about a new theatre.

Choose the **two** correct statements for each section (1–3) and write the letters.

1

A	The theatre will open in seven days' time.
B	The theatre is in the market square.
C	The theatre is located near the church.
D	The church closed two years ago.

2

A	The theatre can seat more than 100 people.
B	10 seats are reserved for disabled people.
C	There is a café on the ground floor.
D	The café will serve hot and cold food.

3

A	It is hoped that the theatre will attract tourists.
B	The nearest theatre used to be 30 km away.
C	The tickets will be moderately priced.
D	Young people will pay less.

6 marks

Conseil

In any multiple-choice task, beware of choosing an option based on a single word or phrase. Read the four sentences for each section carefully and note details such as verb tenses, and positive or negative expressions.

6 You hear this announcement about a shopping centre in La Vallée.

Choose the correct answer and write the letter.

1 The shopping centre is open…

A	five days a week.
B	six days a week.
C	seven days a week.

1 mark

2 This week there are… available.

A	tasting sessions
B	price reductions
C	new types of vegetables

1 mark

3 The cinema…

A	doesn't accept bags.
B	doesn't take reservations.
C	has recently opened.

1 mark

4 You are advised to travel by…

A	car or bus.
B	car or bike.
C	bus or bike.

1 mark

Dictation A

You will now hear **five** short sentences.

- Listen carefully and, using your knowledge of French sounds, write down in French exactly what you hear for each sentence.
- You will hear each sentence **three** times: the first time as a full sentence, the second time in short sections and the third time again as a full sentence.
- Use your knowledge of French sounds and grammar to make sure that what you have written makes sense. Check carefully that your spelling is accurate.

10 marks

Dictation B

You will now hear **five** more sentences.

Write down in French exactly what you hear for each sentence.

10 marks

Test and revise: Higher Speaking

Role play

You are talking to your French friend.

Your teacher will play the part of your friend and will speak first.

You should address your friend as *tu*.

When you see this – ? – you will have to ask a question.

In order to score full marks, you must include at least one verb in your response to each task.

1 Say how you relax at the weekend. (Give **two** details.)

2 Say what you think about TV and why. (Give **one** opinion and **one** reason.)

3 Mention **two** free-time activities you did during your last holidays.

4 Say what you talk about with friends. (Give **one** detail.)

? 5 Ask your friend a question about reading.

10 marks

Conseil

In the role play, you should include at least one verb in your response to each task (1–5) on the card. Keep your responses short and simple and focus on conveying your meaning accurately.

Reading aloud

When your teacher asks you, read aloud the following text **in French**.

Ma grande passion, c'est la natation.

Mon rêve est de devenir célèbre, mais je sais que ce n'est pas facile.

J'ai déjà participé à des concours et j'ai gagné des prix.

Je fais toujours de mon mieux.

Cependant, il y a beaucoup d'autres jeunes qui savent bien nager.

You will then be asked four questions **in French** that relate to the topic of **Celebrity culture**. Make sure you **answer all four questions as fully as you can**.

15 marks

Conseil

Take care with your pronunciation in the reading aloud task. Try to remember all the French sounds and sound combinations you have learnt.

Answer the follow-up questions fully. To extend your sentences, you can give justified opinions and use a range of tenses, with adverbs and intensifiers.

Photo card

- During your preparation time, look at the two photos. You may make as many notes as you wish on an Additional Answer Sheet and use these notes during the task.
- Your teacher will ask you to talk about the content of these photos. The recommended time is approximately **one and a half minutes**. You must **say at least one thing about each photo**.
- After you have spoken about the content of the photos, your teacher will then ask you questions related to **any** of the topics within the theme of **Popular culture**.

25 marks

Conseil

Make sure you say at least one thing about each photo. Give as much information as you can. Try to extend your answers to the follow-up questions as much as possible: you can give and justify opinions, and use a variety of tenses, adjectives, adverbs, pronouns and intensifiers.

Photo 1

Photo 2

Test and revise: Higher Reading

1 You see some headlines (A–E) online. Which headline matches each issue (1–3)? Write the correct letter.

A	Après la pluie, la météo est enfin bonne – profitez-en!
B	Les jeunes ne lisent plus pendant leur temps libre – quel dommage!
C	Faisons la cuisine! C'est moins cher et c'est bon pour la santé.
D	Voulez-vous être plus actif / active? Voici quelques idées pour les vacances.
E	Les séries – est-ce que ça vaut la peine de les regarder?

1 Reading **1 mark**

2 Television **1 mark**

3 Weather **1 mark**

2 You read this online forum. People are talking about Christmas. Who says each statement (a–e)?

Write **L** for **Louise**
A for **Arthur**
Y for **Yasmine**.

Louise Pour nous, Noël est un jour comme les autres. Ma mère est policière et elle doit souvent travailler le 25 décembre. Mais il est évident que mes copines ne sont pas d'accord. Elles aiment bien faire la fête. Elles aiment aussi offrir et recevoir des cadeaux.

Arthur Noël fait partie de notre culture. Je ne peux pas imaginer le 25 décembre sans un repas de fête et sans cadeaux. Pourtant, je sais que Noël peut être triste pour certaines personnes qui n'ont pas de famille. Notre voisine vit seule et cette année, nous allons l'inviter à passer la journée chez nous.

Yasmine Je suis musulmane, mais le 25 décembre, j'aime bien faire la fête. Normalement, ma tante et mon oncle viennent nous voir. Personne ne travaille et tout le monde se relaxe. Les cadeaux n'ont pas beaucoup d'importance pour nous, mais on aime faire un bon repas.

a A neighbour will visit us. **1 mark**

b Christmas is not a special day. **1 mark**

c No one works at Christmas. **1 mark**

d I'm different from my friends. **1 mark**

e Christmas can be a sad time for some. **1 mark**

Conseil

For some questions you will need to infer the answer (work it out based on information from the text). Here, the English statements are not direct translations of the French, but you are given the right information in the text to work out the answers.

3 You read a blog post from a French teenager, Lucie, who is talking about her family's free-time activities.

Complete the sentences (1–4, on page 103). Write the letter for the correct option.

Dans ma famille, nous avons tous des passe-temps différents. Quand on est en vacances, il est difficile de trouver des activités que tout le monde aime!

D'abord mon frère… Lui, quand il était petit, il était très sportif mais depuis quelque temps, il ne participe plus à des concours et il adore la lecture.

En ce qui concerne ma sœur, c'est le contraire. Elle se repose moins qu'avant, mais elle s'est inscrite à un club de natation et elle dit qu'elle va aussi faire du vélo.

Ensuite, la passion de ma mère est de prendre des photos. Elle ne fait jamais de promenade sans son portable et elle est toujours prête à le sortir quand elle voit un bâtiment intéressant – même s'il pleut.

1 For Lucie's family it can be a problem to…

A	please everyone.
B	do something different.
C	find something to do.

1 mark

2 Lucie's brother now…

A	keeps active.
B	competes.
C	reads.

1 mark

3 Lucie's sister used to spend more time…

A	resting.
B	swimming.
C	cycling.

1 mark

4 Lucie's mother…

A	never goes for a walk.
B	photographs buildings.
C	doesn't like wet weather.

1 mark

4 You see an article about the actor and singer Gad Elmaleh.

Answer the questions in **English**.

Gad Elmaleh

Gad Elmaleh est né d'une famille juive au Maroc. Son père travaillait dans le commerce mais pratiquait le théâtre pendant son temps libre. Dès l'âge de cinq ans, il a accompagné son père sur scène pour annoncer ses spectacles. Son rêve était de devenir célèbre.
En 1988, il a quitté son pays d'origine pour vivre et étudier au Québec. Après ses études, il a suivi une formation de théâtre à Paris. Depuis 1994, Gad Elmaleh mène une carrière d'acteur et de chanteur, mais il est surtout humoriste et connu pour ses spectacles. En 2007, il a gagné le titre d'homme le plus drôle de l'année.

a Which **two** things are we told about Gad Elmaleh's father? **2 marks**

b What did Gad Elmaleh start doing when he was five? Give **two** details. **2 marks**

c What did Gad Elmaleh do before moving to Paris? **1 mark**

d Why was 2007 a good year for Gad Elmaleh? **1 mark**

Conseil

In this type of question, you need to note the number of points required. If the question says **'two** things' or **'two** details', then you must convey **two** separate points, even if they are part of the same sentence.

5 Translate these sentences into English.

a Cette année, j'ai de la chance car mon anniversaire tombe un dimanche.

b Quand j'étais petite, ma tante passait les vacances chez nous.

c Il y aura un grand défilé et on dansera toute la nuit.

d Après avoir joué au festival, il a continué sa tournée internationale.

e Elle s'est inspirée de la jeune chanteuse marocaine. **10 marks**

6 Translate these sentences into English.

a Je serai heureuse d'assister à ce nouveau festival.

b J'aime offrir des cadeaux à des personnes que je ne vois pas souvent.

c Il est membre de l'équipe française depuis plusieurs années.

d Avant de créer son blog, elle a fait des recherches en ligne.

e À cette époque, nous habitions au Canada et nous faisions beaucoup de sport. **10 marks**

Conseil

You need to take account of every detail in each French sentence, including words like *nouveau* and *beaucoup* that could easily be forgotten. If there is a word or expression that you do not understand, make a logical guess – write something that makes sense in the context.

Test and revise: Higher Writing

1 Translate the following sentences into French.

a It's a good festival but the tickets are too expensive.

b When I was ten, I used to swim every day.

c She became famous after winning her first prize.

d Unfortunately, I was unable to go to the birthday party.

e In the future, he will work hard as he would like to travel round the world.

10 marks

Conseil

The priority in the translation task is to convey the correct meaning. It is crucial to get the verb tense right and to distinguish correctly between the subject pronouns ('I', 'you', etc.).

Either question 2.1 or question 2.2

2.1 You are emailing your French friend about your free-time activities.

Write approximately **90** words in **French**.

You must write something about each bullet point.

Describe:

- what you normally do in the evening
- how you spent last weekend
- your free time activities in the future.

15 marks

Conseil

For this task, you must write something about all the bullet points, but there is no need to cover them equally. Try to convey a lot of information clearly and use varied vocabulary and grammar. You should also make accurate references to all three time frames. Try to develop your ideas and use different linking words such as *mais*, *quand* and *si*.

2.2 You are emailing your Canadian friend about celebrities.

Write approximately **90** words in **French**.

You must write something about each bullet point.

Describe:

- the advantages and disadvantages of being famous
- a celebrity that you saw on screen or in person recently
- why you would like (or not like) to be famous one day.

15 marks

Either question **3.1** or question **3.2**

3.1 You are writing a post for your blog. Your post is about festivals.

Write approximately **150** words in **French**.

You must write something about both bullet points.

Describe:

- the positive and negative aspects of festivals
- a festival you have seen, either in person or on screen.

25 marks

3.2 You are writing a post for your blog. Your post is about sport.

Write approximately **150** words in **French**.

You must write something about both bullet points.

Describe:

- the importance of sport
- sports you intend to do and watch.

25 marks

Conseil

Remember to write something about both bullet points and make sure what you write is relevant. There is no need to cover the bullet points equally and you can use a variety of tenses in response to them both. Aim to develop your ideas as much as possible, using complex, varied language, and ensure you communicate your message clearly.

Theme 3
Communication and the world around us

Travel and tourism

1 **Read the statements about travel. Choose the correct opinion, means of transport and reason for each one.**

1 Quand je vais en vacances, j'aime voyager en avion car c'est rapide.
2 Pour partir en vacances, je préfère prendre le train parce que ce n'est pas cher.
3 J'adore voyager en bateau quand je vais en vacances mais j'ai le mal de mer.
4 Je déteste voyager à vélo parce que ce n'est pas rapide.
5 Je n'aime pas voyager en voiture car c'est mauvais pour l'environnement.
6 J'aime beaucoup voyager en car parce que c'est pratique.

Opinion	Transport	Reason
a I really like	a 	a It is bad for the environment.
b I hate	b 	b It is quick.
c I do not like	c 	c I get seasick.
d I like	d 	d It is convenient / practical.
e I love	e 	e It is not quick.
f I prefer	f 	f It is not expensive.

rapide	quick / fast	*mauvais*	bad
cher	expensive	*le mal de mer*	seasickness
pratique	convenient / practical		

2 **Listen (1–4) and match each speaker to their perfect holiday (a–d).**

a 

b  

c  

d  

il fait chaud	it's hot
il fait froid	it's cold
il y a du soleil	it's sunny
il pleut	it's raining

3 **Read the forum. Write down in English the activities each person does on holiday. Add whether they love, like, dislike or hate each activity.**

Marion
Quand il fait beau, j'aime bien marcher dans la campagne et faire du vélo. J'adore faire de la natation dans la mer et jouer sur la plage avec mon frère.

Thomas
Quand je suis en vacances avec ma famille, j'aime faire du shopping dans les magasins en ville mais je déteste visiter des sites historiques. C'est ennuyeux, surtout quand il fait chaud.

a shopping
b walking
c visiting sites
d cycling
e swimming
f playing on the beach

marcher	to walk
passer du temps	to spend time
la campagne	the countryside
la plage	beach
les magasins	shops

Media and technology

1 Match the phrases (1–5) to the pictures (a–e).

1 un journal
2 les réseaux sociaux
3 la radio
4 une émission
5 les devoirs

a

b

c

d

e
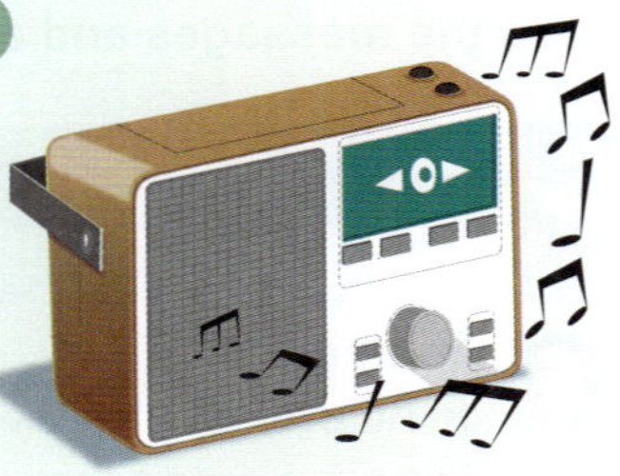

2 Listen (1–4) and choose the *two* activities (a–f) mentioned by each person.

a read newspapers
b use social media
c watch TV
d download music
e listen to the radio
f do homework online

regarder	to watch
écouter	to listen to
poster	to post
télécharger	to download

3 Listen again (1–4) and decide whether their opinion of each activity is positive (P) or negative (N).

4 Read the posts and decide who says each statement (a–f).

Abdel
J'ai un ordinateur dans ma chambre. Je recherche des informations sur Internet et je fais mes devoirs mais je ne vais pas souvent sur les réseaux sociaux.

Suzanne
Normalement, je télécharge de la musique sur Internet mais j'aime aussi écouter la radio.

Karim
Je passe tous les soirs deux heures en ligne car j'aime parler avec mes amis sur les réseaux sociaux et partager mes photos sur Internet.

a I download music.
b I have a computer.
c I share photos online.
d I don't use social media often.
e I go online every evening.
f I listen to the radio.

un ordinateur	a computer
la chambre	bedroom
souvent	often
en ligne	online
tous les soirs	every evening
partager	to share

The environment

1 Read the sentences and decide if each one has a positive (P) or negative (N) impact on the environment.

a J'utilise tous les jours ma voiture.
b Je vais au collège à pied.
c Je prends le bus.
d Je ne prends jamais de bain, je préfère la douche.
e Je fais du recyclage.
f Je mange de la viande à chaque repas.

utiliser	to use
prendre	to take
un bain	a bath
une douche	a shower
un repas	a meal
le recyclage	recycling
à pied	on foot

2 Read the messages and answer the questions (a–h).

Amis

Ahmed
Je ne prends pas l'avion car c'est mauvais pour l'environnement. Je préfère utiliser les transports publics.

Issa
Le plastique est dangereux pour les animaux. Je fais souvent du recyclage car je ne jette pas le plastique dans la poubelle.

Martin
La pollution est un problème. Il y a trop d'usines et de voitures et le réchauffement du climat est de plus en plus dangereux.

mauvais	bad
les transports publics	public transport
jeter	to throw away
la poubelle	dustbin
une usine	a factory
le réchauffement du climat	global warming

a Which means of transport does Ahmed **not** use?
b Why doesn't he use it?
c What does he use instead?
d What does Issa say plastic is dangerous for?
e What does she do with plastic?
f What does Martin think is a problem?
g What does he say there are too many of? Give **two** details.
h What is becoming more dangerous?

3 Listen to three people's aims for environmental actions (1–3) and choose the correct picture (a–c).

a

b

c

4 Listen again (1–3) and write down the order in which the actions (a–f) are mentioned.

a Do more recycling.
b Eat less meat.
c Don't have a bath.
d Eat more fruit and vegetables.
e Use public transport.
f Don't travel by plane.

Where people live

1 **Match each property advert (1–3) to a potential tenant (a–c).**

1
C'est une maison avec un étage, à la campagne. Il y a une cuisine, un salon, une salle de bains et un grand jardin.

2
La maison est au centre-ville et elle a deux étages. Il y a trois chambres et deux salles de bains. Il n'y a pas de jardin.

3
C'est un appartement au bord de la mer. Il y a une grande pièce pour la cuisine, la salle à manger et le salon. Il y a une chambre.

- a a couple, looking for a seaside location
- b a family, looking for a rural location with lots of outdoor space
- c three students who don't want to do any gardening

un étage	floor, storey
le jardin	garden
la cuisine	kitchen
le salon	living room
la salle à manger	dining room
la salle de bains	bathroom
la chambre	bedroom
à la campagne	in the countryside
au bord de la mer	by the seaside
au centre-ville	in the town centre

2 **Read the adverts again and answer the questions.**

- a Where is property 1 situated?
- b How many floors are there in property 2?
- c What is the main room in property 3?

3 **Listen to Isabelle talking about her city, Lausanne in Switzerland. Choose the *five* activities people can do there.**

- a walk in the mountains
- b eat out
- c play football
- d go to museums
- e go to the lake
- f visit the castle
- g walk around the town
- h do shopping

la montagne	mountain
le restaurant	restaurant
le musée	museum
le lac	lake
le château	castle
le magasin	shop
les courses	food shopping

4 **Listen again and answer the questions.**

- a How big is Lausanne?
- b Where is it? Give **two** details.
- c What are there a lot of? Give **two** details.
- d Where can you walk? Mention **two** places.
- e Where can you go shopping? Give **two** details.

7.1F Les îles francophones

OBJECTIVES
- Places where we used to live
- Revising adjective agreement
- The imperfect tense of *être*, *avoir* and *faire*
- Phonics: *è*, *ê*, *ai* and *a*

1 **Read the forum about where people used to live and match the posts (1–4) to the pictures (a–d).**

ACCUEIL | NOUVEAU | RÉPONSES | FAVORIS

1 Quand j'étais jeune, j'habitais entre mer et montagne, sur une île située dans l'océan Indien. Il faisait souvent beau mais parfois, il y avait du vent. L'île avait une histoire intéressante. J'aimais découvrir la culture, les traditions et les religions de l'île. Par contre, la vie était chère.
Posté par Aurélien

2 Quand j'avais huit ans, je vivais sur une île calme située dans l'océan Atlantique. Il faisait vraiment froid, surtout en hiver, et il y avait beaucoup de neige. C'était vraiment comme l'Europe mais dans le nord de l'Amérique! On utilisait l'euro, on parlait français mais on était très près de la frontière canadienne.
Posté par Laëtitia

3 Quand j'étais plus jeune, j'habitais sur une île, dans l'océan Indien. Il y avait beaucoup de longues plages et il faisait assez chaud toute l'année, surtout sur la côte. La vie était calme et je trouvais les gens très gentils. J'ai appris la cuisine traditionnelle et la langue de l'île. La capitale était une ville historique.
Posté par Marinette

4 Quand j'avais dix ans, je vivais sur une île des Caraïbes. Il y avait deux pays sur l'île. Dans mon pays, on parlait français et dans l'autre pays, on parlait espagnol! La cuisine locale était très fraîche et on mangeait beaucoup de fruits. La vie culturelle était riche et la mer était toujours chaude.
Posté par Adrien

a Haïti

b La Réunion

c St Pierre et Miquelon

d Madagascar

2 **Read the texts again. Copy and complete the sentences.**

a On La Réunion, the weather was often ___ but sometimes, it was ___.
b Aurélien liked discovering the culture, ___ and religions of the island.
c In St Pierre and Miquelon, it was really ___ in winter.
d The island was very close to ___.
e In Madagascar, the beaches were ___ and life was ___.
f The ___ city was historic.
g In Haïti, the local cooking was ___ and people ate lots of ___.

Culture

Due to a diverse, and sometimes difficult, history, there are many francophone islands across the world. Some are overseas French territories, governed by the French government, with French as their official language. Others maintain a more distant link with France but still use French as one of their languages.

Phonétique

è*, *ê*, *ai*, and *a

è, *ê* and *ai* all sound the same:

très	*près*	*frontière*	*chère*
fête	*tête*	*arrêter*	*vous êtes*
vrai	*j'ai*	*j'aimais*	*vraiment*

Compare *ai* with *a*:

la capitale	*il y avait*
canadienne	*j'habitais*

3 Copy and complete the sentences, using the correct form of *être*, *avoir* or *faire* in the imperfect tense.

a Au nord de l'île, il y ___ une grande forêt.
b Il ___ beau tous les jours.
c L'histoire de l'île ___ intéressante.
d Quand mon frère ___ 12 ans, il habitait en Guadeloupe.
e Il ___ souvent froid, surtout en hiver.
f La cuisine locale ___ fraîche.

4 Translate the sentences (activity 3) into English.

Les verbes

The imperfect tense of *être*, *avoir* and *faire*

Use the imperfect tense to talk or write about what you used to do or were doing in the past. *Avoir*, *être* and *faire* are often used in the imperfect to set the scene of an action or to express feelings and opinions.

*J'**avais** faim.* I was hungry.

*Tu **étais** jeune.* You were young.

*Il **faisait** du vélo.* He went / used to go cycling.

*Il **faisait** beau.* The weather was fine.

*Il y **avait** du vent.* It was windy.

5 Listen to the podcast about Sylvain's experience of living in New Caledonia (*Nouvelle-Calédonie*), in the South Pacific. Write down the order in which the topics (a–f) are mentioned.

a the weather
b the activities he did there
c where the island is located
d what the landscape was like
e what the people were like
f how long he lived there

6 Listen again and choose the correct option to complete each sentence.

a Sylvain is **22** / **32** / **25**.
b He lived in New Caledonia for **5** / **10** / **15** years.
c The weather was **too hot** / **too cold** / **just right**.
d Sylvain used to go **swimming** / **horse riding** / **climbing**.
e He found that the culture was **ancient** / **varied** / **interesting**.
f He hopes to return to New Caledonia **next year** / **one day** / **next summer**.

7 In the text in activity 1, find *one* example of a noun with an adjective in these forms:

- masculine singular
- masculine plural
- feminine singular
- feminine plural.

Grammaire

Revising adjective agreement

Adjectives (describing words) must agree in gender and number with the noun they describe. For most adjectives, add an *-e* for feminine and an *-s* for plural:

un pays français   *une île français**e***   *des villes français**es***

Some adjectives are irregular and you need to learn their endings:

nouveau – nouvelle   *gentil – gentille*   *blanc – blanche*

8 In pairs, take turns to ask and answer the questions. Use the profile cards for ideas.

- Tu habitais où avant?
- Tu avais quel âge?
- Comment était le temps?
- La vie était comment?
- Qu'est-ce que tu faisais le week-end?

9 Write a paragraph (90 words) using one of the profile cards.

Example: Quand j'avais huit ans, j'habitais avec mon frère, ma mère et mon beau-père dans un village à la montagne…

Where: small town near Paris
At age: 12
Weather: quite cold in winter; sunny and nice in summer
Life: found the people nice
Activities: walks and swimming

Where: village in the mountains
At age: 8
Weather: foggy and windy in winter; very hot in summer
Life: very quiet
Activities: cycling and cooking

7.1H Mon blog de voyage

OBJECTIVES
- A gap year abroad
- *dans* and *en*
- Two tenses together: future and near future

1 **Read the blog posts. Who says what (a–f): Amadou or Angélique?**

Amadou

Je ne vais pas abandonner mes études mais je vais prendre une année sabbatique. Pour gagner un peu d'argent, je vais travailler dans un café près de chez moi pendant deux mois et puis je voyagerai au Togo avec mon sac à dos. Le Togo est un pays francophone situé dans l'ouest de l'Afrique. Là-bas, je chercherai un travail dans une ferme et je vais contribuer à l'agriculture locale. J'y passerai trois mois et j'habiterai dans un appartement avec d'autres jeunes, dans le centre de la capitale, Lomé, dans un quartier très vivant.

On va apprendre à être indépendants et on communiquera avec les habitants du pays dans leur langue. Nous allons profiter de ce pays et j'espère que nous arriverons aussi à nous relaxer un peu. Je vais écrire un blog pour d'autres jeunes et je donnerai des conseils pour voyager et travailler en même temps.

Angélique

Après mes examens, je ne vais pas aller à l'université. Je rêve d'acheter un billet d'avion direct pour le Vietnam, en Asie, où je pratiquerai la photographie. Mon rêve est d'écrire un blog de voyage où je partagerai mes photos de la culture du Vietnam – des photos des défilés, des festivals, des spectacles et des temples. Le paysage sera si différent!

Le plus important pour moi, pendant mon séjour, va être de me perdre dans des villes et des villages pour découvrir les traditions, pour manger la nourriture locale et comprendre l'identité du pays. Je nagerai dans des rivières et dans des lacs. Je dormirai dans une chambre pas chère au bord de la mer. Évidemment, je vais partager mon expérience avec beaucoup de personnes sur mon blog!

a I will share my photos on my blog.
b It will be great to learn independence.
c I will look for a job on a farm.
d I will work before travelling to earn money.
e I am not going to go to university.
f I will stay by the sea.

2 **Read the blogs again. Copy and complete the sentences.**

a First, Amadou will ___ for two months near his home.
b He will spend ___ months working in Togo.
c He will live with other ___.
d He will give advice for travelling and ___ abroad.
e Angélique will travel to Vietnam by ___.
f She wants to lose herself in the ___ and ___.
g She's looking forward to the local ___.
h She also wants to understand the ___.

3 **Find the verbs in the future in the blogs (activity 1). Write two lists: future tense and near future tense.**

4 **Translate the sentences into French.**

a We're going to take a gap year.
b They are going to start a travel blog.
c My sister will share her photos.
d I'm going to discover the local traditions.
e My blog is going to give advice about travelling.
f Will you (*tu*) communicate with the residents of the country?

5 **Listen to the report about *votretourdumonde*, a travel blog written by Bruno. Choose the correct option to complete each sentence.**

a Bruno's blog has been active since **2002 / 2012 / 2022**.
b He wants to share his love of **travelling / cooking / the internet**.
c Through his blog, Bruno will help people **discover the world / book flights / see animals**.
d He will offer **prizes / plane tickets / advice and ideas**.
e The blog will help people **plan trips / book train tickets / learn a language**.

6 **Listen (1–5) and write down the sentences you hear.**

7 **Copy and complete the sentences with *dans* or *en*.**

a Je voyagerai ___ Amérique.
b On va dormir ___ un hôtel.
c Ils mangeront ___ un restaurant.
d Pour mon année sabbatique, je vais aller ___ Afrique.

8 **In pairs, take turns to ask and answer the questions for yourself. You can talk about a real trip, or a fictional one. Use the blogs (activity 1) for support.**

- Tu vas prendre une année sabbatique? Pourquoi (pas)?
- Tu voyageras ou tu continueras tes études? Pourquoi?
- Qu'est-ce que tu feras pendant ton voyage?

Les verbes

Two tenses together: future and near future

The near future tense and the future tense can both express ideas about the future.

The near future is formed from the present tense of ***aller*** + a verb in the infinitive:

*Je **vais** manger la nourriture locale.*
I**'m going to** eat local food.

*Nous **allons** regarder des défilés.*
We**'re going** to watch the processions.

The future tense is formed from a future stem (usually the infinitive) + the future tense endings:

manger **(to eat)**	
*je manger**ai***	*nous manger**ons***
*tu manger**as***	*vous manger**ez***
*il / elle / on manger**a***	*ils manger**ont***

*J'**écouterai** de la musique.* I**'ll listen** to music.

Some verbs are irregular, so you need to learn their future stem, shown in bold here:

*avoir: j'**aur**ai* *être: je **ser**ai* *aller: j'**ir**ai* *faire: je **fer**ai*

Culture

Travel blogs are a popular source of both general and specific advice about travelling. *sea&seed* is a French blog offering advice about green and eco-friendly travel, while *voyagesetvagabondages* gives insight into travel for solo women. Do you know any other French-language travel blogs?

Grammaire

Using *dans* and *en*

Dans and *en* both mean 'in'. *Dans* is followed by an article but *en* is not.

*Je dormirai **dans un** hôtel.*

*Nous voyagerons **en** Europe.*

9 **Write a blog entry (150 words) about a new town, city or country you are going to visit. Describe:**

- where you will go, for how long and where you will stay
- what you will do, see and learn while you are there.

7.2F Vacances de rêve

OBJECTIVES
- Holiday stories
- *pour* and *sans* + infinitive
- Two tenses together: perfect and imperfect
- Phonics: open *o*

1 **Read the email and answer the questions in English.**

eponine@monmail.fr

Chère Séverine,

L'été dernier, ma famille et moi, nous avons quitté notre maison pour aller en vacances dans le sud de la France. Nous avons pris notre voiture.

Nous sommes partis le samedi matin. Quand nous sommes arrivés dans le sud, il faisait très chaud.

Nous avons dormi dans un hôtel dans une petite ville près de Nice. L'hôtel n'était pas loin d'une synagogue. Dans le jardin, il y avait une piscine et c'était parfait pour faire de la natation et pour se relaxer.

Le lundi, comme il ne faisait pas très beau, mon père a réservé une visite de Nice en bus. C'était génial de visiter la ville sans marcher! J'ai appris l'histoire de la ville et j'ai acheté un livre pour mes parents. Plus tard, nous avons fait les courses dans des magasins sans passer trop de temps en ville.

Et toi, tu es allée en vacances récemment?

À bientôt!

Éponine

a When did Éponine go on holiday?
b When did they leave home?
c What was the weather like when they arrived?
d Where did they stay during the holiday?
e Give **two** details about the hotel.
f Why did her dad book a tour of the city?
g What did they do later?

2 **Find the French for the English phrases in the email.**

a we left our house to go on holiday
b the weather was very hot
c there was a swimming pool
d my dad booked a visit
e I bought a book
f we went shopping
g did you go on holiday?

Les verbes

Two tenses together: perfect and imperfect

The perfect and imperfect tenses are often used alongside each other. The **imperfect tense** is used to describe continuous actions or events in the past, settings and emotions, while the perfect tense is used for completed actions.

Il faisait *beau alors je suis allée en ville.*
It was nice so I went into town.

J'avais *faim donc j'ai mangé des frites.*
I was hungry so I ate some chips.

3 **Translate the sentences into French.**

a Last summer, I went on holiday.
b We left on Sunday morning.
c It was sunny every day.
d The hotel was in the countryside.
e There were lots of restaurants.

Attention

Think carefully about whether you need to use the perfect or imperfect tense.

4 Find *five* examples of *pour* or *sans* + infinitive in activity 1 and translate them into English.

5 Listen to Josse talking about his disastrous holiday. Write down the order in which the statements (a–f) are mentioned.

a The meal was cold.
b The waiter was not nice.
c They slept on a boat.
d Josse got lost while on a walk.
e The weather was awful when they arrived.
f Josse went on holiday last year.

Grammaire

Using *pour* and *sans* + infinitive

Use *pour* or *sans* + infinitive to say 'in order to' do something or 'without' doing something:

***Pour** aller en France, j'ai pris le bus.* **In order to** go to France, I took the bus.

*Je suis parti **sans** payer.* I left **without** paying.

6 In pairs, complete the role play. Take turns to ask and answer the questions.

Phonétique

open *o*

dormi *logement* *Portugal*

You are talking to your Canadian friend about a recent holiday.

1 *Alors, tes vacances l'année dernière?*
Say where you went on holiday last year. (Give **one** detail.)
2 *Et le temps?*
Say what the weather was like there. (Give **one** detail.)
3 *Et ton logement?*
Say where you stayed. (Give **one** detail.)
4 *Et tes activités?*
Say what you did. (Give **one** detail.)
5 Ask your friend a question about their holiday.
Say something about your holiday.

7 Write an email (90 words) to your Belgian friend about your worst holiday. This can be real or fictional. Describe:

- when, where you went and with whom
- what you did and where you stayed
- something that went wrong.

L'année dernière, L'été dernier,	je suis allé(e) je suis parti(e)	en vacances	en France en Suisse au Portugal	avec ma famille. avec mes amis.
On est parti(e)s Je suis parti(e)	le samedi matin le dimanche après-midi	en voiture. en avion. en train.		
On a dormi J'ai dormi	dans un hôtel dans un appartement	près de la mer. à la campagne.		
Il y avait	un restaurant / une grande piscine.			
Il faisait	beau mauvais	alors donc	nous avons j'ai	fait de la natation. visité des monuments historiques.
Malheureusement,	au restaurant, le serveur n'était pas sympa. au restaurant, le repas était froid. il faisait mauvais tous les jours.			

7.2H Découvrir de grandes villes

OBJECTIVES
- Descriptions of a city
- Revising *y* and *en*
- The passive voice

1 Read the article about Dakar in Senegal and find the French for the English phrases (a–g).

Dakar

L'histoire

Au XVIe siècle, Dakar est colonisée par les Portugais et elle est utilisée comme centre d'esclavage. Au XIXe siècle, Dakar devient une partie de l'empire français et la capitale de l'Afrique de l'ouest française. C'est en 1960 que Dakar devient la capitale du Sénégal, un pays africain francophone.

Une ville pour les touristes

Dakar se situe sur la côte Atlantique. Aujourd'hui, c'est la plus grande et l'une des plus belles villes du Sénégal. Dakar profite d'un climat chaud toute l'année et il ne pleut pas souvent. Des fêtes, des festivals et des spectacles nationaux et internationaux sont organisés chaque année par la ville de Dakar. Ils offrent une expérience unique!

Dakar mérite sa réputation de lieu historique. Les habitants vous font bon accueil et les marchés et les traditions contribuent à une ambiance vivante. Dans la culture sénégalaise, les vêtements, la cuisine, la danse et la musique nous font voyager dans un endroit loin du monde occidental. La vie y est moins chère qu'en Europe.

l'esclavage slavery

a the capital of French western Africa
b Dakar enjoys a warm climate
c all year round
d Dakar deserves
e the markets and traditions contribute to a lively atmosphere
f make us travel
g life there is cheaper

Les verbes

The passive voice

The passive voice focuses on something or someone receiving the action of the verb, rather than doing it.

In French, the passive is made up of part of *être*, plus a past participle and *par* (by). The past participle agrees with the noun.

Passive voice: *La ville* ***est visitée par*** *les touristes.* The city is visited by tourists.
Active voice: *Les touristes* ***visitent*** *la ville.* Tourists visit the city.

An alternative to the passive in French is to use a phrase with *on*:
On visite *la ville*. People visit the city.

2 Read the article again and choose the correct option to complete each sentence.

a Dakar was colonised by **the Portuguese / the Spanish / the Canadians**.
b In 1960, Dakar became **a tourist town / a famous port / the capital** of Senegal.
c Dakar is located **in the countryside / on the coast / in the mountains**.
d The weather in Dakar is often **hot and dry / cold and wet / warm and wet.**
e Dakar is known to be **an industrial / a historical / a modern** city.
f Life in Dakar is **cheaper than / more expensive than / as expensive as** life in Europe.

3 **Decide which sentences (a–e) are in the passive voice.**

a Dakar est colonisée par les Portugais.

b Les Portugais colonisent le Sénégal.

c La ville organise des festivals.

d Des spectacles sont présentés par la ville.

e Au restaurant, les touristes commandent des plats traditionnels.

4 **Rewrite the active sentences from activity 3, using the passive voice.**

Grammaire

Revising the pronouns *y* and *en*

The pronoun *y* replaces *à* + noun. It often means 'to it', 'at it' or 'there'.

*J'adore le Sénégal. La vie **y** est moins chère qu'en Europe*

The pronoun *en* replaces *de* + noun. It often means 'of it' or 'of them'.

*J'aime les sites historiques. J'**en** visite un par jour.*

5 **Listen and answer the questions.**

a Who did Cara go to Dakar with?

b Why did they arrive in the evening?

c What did Cara find difficult?

d What was their hotel like? Give **two** details.

e What did Cara visit several of?

f What did they eat every evening?

6 **Listen (1–5) and write down the sentences you hear.**

7 **In pairs, look at the photo and take turns to ask and answer the questions.**

- Parle-moi de la photo.
- Quelle est ta ville préférée? Pourquoi?
- Parle-moi de ton dernier voyage scolaire.
- Où iras-tu pour tes prochaines vacances?

<table>
<tr><td rowspan="2">Ma ville préférée, c'est…</td><td rowspan="2">parce que / qu'</td><td>c'est</td><td>intéressant / beau. passionant.</td></tr>
<tr><td>on peut</td><td>faire / aller / visiter / voir…</td></tr>
<tr><td colspan="2" rowspan="2">Pour mon dernier voyage scolaire, on</td><td colspan="2">est allés…</td></tr>
<tr><td colspan="2">a visité / fait / vu…</td></tr>
<tr><td colspan="4">Pour mes prochaines vacances, j'irai / je resterai / on ira / on restera…</td></tr>
</table>

8 **Translate the sentences into French.**

a The city is visited by many tourists.

b Traditional dishes are prepared by restaurants.

c The festivals are celebrated by the tourists.

d I love Dakar. You find lots of historic sites there. I visit them every day.

9 **Write a post (150 words) about holidays for a French-speaking tourist website. Describe:**

- a francophone city that you have visited, heard of or read about
- a real or fictional future holiday or visit to a city.

8.1F Le monde avant et après Internet

OBJECTIVES
- Evolution and uses of the internet
- Opinion / modal verbs + infinitive
- Present and past tenses together
- Phonics: *au, eau,* closed *o* and *ô*

1 **Read the article and find the French for the English phrases (a–h).**

Dans les années 1990, Internet est arrivé sur le marché mais tout d'abord, il n'était pas facile d'aller sur Internet. Aujourd'hui, 64,4% de la population mondiale peut aller sur Internet tous les jours.

Avant, on utilisait les smartphones pour travailler seulement, mais maintenant, beaucoup de gens utilisent leur smartphone dans la vie quotidienne.

Dans les années 2000, la technologie a fait des progrès rapides: on a développé les réseaux sociaux et aujourd'hui, on peut toujours trouver une nouvelle appli ou un nouveau site en ligne.

Internet a changé notre façon de communiquer mais aussi notre société. Cependant, avec Internet, de nouveaux dangers sont présents et nous devons faire attention.

- **a** on the market
- **b** at first
- **c** it wasn't easy
- **d** in order to work
- **e** in daily life
- **f** in the 2000s
- **g** made rapid progress
- **h** we must pay attention

2 **Read the article again. Choose the correct option to complete each sentence.**

- **a** The internet arrived on the market **in the 1980s** / **quickly** / **in the 1990s**.
- **b** To start with, the internet was **easy** / **difficult** / **slow** to use.
- **c** Smartphones were originally used **for work** / **in everyday life** / **rarely**.
- **d** In the 2000s, **websites** / **online shops** / **social media** were developed.
- **e** People communicate **differently** / **sometimes** / **slowly** with the internet.
- **f** New **technologies** / **dangers** / **computers** have appeared.

3 **Read the article again. Make three lists of all the verbs in the perfect, imperfect and present tense.**

4 **Choose the correct verb to complete each sentence.**

- **a** Aujourd'hui, les gens **utilisent** / **ont utilisé** tous les jours Internet.
- **b** Avant, on **ne va pas** / **n'allait pas** sur Internet aussi souvent.
- **c** Dans les années 2000, les réseaux sociaux **deviennent** / **sont devenus** plus populaires.
- **d** Maintenant, **il y a** / **il y avait** de nouveaux dangers.
- **e** **J'ai découvert** / **Je découvrais** Internet quand **j'avais** / **j'ai** dix ans.

Les verbes

Present and past tenses together

Use present and past tenses together to say how things have changed, or to compare what you do now with what you used to do.

Adding a time phrase makes the time frame clear.

*Le week-end dernier, je **suis allé** sur Internet mais aujourd'hui, je **passe** moins de temps en ligne.*

*Avant, on **utilisait** des smartphones seulement pour le travail mais maintenant, beaucoup de gens **ont** un smartphone.*

Attention

Use time phrases such as *aujourd'hui* (today), *maintenant* (now), and *avant* (before) to help you work out which tense to use.

5 **Listen to Audrey, Sofiane and Kévin. Note the order in which the statements (a–e) are mentioned.**

- a I'm reading today.
- b I never used the internet when I was younger.
- c I want to spend less time online.
- d I have a laptop.
- e I didn't have a computer before.

6 **Listen again and answer the questions.**

- a How often does Audrey use the internet?
- b What does she like to do on her laptop? Give **two** details.
- c What did Sofiane do on his phone yesterday?
- d Why does he like to go online?
- e Why does Kévin use the internet every day?
- f What does he prefer to do online?

7 **Read the text and find:**

- a **two** phrases containing a modal verb + infinitive
- b **three** phrases containing a verb of liking / disliking + infinitive.

Aujourd'hui, on peut aller sur Internet tous les jours. Moi, je n'aime pas utiliser Internet trop souvent mais je dois faire mes devoirs en ligne. De plus, ma famille et moi adorons regarder des films en ligne car ce n'est pas cher. Par contre, je déteste jouer à des jeux vidéo. Je trouve ça très ennuyeux.

Les verbes

Opinion verbs, modal verbs + infinitive

When you use a **conjugated verb** + another verb, the second verb needs to be in the infinitive. You will often find this infinitive construction after an opinion verb or a modal verb. Be careful, as it does not always translate as an infinitive in English.

*Je **peux** regarder la télé en ligne.* I **can** watch TV online.

*On **aime** télécharger de la musique.* We **like** downloading music. / We **like** to download music.

8 **Translate the text (activity 7) into English.**

9 **In pairs, look at the photo and take turns to ask and answer the questions.**

- Parle-moi de la photo.
- Comment tu utilises les ordinateurs à l'école?
- Qu'est-ce que tu as fait en ligne hier?

10 **Write a blog entry (90 words) about how you use the internet. Describe:**

- what you usually do online
- what you did online yesterday.
- what you dislike about the internet and why.

Normalement, je j'	regarde / fais / télécharge écris / lis discute envoie consulte télécharge / écoute joue fais recherche	des vidéos / photos / films. mes e-mails / mon blog. avec mes amis. des photos. des sites web. de la musique / des podcasts. à des jeux vidéo. mes devois. des informations.	
Hier, j'ai	regardé / fait / lu / joué / téléchargé / écouté…		
Je déteste Je n'aime pas	les reseaux sociaux les applis de…	parce que c'est	ennuyeux. dangereux. cher.

Phonétique

au, eau,* closed *o* and *ô

au, eau, closed *o* and *ô* all sound the same:

***au**jourd'hui*	***au**ssi*
***beau**coup*	*nouv**eau***
*vidé**o***	*tr**o**p*
*h**ô**tel*	*dr**ô**le*

8.1H Ma vie dans le monde numérique

OBJECTIVES
- The influences of the digital world
- *personne ne …* and *rien ne …*
- Modal verbs in the perfect tense

1 **Read Candice's blog entry. Copy and complete the sentences (a–e).**

Ma vie d'influenceuse

Ma_vie_verte

À l'âge de 17 ans, j'ai commencé à lire des blogs et à regarder des vidéos d'influenceurs sur YouTube. Avec ces outils numériques modernes, j'ai pu découvrir de bonnes idées et j'ai aussi reçu de bons conseils. Je trouvais toujours le contenu et les dialogues entre les influenceurs et leur public puissants. Alors, j'ai su que moi aussi, je voulais partager en ligne mes connaissances et ma passion pour un mode de vie vert. À mon avis, rien n'est plus important que l'environnement.

D'abord, j'ai dû créer un profil sur les réseaux sociaux. Je l'ai appelé Ma_vie_verte. Je postais deux fois par jour, parfois plus. Au début, je n'avais pas beaucoup d'abonnés mais en quelques semaines, leur nombre a augmenté. Après quelques mois à poster régulièrement, j'ai eu plus de 2000 abonnés. Personne ne pouvait m'arrêter!

Tous les jours, j'ai pu discuter avec les personnes qui me suivaient sur les réseaux sociaux. J'ai voulu améliorer mon contenu et je l'ai adapté aux idées de mes divers abonnés. J'ai su que faire de la publicité pour de nouvelles marques de produits verts était une bonne façon de recevoir de l'argent. Je travaille avec des marques que je respecte et aujourd'hui, je peux gagner ma vie comme ça.

les abonnés	followers
faire de la publicité	to advertise

a When she was 17, Candice started reading ___.
b She found good ___ and ___ online.
c At the start, she didn't have many ___.
d She wanted to improve and adapt her ___.
e She used her followers' ___.

2 **Read the text again and answer the questions.**

a Where did Candice start to watch influencers' videos?
b How did she find the content and discussions of these blogs and videos?
c What passion did Candice decide to share online?
d What did she do first?
e How often was she posting messages, to start with?
f When did she reach 2000 followers?
g What does she do to earn money?

Les verbes

Modal verbs in the perfect tense

Modal verbs take *avoir* in the perfect tense and all have an irregular past participle:

vouloir (to want to) → *voulu*

pouvoir (to be able to) → *pu*

devoir (to have to) → *dû*

savoir (to know) → *su*

A modal verb is usually followed by an infinitive.

Ma sœur ***a dû*** *créer un profil.* → My sister **had** to create a profile.

*J'****ai voulu*** *devenir influenceur.* → I **wanted** to become an influencer.

3 **Copy and complete the sentences with the past participle of the modal verb given in brackets.**

a J'ai ___ devenir influenceur. (*pouvoir*)
b Mon frère a ___ regarder des vidéos. (*vouloir*)
c Tu as ___ comment créer du contenu? (*savoir*)
d Nous avons ___ acheter un nouvel ordinateur. (*devoir*)

4 **Translate the sentences into French. Use the perfect tense.**

a He wanted to share my passion.
b We were able to discover good advice.
c I wanted to create interesting content.
d She knew that posting messages was important.
e They had to talk to people.

5 **Find in the text in activity 1 and translate into English:**

- **one** sentence containing *rien ne …*
- **one** sentence containing *personne ne …*

Grammaire

Personne ne … and rien ne …

Personne ne … and *rien ne …* are used to express the idea of 'nobody' and 'nothing'. They are always followed by a verb in the *il / elle / on* form:

Avant, ***personne n'****utilisait les réseaux sociaux.* Before, nobody used to use social media.

Rien n'*est aussi facile qu'Internet.* Nothing is as easy as the internet.

6 **Listen (1–5) and write down the sentences you hear.**

7 **In pairs, take turns to read out the text.**

Je lis des blogs et j'aime suivre des influenceurs sur les réseaux sociaux.

Je trouve que rien n'est meilleur pour partager son avis et pour réagir à certaines publicités.

J'aime surtout les influenceurs qui parlent des derniers jeux en ligne.

8 **In pairs, ask and answer the questions.**

- Tu aimes lire des blogs ou suivre des influenceurs? Pourquoi (pas)?
- Tu crois que c'est une bonne façon de partager une opinion? Pourquoi (pas)?
- Qu'est-ce que tu as fait sur les réseaux sociaux récemment?

9 **Write a blog post (150 words) about the influence of blogs and influencers on today's digital world. Describe:**

- whether you read blogs, follow influencers or write your own blog
- what you read or wrote about recently online.

À l'âge de … ans, Il y a un an,	j'ai commencé à	lire des blogs suivre des influenceurs regarder des vidéos d'influenceurs		en ligne. sur Internet.	
J'aime Je préfère	poster des conseils écrire des articles lire des blogs	sur	la musique le cinéma la vie verte l'environnement	tous les jours. deux fois par semaine. de temps en temps.	
Hier, Récemment, Le week-end dernier,	j'ai pu j'ai voulu	découvrir lire suivre	un nouveau blog un nouvel influenceur	qui parlait de	musique cinéma.
J'ai su que c'était	un bon blog un profil parfait		pour	recevoir trouver	de bons conseils. de nouvelles idées.
				parler avec des nouvelles personnes.	

8.2F J'utilise la technologie!

OBJECTIVES
- Technology use in the past, present and future
- Adjectives beginning with *in-* or *im-*
- Three time frames
- Phonics: *en/an/em/am, on/om, ain/in/aim/im and un*

1 **Read the email and write down the order in which the statements (a–g) are mentioned in the text.**

tombeaupré18@monmail.fr

Quand j'avais dix ans, je n'avais pas de portable. Par contre, avant, on avait un ordinateur à la maison mais il était dans le salon et toute la famille l'utilisait. Sur l'ordinateur, j'écoutais parfois de la musique mais c'était presque impossible car Internet n'était pas rapide et l'ordinateur était inaccessible.

Pour mon dernier anniversaire, mes parents m'ont acheté un portable et je l'adore! **En ce moment, je télécharge beaucoup d'applis** et elles m'aident pour mes devoirs. De plus, j'envoie des messages à mes amis et j'adore prendre des photos.

Cependant, **maintenant, mes parents disent que je passe trop de temps en ligne. C'est injuste, mais le week-end prochain, je vais réduire mon temps en ligne. À l'avenir, je vais aussi passer plus** de temps dehors!

Thomas

- **a** My parents bought me a mobile phone.
- **b** My whole family used the computer.
- **c** I use my phone for homework.
- **d** I will spend more time outside.
- **e** My parents think I spend too long online.
- **f** I download apps.
- **g** I use my phone to take photos.

2 **Read the email again and answer the questions.**

- **a** At what age did Thomas **not** have a mobile phone?
- **b** How did he go online instead?
- **c** Why was it difficult to listen to music on the computer? Give **two** details.
- **d** When did Thomas' parents buy him a phone?
- **e** Who does he send messages to?
- **f** What is he going to do next weekend?

3 **Sort the verbs into three categories: past, present and future.**

- **a** j'ai téléchargé
- **b** je n'avais pas
- **c** je vais utiliser
- **d** je découvre
- **e** je joue
- **f** j'ai recherché
- **g** j'étais
- **h** je vais réduire

Les verbes

Three time frames

It is important that you can identify which time frame or tense is being used (through verbs and time phrases) and that you can use them in your own work. Using an appropriate <u>time phrase</u> will help you use the correct **verb tense**.

*<u>Maintenant</u>, **j'ai** un ordinateur dans ma chambre mais <u>avant</u>, **il était** dans le salon.*

<u>Now</u>, **I have** a computer in my bedroom but <u>before</u>, **it was** in the living room.

*<u>Hier</u>, **j'ai envoyé** un SMS à ma sœur mais <u>demain</u>, **je vais l'appeler**.*

<u>Yesterday</u>, **I sent** a message to my sister but <u>tomorrow</u>, **I'm going to ring her**.

4 **Identify the time phrase and the tense used in the phrases in bold in the email in activity 1.**

5 **Copy and complete the sentences, putting the verb into the correct tense. Use the time phrases to help you decide which tense to use.**

a Hier, ma sœur ___ une nouvelle chanson. (*télécharger*)
b À l'avenir, je ___ mon temps en ligne. (*réduire*)
c Maintenant, mon frère ___ son portable tous les jours. (*utiliser*)
d Mes copains et moi, on ___ tous les soirs à des jeux en ligne. (*jouer*)
e Quand j'avais dix ans, je ne ___ pas de films sur Internet. (*regarder*)

6 **Listen to Lisa, Amadou and Marc talking about their use of technologies. Decide whether each one is talking about the past, present or future.**

7 **Listen again and answer the questions.**

a What does Lisa think is a problem online?
b What does she say is important?
c How does Amadou describe his mobile phone? Give **two** adjectives.
d What has he used the new app for?
e Who does Marc say lives in Switzerland?
f Name **two** activities they will do together.

8 **Copy and complete the table.**

French	Noun or adjective?	+ *in-* or *im-*	English
complet			
		indifférent	
	noun		*inactivity*
		indépendance	

9 **In pairs, take turns to ask and answer the questions.**

- Comment tu as utilisé les technologies hier?
- Normalement, comment est-ce que tu utilises les technologies?
- Comment vas-tu utiliser les nouvelles technologies demain?

10 **Translate the sentences into French.**

a Last year, I bought a new phone.
b Now, I use my mobile every day.
c Tomorrow, I'm going to play online with my friend.
d When I was ten, I did not use the internet.
e Yesterday, my mum watched a film on TV.

Attention

The verb tense and time phrases such as *l'année dernière*, *maintenant* or *la semaine prochaine* will help you work out the time frame of a sentence.

Remember that the perfect tense is used for completed actions and the imperfect tense for ongoing actions in the past.

Phonétique

en / an / em / am, on / om, ain / in / aim / im* and *un

These groups of letter combinations all sound similar:

en/an/em/am:
*pr**en**dre* *av**an**t* *t**em**ps* *ch**am**bre*

on/om:
*sal**on*** *c**on**tre* *c**om**me* *t**om**ber*

ain/in/aim/im:
*proch**ain*** ***in**juste* *f**aim*** ***im**possible*

un:
*l**un**di* *empr**un**ter*

Practise reading aloud this question:
Mais cependant, comment tu passes ton temps en ce moment, maintenant?

Grammaire

Adjectives beginning with *in-* or *im-*

Some French adjectives can have *in-* or *im-* added, to give the opposite meaning or make them negative. It applies to some nouns and adverbs too. The English equivalent is *in-* or *un-*.

juste (fair) → *injuste* (unfair)

accessible (accessible) → ***in**accessible* (inaccessible)

possible (possible) → ***im**possible* (impossible)

8.2H Attention aux dangers en ligne!

OBJECTIVES
- Discussing risks and staying safe online
- *après avoir / être* + past participle
- The imperative

1 Read the problem page and find the French for the English phrases (a–h).

Tu as eu des problèmes sur Internet?

30 juin | **Pose tes questions à notre expert!**

Manon

Problème:

Sur Internet, il y a des risques mais je n'ai jamais réalisé que ça pouvait être aussi dangereux. L'année dernière, j'ai cliqué sur un lien dans un e-mail. Ce lien était un virus et il a attaqué mon ordinateur. Après avoir cliqué sur le lien, j'ai perdu tous mes documents, mes photos et mes informations personnelles. J'étais vraiment très inquiète.

Réponse:

Les nouvelles technologies et Internet facilitent vraiment notre vie quotidienne. Mais attention! Sois vigilant! Après avoir reçu un e-mail, regarde l'adresse d'origine avant de l'ouvrir. De plus, ne télécharge rien de dangereux.

Karim

Problème:

La fraude en ligne est un problème de plus en plus courant. Après être allé en ligne pour acheter quelque chose, j'ai été victime de fraude. Des pirates informatiques ont volé mes informations personnelles et ensuite, ils les ont utilisées pour faire leurs propres achats en ligne avec mon argent. Ce n'est vraiment pas juste mais malheureusement, ça peut arriver si nous ne sommes pas vigilants.

Réponse:

Les réseaux sociaux offrent de nombreuses possibilités positives, mais également négatives. Malheureusement, le nombre de fraudes en ligne augmente depuis plusieurs années. Soyons attentifs! Faisons attention aux sites que nous visitons, ne partageons pas nos informations personnelles et changeons régulièrement de mots de passe.

a I have never realised
b after clicking on the link
c our daily life
d after receiving an email
e before opening it
f after going online
g I was a victim
h it can happen

2 Read the problem page again and answer the questions.

a What did Manon lose when she clicked on the link? Give **three** details.
b What should we do before opening an email?
c What should we **not** download?
d What can fraudsters do once they have your personal details?
e What kind of opportunities do social media offer? Give **two** details.
f Which problem has increased online recently?

3 Find examples of phrases containing an imperative verb on the problem page and translate them into English.

Example: Pose tes questions à notre expert! – Put your questions to our expert!

4 Choose the correct imperative verb to match the English translation.

a **Es / Sois / Être** plus gentil avec ton petit frère!
Be kinder to your little brother!

b **Parlez / Parlons / Parler** de vos problèmes avec un adulte.
Talk about your problems with an adult.

c Ne **clique / cliquer / cliquons** pas sur un lien dans un e-mail.
Don't click on a link in an email.

d **Prenons / Prenez / Prends** le temps de protéger les jeunes en ligne.
Let's take the time to protect young people online.

5 Listen. Copy and complete the sentences.

a Chantal Ducarré is an expert in ___.

b Jean asks Chantal to talk about the ___ that exist online.

c Chantal says we use the internet for doing ___, ___ online, ___, and ___ our daily life.

d She says no one can avoid the ___ world.

6 Listen (1–5) and write down the sentences you hear.

7 Translate the sentences into French.

a After using the internet, I received an email.

b There are many risks in the digital world.

c After going on a website, I shared my personal details.

d Let's use safe sites.

e Let's not share too much information on the internet.

8 In pairs, take turns to give advice about these online issues.

a la fraude en ligne

b le vol d'identité

c parler à des personnes qu'on ne connaît pas

9 Write a blog entry (90 words) about online safety. Describe:

- what you used the internet for recently
- some of the dangers online
- advice to stay safe online.

Les verbes

The imperative

The imperative is used to give advice or instructions, in the *tu*, *vous* or *nous* form.

Use the present tense of the verb, but drop the subject pronoun. You also need to drop the final *-s* for *-er* verbs in the *tu* form.

***Regarde** cet e-mail.* Look at this email.

***Faites** attention en ligne.* Watch out online.

***Parlons** de nos problèmes.* Let's talk about our problems.

être is irregular and does not follow the same pattern:

tu → *sois*	***Sois** gentil!* (Be kind!)
vous → *soyez*	***Soyez** calmes!* (Be quiet!)
nous → soyons	***Soyons** vigilants!* (Be alert!)

Les verbes

après avoir / être + past participle

après avoir / être + a past participle is used to say 'after doing something.'

Use *avoir* or *être* depending on the verb, just as you would in the perfect tense. If the verb uses *être*, make the past participle agree.

***Après avoir** volé mon identité, ils ont fait des achats.* After stealing my identity, they made some purchases.

***Après être** allée en ville, ma sœur a fait des recherches sur Internet.* After going to town, my sister did some research on the internet.

9.1F Sauvons la planète!

OBJECTIVES
- A positive impact on the planet
- Infinitives used as nouns
- *je voudrais*

1 **Listen and read the texts. Choose the correct verbs to fill the gaps.**

devenir utiliser fabriquer voudrais réduit
utilise aider coupe fabrique créer

Solène

On **1** ___ les arbres et ça **2** ___ l'oxygène. Ça peut **3** ___ un problème alors je **4** ___ planter des arbres et **5** ___ de nouvelles forêts pour les futures générations.

Timothée

Dans ma famille, on **6** ___ nos propres produits ménagers alors on **7** ___ moins de plastique. C'est meilleur pour la santé et pour l'environnement. Je voudrais aussi **8** ___ mon propre savon pour me laver.

Amandine

Sur la Terre, il y a des ressources naturelles, comme l'énergie du vent ou du soleil. Je voudrais **9** ___ ces ressources pour **10** ___ notre planète.

les produits ménagers	household products
le savon	soap

2 **Read the texts again and answer the questions.**

a What does Solène say can be a problem?
b What does she want to do? Give **two** details.
c What results does Timothée say making their own household products has? Give **three** details.
d What else would he like to make?
e What does Amandine say planet Earth has?
f What would she like to do?

3 **Translate Solène and Timothée's texts into English.**

4 **Listen (1–4) and write down the sentences you hear.**

Attention

In dictation tasks, use your knowledge of grammar to check that what you have written is correct French. Look at adjective agreements and verb endings, for example.

Les verbes

je voudrais

je voudrais (I would like) is often followed by an infinitive:

***Je voudrais** utiliser moins de plastique.*
I would like to use less plastic.

It can also be followed by a noun:

***Je voudrais** des arbres dans la nature.*
I would like trees in nature.

5 Read the blog post about veganism. Choose the correct heading (a–e) for each paragraph (1–5).

a Fashion or lifestyle?
b Life without animal-based products
c A significant day for veganism
d More than just food!
e Environmental worries

Le véganisme: un nouveau mode de vie?

124

1 Protéger l'environnement est un souci pour tous et beaucoup de gens essayent de faire une différence.

2 Pour certains, par exemple, manger et boire des produits qui ne viennent pas des animaux est un mode de vie. Selon les experts, le véganisme encourage le respect parce qu'il n'utilise pas les animaux dans la nourriture, les vêtements et les expériences scientifiques.

3 Tu voudrais savoir si le véganisme est seulement une mode? Mais non, pour les végans, ce n'est pas une mode mais un moyen de vivre qui aide à protéger l'environnement et qui est meilleur pour la santé. Moi, je voudrais essayer de vivre de cette façon.

4 De plus en plus populaire dans un climat inquiétant, le véganisme donne des idées sur la nourriture mais aussi sur beaucoup d'autres choses. Par exemple, il est normal de fabriquer des produits ménagers sans produit animal.

5 Le 1er novembre 1994, la journée du véganisme a eu lieu pour la première fois. Chaque année, ce jour-là, on célèbre les droits des animaux. Même si c'est un choix moins populaire que le végétarisme en ce moment, deux pour cent des Français sont végans.

6 Read the text again. Find the French for the English phrases (a–i).

a protecting the environment
b a worry for all
c to make a difference
d eating and drinking
e a way of life
f better for your health
g I would like to try
h making products
i without animal products

7 Translate the sentences into French.

a I would like to plant trees.
b Eating less meat is better for our health.
c I would like to make my own products.
d Drinking vegan products is a way of life.

8 In pairs, take turns to read aloud the problems (a–d) and say what you would do to solve each problem, using *je voudrais*...

a couper trop d'arbres
b utiliser toutes les ressources
c manger trop de produits animaux
d utiliser des produits ménagers qui ne sont pas naturels

Les verbes

Using infinitives as nouns

An infinitive can be used as a noun. It translates as a noun ending in '-ing' in English.

Couper *les arbres diminue l'oxygène.*
Cutting down trees decreases the oxygen.

Protéger *l'environnement, c'est important.*
Protecting the environment is important.

9 Write an article (90 words) for your school's newsletter. Describe:

- which environmental problems you find worrying
- what you would like to do to help
- whether you would like to become a vegan one day.

9.1H L'environnement local

OBJECTIVES
- The local environment
- Partitive articles: *du, de la, de l', des*
- Negatives

1 **Read the article about recycling in Essaouira, Morocco. Write the order in which the statements (a–g) are mentioned in the text.**

Essaouira: experte en recyclage?

La ville d'Essaouira, au Maroc, a un problème avec le recyclage. Il y a des déchets dans les rues et sur les plages, et personne ne recycle. Mais pourquoi pas? Malheureusement, il n'y a ni centre de recyclage, ni poubelles de recyclage dans cette grande ville située sur la côte du Maroc. Il y a donc beaucoup d'habitants qui ne peuvent pas recycler ou qui ne savent pas comment faire.

Et à Essaouira, le plastique est toujours très populaire: comme il est plus pratique et moins cher, il est toujours utilisé par les restaurants et hôtels – les « riads » – de la ville.

Chaque année, le Maroc produit 6,9 millions de tonnes de déchets. Dans les prochaines années, le Programme national de gestion des déchets ménagers (PND) voudrait en recycler 20%, mais l'an dernier, le PND n'a réussi à trier et recycler que 7% des déchets. Il n'y a que 11% du plastique qui est recyclé chaque année et le reste finit souvent dans la nature.

Youssef Chaqor, un entrepreneur, a peut-être une solution: il voudrait transformer Essaouira en experte du recyclage en Afrique. C'est l'objectif du programme Mogagreen. Youssef Chaqor explique qu'avec les nouvelles technologies, il voudrait créer un modèle qui encouragerait l'économie et la durabilité des villes. C'est un projet nécessaire qui pourrait transformer le paysage de cette belle ville.

les déchets (ménagers)	(household) waste
la gestion	management
trier	to sort
la durabilité	sustainability

a Most of the rubbish ends up in nature.

b There are problems with recycling rubbish in Essaouira.

c Plastic is still used in restaurants and hotels.

d The Mogagreen project could change the look of the town.

e Essaouira is on the coast of Morocco.

f Only 7% of rubbish was sorted and recycled last year.

g They are hoping that new technologies will help.

2 **Read the article again and choose the correct option to complete each sentence.**

a Essaouira is a **large** / **medium-sized** / **small** town.

b There is no **recycling centre** / **litter** / **beach** in the town.

c Many of the residents do not **need** / **want** / **know how** to recycle.

d Plastic is used by restaurants because it is **cheap** / **lightweight** / **readily-available**.

e Only **20%** / **7%** / **11%** of plastic is recycled each year.

f Youssef Chaqor's plan could make the city an expert on **recycling** / **the landscape** / **the economy** in Africa.

3 Find *four* phrases containing a negative construction in the article in activity 1.

4 Translate the first paragraph of the article into English (as far as: *comment faire*).

5 Listen (1–4) and decide if each speaker presents their town in a positive (P) or negative (N) light, or both positive and negative (P+N).

6 Listen again and answer the questions.

a According to Rachel, why is pollution becoming a problem in Lomé?
b How does Rachel describe Lomé's city centre?
c What does Yvan say about nature in Québec?
d What does Yvan say contributes to air pollution in Québec?
e According to Martin, which cars are allowed in Paris?
f According to Chantal, what does public transport reduce? Give **two** details.

7 Copy and complete the sentences with the correct partitive article.

a Dans ma région, il y a ___ pollution.
b Chez moi, on recycle ___ papier.
c Les usines produisent ___ gaz qui polluent l'air.
d Ici, les gens recyclent ___ plastique.

8 In pairs, take turns to read aloud the first paragraph of the article (activity 1).

9 In pairs, ask and answer the questions.

- Comment est l'environnement de ta ville?
- Quel est le plus grand problème de l'environnement dans ta ville?
- Qu'est-ce que tu fais pour aider l'environnement près de chez toi?

10 Write an article (150 words) about the environment where you live. Describe:

- problems with the environment where you live
- what could be done to improve the environment.

Grammaire

ne … plus, ne … que, ne … pas encore, ne … ni … ni

With negative constructions, the two parts sandwich around the verb:

*Nous **n'**achetons **pas** de plastique.*
We **don't** buy plastic.

*Il **n'**y a **plus** de déchets dans les rues.*
There is **no more** rubbish in the streets.

*La ville **n'**a **qu'**un centre de recyclage.*
The town **only** has one recycling centre.

*On **ne** sait **pas encore** comment faire du recyclage.*
People **do not yet** know how to recycle.

ne … ni … ni (neither … nor) has three parts to it in French:

*Ils **ne** recyclent **ni** le plastique **ni** le papier.*
They recycle **neither** plastic **nor** paper.

Grammaire

Partitive articles

Partitive articles (*du*, *de la*, *de l'*, *des*) often correspond to 'some' or 'any' in an English translation, as in: *du café* (some coffee). A partitive article is often required in French when it is not needed in English.

*Dans ma ville, il y a **de la pollution**.* There is **pollution** in my city.

*Je bois souvent **de l'eau**.* I often drink **water**.

Remember that the partitive article must agree with the noun in gender and number.

9.2F Un guide de ma ville

OBJECTIVES
- Describing your town
- *si* and *quand*
- Modal verbs in the present tense
- Phonics: *h*

1 **Read the review of Sarlat and choose a heading (a–d) for each paragraph (1–4).**

Sarlat (Dordogne)

Accueil | **Lieux** | Hôtels | Transport | Restaurants | Météo

1 J'habite à Sarlat, en Dordogne, dans le sud-ouest de la France. Je sais qu'aujourd'hui il y a environ 10 000 habitants à Sarlat. La Dordogne est une région qui reçoit beaucoup de touristes.

2 C'est une très jolie ville médiévale, avec beaucoup de vieilles maisons et de bâtiments historiques. Dans le centre-ville, il n'y a pas beaucoup de voitures et on peut faire du shopping au marché et dans les petits magasins indépendants.

3 J'adore ma ville parce qu'il y a beaucoup à faire, pour les jeunes et pour les familles. Cependant, en juillet et août, il y a vraiment trop de gens et à mon avis, on doit réduire le nombre de visiteurs.

4 Les touristes peuvent visiter les églises, les petites rues, les places et les jardins. Ils peuvent aussi manger dans les restaurants locaux car la cuisine de la région est délicieuse. Quand il fait beau, ils peuvent faire de la natation dans la rivière. Et quand il pleut, ils peuvent aller au cinéma.

a Sarlat, a historic town
b Location
c What's offered for tourists
d My opinion

2 **Read the review again. Copy and complete the sentences.**

a Sarlat is situated in the ___ of France.
b The Dordogne attracts many ___.
c It is a very ___ town, with lots of ___ houses.
d There are not many ___ in the town centre.
e There are too many ___ in Sarlat in the summer.
f Tourists can visit the ___ and they can also try the ___.

Culture

La Dordogne in the south-west of France is one of the most popular tourist regions in France. It is famous for its rivers, castles and picturesque villages. The region also boasts rich cuisine and a warm climate.

Les verbes

Modal verbs in the present tense

Devoir, *pouvoir*, *savoir* and *vouloir* are irregular modal verbs. They are often followed by an infinitive.

*On **peut** faire du shopping dans le centre-ville.*
We **can** go shopping in the city centre.

*Je **sais** qu'il y a 5 000 habitants dans ma ville.*
I **know** there are 5,000 inhabitants in my city.

devoir **(to have to / must)**	
je dois	*nous devons*
tu dois	*vous devez*
il / elle / on doit	*ils / elles doivent*
pouvoir **(to be able to / can)**	
je peux	*nous pouvons*
tu peux	*vous pouvez*
il / elle / on peut	*ils / elles peuvent*
vouloir **(to want)**	
je veux	*nous voulons*
tu veux	*vous voulez*
il / elle / on veut	*ils / elles veulent*
savoir **(to know)**	
je sais	*nous savons*
tu sais	*vous savez*
il / elle / on sait	*ils / elles savent*

3 **Choose the correct option to complete each sentence.**

a Je **dois** / **doit** / **devoir** aller en ville à pied.
b Mon frère **peux** / **peut** / **pouvons** visiter le château.
c On **voulez** / **veux** / **veut** essayer les restaurants locaux.
d Si on **sait** / **savons** / **savoir** faire du vélo, il y a un parc pas loin.
e Je **veut** / **veux** / **voulez** faire du shopping dans les magasins.

4 **Translate the sentences (activity 3) into English.**

5 **Listen (1–5) and decide whether Aurélie's opinions are positive (P), negative (N) or positive and negative (P+N).**

6 **Listen (1–6) and answer the questions.**

1 What does Aurélie say about the weather in the mountains?
2 How does Aurélie describe the houses?
3 What does Aurélie say are expensive? Give **two** details.
4 Why is the shopping not good for young people? Give **two** details.
5 What is the problem when it's cold?
6 Which **two** cultural places do Aurélie's parents go to?

7 **Listen (1–4) and write down the sentences you hear.**

8 **Translate the sentences into French.**

a There are lots of restaurants.
b We can visit the church.
c I know that my town is historic.
d When it is cold, I can go to the shopping centre.
e If you (*tu*) want to see a film, you can go to the cinema.

Grammaire

si **and** ***quand***

Si *on aime l'histoire, on peut visiter le château.*
If you like history, you can visit the castle.

Quand *il fait froid, il n'y a rien à faire.*
When it is cold, there is nothing to do.

9 **In pairs, take turns to read aloud paragraph 2 of the review (activity 1).**

10 **In pairs, ask and answer the questions.**

- Comment s'appelle ta ville? C'est où?
- Qu'est-ce qu'il y a pour les jeunes?
- Qu'est-ce qu'il y a pour les touristes?
- Tu aimes ta ville? Pourquoi (pas)?

Phonétique

h

***h**ôtel*	*à l'**h**ôtel*
***h**istorique*	*j'**h**abite*

11 **Write an article (90 words) for a tourist website where you live.**
Describe:

- what your town / city / village is like
- what there is to see and do there
- something you have done there recently.

Example: Ma ville s'appelle… C'est dans le nord de… Il y a beaucoup de… Il n'y a pas de… On peut visiter… et aller… Le weekend dernier, j'ai…

9.2H Ma ville idéale

OBJECTIVES
- Comparing real and ideal homes
- Indirect object pronouns (plural forms)
- Revising the conditional of regular *-er* verbs
- Phonics: *-ill-* and *-ille*

1 **Read the texts. Copy and complete the sentences (a–h).**

Margaux

Posté le 3 octobre

J'habite dans un tout petit village à la campagne. Malheureusement, il n'y a jamais rien à faire pour les jeunes et je trouve souvent la vie ici ennuyeuse. Par contre, j'adore ma maison parce qu'elle est belle, avec un grand jardin qui donne sur une forêt. Les voisins ne font jamais de bruit et j'ai ma propre chambre.

À l'avenir, si je pouvais, **j'aimerais habiter en ville** car c'est beaucoup plus intéressant. **J'adorerais vivre dans une capitale comme Paris ou Rome car je préfère les villes vivantes** où il y a plein de choses à faire et beaucoup de magasins. Comme j'aime vraiment ma maison actuelle, **j'achèterais une maison pareille** ou peut-être un grand appartement.

Martin

Posté le 17 Septembre

Moi, je vis dans un appartement en ville avec mes parents. Nous vivons près des magasins, de la gare, des cafés et du cinéma. Même si j'apprécie d'y vivre la plupart du temps, il y a des inconvénients. Par exemple, il y a trop de circulation et on entend toujours du bruit, même la nuit. Et puis en été, comme notre appartement est au soleil et qu'il n'est pas très grand, il y fait souvent très chaud.

Je pense que plus tard, **je préférerais quitter la ville** et si c'était possible, **j'habiterais à la campagne**, dans un petit village pas loin de la mer et de la montagne. Comme l'air frais est très important pour la santé, **je marcherais tous les jours dans la nature** et **je nagerais tous les week-ends dans la mer pour me relaxer**. Voilà, c'est mon rêve!

a Margaux lives in a ___ in the ___.
b She has her own ___.
c She prefers ___ towns.
d Her ideal town would have ___ and ___.
e Martin lives with ___.
f There are cafés, a cinema, ___ and a ___ nearby.
g Martin's ideal village would be near the ___ and the ___.
h He would go ___ every day.

2 **Read the texts again and answer the questions.**

a Why is Margaux often bored?
b Why does Margaux love her house? Give **two** details.
c What does she say about the neighbours?
d What would her new house be like? Give **two** details.
e Name **two** disadvantages of Martin's area.
f What is the problem with his flat? Give **three** details.
g What does Martin feel is important for his health?
h Why would he swim every weekend?

3 **Translate the bold phrases in the texts in activity 1 into English.**

Les verbes

Revising the conditional of regular *-er* verbs

The conditional is used to say what someone **would** do or what **would** happen in the future, or to express a wish (I would like to…).

It is made up of a stem (the same as the infinitive, for *-er* verbs) and an **ending** (the same as imperfect tense endings).

*Elle habiter**ait à Marseille***. She **would live** in Marseille.

habiter **(to live)**	
*j'habiter**ais***	*nous habiter**ions***
*tu habiter**ais***	*vous habiter**iez***
*il/elle/on habiter**ait***	*ils/elles habiter**aient***

4 **Copy and complete the sentences, using the conditional form of the verb in brackets.**

a J'___ dans un appartement moderne. (*habiter*)

b S'il faisait beau, ma sœur ___ tous les matins dans la mer. (*nager*)

c Nous ___ habiter à la campagne si c'était possible. (*adorer*)

d Mes parents ___ une belle maison. (*préférer*)

e Tu ___ habiter en ville si c'était moins cher? (*aimer*)

5 **Listen (1–2). Copy and complete the table in English.**

	Prefers town or country?	Three reasons
1		

6 **Listen to Louane's opinions and choose the correct answer to complete each sentence.**

a A city offers more **restaurants** / **theatres** / **possibilities** than the countryside.

b In town, you can **cycle** / **walk** / **take the bus** everywhere.

c It is easy to go to the **theatre** / **countryside** / **park**.

d In the countryside, you can have **more to do** / **a bigger garden** / **a better life**.

7 **Listen (1–5) and write down the sentences you hear.**

8 **Translate the sentences (activity 7) into English.**

9 **Translate the sentences into French.**

a I would like to live in the city.

b I would prefer to swim in the sea every day.

c My sister would buy an apartment in town.

d The city offers us more possibilities than the countryside.

e Would you live in the countryside or in the city? (use *tu*)

10 **In pairs, look at the photo and take turns to ask and answer the questions.**

- Parle-moi de la photo.
- Quels sont les avantages d'habiter en ville?
- Et quels sont les inconvénients?
- Tu préférerais habiter en ville ou à la campagne? Pourquoi?

11 **Write (150 words) about places to live. Describe:**

- the advantages of living in the countryside and in the city
- where you would like to live in the future and why.

Phonétique

-ill-* and *-ille

*vi**ll**age*	*mi**ll**ion*	*tranqu**ill**ité*
*v**ille***	*tranqu**ille***	
*fam**ille***	*par**eille***	*vi**eille***

Grammaire

Indirect object pronouns (plural forms)

Indirect object pronouns replace a noun that is normally introduced with the preposition *à* (meaning 'to'). They go before the verb. When the verb is in the perfect tense, the pronoun goes before the auxiliary verb (part of *avoir* or *être*).

Present tense: *Je **leur** explique les réponses.* I explain the answers **to them**.

Future tense: *Je **vous** donnerai des instructions.* I will give **you** some directions.

Perfect tense: *Ils **nous** ont montré le bon chemin.* They showed **us** the right way.

Theme 3

Culture

Les logements traditionnels dans le monde francophone

1 Match each house (1–6) with the correct photo (a–f).

1 Une maison sur pilotis au Vietnam
2 Un faré, une maison tahitienne
3 Un banga, une habitation traditionnelle à Mayotte
4 Une case en Afrique subsaharienne
5 Une habitation traditionnelle marocaine
6 Une maison à colombages, un logement traditionnel d'Alsace

a

b

c

d

e

f

Culture

The francophone world boasts a broad range of traditional accommodation types. This variation can be explained by the construction materials available in each country. The climate and natural environment are also big considerations when choosing construction methods.

2 Listen (1–3) and choose *two* correct statements for each house type.

a Volcanic rocks can be used to build them.
b They occupy a central position in the village.
c They can be made of wood, stone or earth.
d Several generations usually live in it.
e They can be round, rectangular or square.
f Coral may be used for the walls.

3 In pairs, discuss in English the house types in activity 1.

- What are the advantages and disadvantages of these house types?
- Can you think of any house types that are specific to your local area, or your country in general?

4 Read the description of this traditional type of house in Morocco. Find the French for the English expressions (a–g).

La maison au *Maroc*

Avec la mondialisation, les logements de style occidental sont de plus en plus populaires au Maroc. Cependant, les maisons traditionnelles marocaines, comme dans les médinas, sont toujours bien présentes, même dans les grandes villes comme Marrakech. Ces constructions simples et modernes font le charme des villes de l'Afrique du Nord.

En général, les maisons en bois sont rares au Maroc parce que le bois y est cher. C'est pour cette raison que la maison traditionnelle est construite de matériaux directement disponibles. La brique est donc principalement utilisée: facile à produire, elle est une solution très écologique puisqu'aucun produit chimique n'est utilisé dans sa fabrication.

Dans certains villages, on utilise des briques traditionnelles faites à partir d'un mélange de boue et de paille. De l'extérieur, les maisons traditionnelles du Maroc ressemblent à de simples blocs en forme rectangulaire. Comme il n'y a pas de toit d'angle sur la maison, cela permet d'avoir une terrasse.

la mondialisation	globalisation
une médina	north-African city
principalement	mainly
chimique	chemical
la boue	mud
la paille	straw
le toit	roof

- **a** are more and more popular
- **b** even in the cities
- **c** give charm to
- **d** with directly available materials
- **e** is a very eco-friendly solution
- **f** made from a mixture of mud and straw
- **g** of a rectangular shape

5 Read the text again and answer the questions.

- **a** What has caused western-style accommodation to become more and more popular in Morocco?
- **b** Where can traditional houses still be seen?
- **c** Why are wooden houses not common in Morocco?
- **d** Give **two** reasons why brick is the main building material in Morocco.
- **e** Why are bricks an eco-friendly building material?
- **f** What are bricks traditionally made from in Morocco?

6 Translate the final paragraph into English.

7 Research a traditional type of accommodation in the francophone world and write a short paragraph. Include:

- where in the world it is
- what shape or distinctive features it has
- the construction materials
- your opinion.

Grammar practice

The imperfect tense

1 Copy and complete the sentences with the correct imperfect tense form of the verb. Then translate the sentences into English.

a L'année dernière, il ___ beau quand on est allés en vacances. (*faire*)

b Il y ___ beaucoup de magasins en ville. (*avoir*)

c Au café, j'ai bu de l'eau. Elle ___ froide! (*être*)

d Nous avons voyagé en avion mais c'___ cher. (*être*)

e Il y ___ beaucoup de touristes quand nous avons visité la capitale. (*avoir*)

f Mon frère ___ du vélo dans le jardin quand il ___ cinq ans. (*faire*, *avoir*)

Agreement of adjectives

2 Choose the correct adjective to complete each sentence.

a C'est une **grand / grande / grandes** île située dans l'océan Atlantique.

b Il y a de **nouvelles / nouveaux / nouvelle** rues (*f*) dans mon village.

c Dans ma région, on peut faire de **longues / long / longue** promenades (*f*).

d Le temps est **idéale / idéals / idéal** pour faire de la natation.

e Les sites (*m*) **culturels / culturelles / culturel** de ma ville sont **intéressantes / intéressante / intéressants**.

Grammaire

Adjectives need to agree in gender and number with the noun they describe.

Future and near future tenses

3 Copy and complete the sentences, putting the verb in the near future (a–c) and the future tense (d–f).

The near future tense:

a Après mes examens, je ___ une année sabbatique. (*prendre*)

b Pour aider l'environnement, mon frère ___ moins de viande. (*manger*)

c Avant de dormir, on ___ de regarder le film sur notre portable. (*finir*)

The future tense:

d La ville ___ les transports pour les touristes. (*améliorer*)

e Nous ___ avant de voyager. (*travailler*)

f Mon copain ___ à Paris pendant quinze jours. (*rester*)

dans and *en*

4 Choose *dans* or *en* to complete each sentence.

a Je voyage souvent **dans / en** France.

b Nous habitons **dans / en** le sud du Québec.

c **Dans / En** hiver, il fait froid.

d **Dans / En** le passé, j'ai voyagé **dans / en** Europe.

e Avec cette appli, on peut parler **dans / en** espagnol.

f Nous avons dormi **dans / en** un hôtel au bord de la mer.

Grammaire

Dans and *en* both mean 'in'. *Dans* is followed by an article but *en* is not.

Perfect and imperfect tenses

5 Copy and complete the sentences, putting the verbs in the perfect or imperfect tense.

a Nous ___ tôt en voiture. (*partir*)
b Il y ___ une piscine dans le jardin. (*avoir*)
c La viande ___ froide. (*être*)
d Mes parents ___ des musées. (*visiter*)
e Mon frère ___ des films en ligne. (*regarder*)
f Les films ___ ennuyeux. (*être*)

Les verbes

The **imperfect tense** is used to describe continuous actions or events in the past, settings and emotions, while the **perfect tense** is used to describe completed actions.

pour and *sans* + infinitive

6 Copy and complete the sentences with *sans* or *pour*.

a Je ne peux pas vivre ___ avoir un portable.
b ___ aller en vacances, nous préférons prendre le train.
c ___ visiter les sites historiques, on n'apprend pas la culture d'une région.
d On utilise les réseaux sociaux ___ communiquer avec notre famille.
e ___ faire mes devoirs, je vais sur Internet.
f Je ne peux pas dormir ___ regarder la télé avant.

Attention

Think about the meaning of the sentence to work out whether *sans* or *pour* makes most sense.

Present, perfect and imperfect tenses

7 Choose the correct verb to complete each sentence.

a Dans les années 1990, Internet **n'est / n'était** pas très rapide.
b Tout le monde **a / avait** un portable maintenant.
c L'année dernière, on **est allés / va** en France.
d Maintenant, mon frère **a habité / habite** en Algérie.
e Quand j'étais au Maroc, il **fait / faisait** trop chaud.
f Dans le passé, on **utilisait / utilise** plus de plastique mais aujourd'hui, on **a préféré / préfère** les sacs qui ne sont pas en plastique.

Attention

Use the adverbs of time and the meaning of the rest of the sentence to help you decide which tense is correct.

Opinion / modal verbs + infinitive

8 Rewrite the sentences in the correct order. Then translate them into English.

a regarder | J'adore | en ligne | la télé | .
b aimes | en vacances | Tu | aller | ?
c écouter | préfère | de la musique | Elle | .
d n'aime pas | à mes amis | Je | en ligne | parler | .
e peux | Je | suivre | sur l'appli | mes progrès | .
f en ville | peuvent | les musées | visiter | Mes parents | .

Les verbes

After a conjugated opinion verb or modal verb, the second verb needs to be in the infinitive form.

Grammar practice

Modal verbs in the perfect tense

9 Copy and complete the sentences with the perfect tense of the modal verb given in brackets.

a J'___ passer moins de temps sur les réseaux sociaux. (*vouloir*)
b Nous ___ protéger l'environnement. (*pouvoir*)
c Mon meilleur ami ___ m'écouter. (*savoir*)
d Pour rentrer, il ___ prendre le train. (*pouvoir*)
e Elle ___ appeler ses parents car elle était en retard. (*devoir*)
f Nous ___ voyager en bus car c'était moins cher. (*vouloir*)

après avoir / être + past partiple

10 Copy and complete the sentence with *après avoir* or *après être* and the past participle of the verb in brackets.

a Mon frère a trouvé un travail ___ une année sabbatique. (*prendre*)
b ___ en France, nous avons visité la Suisse. (*aller*)
c ___ un film, on le regarde à la télé. (*télécharger*)
d Les jeunes peuvent aller au centre commercial ___ le château. (*visiter*)
e ___ chez nous, on a dormi. (*rentrer*)
f ___ du bus, ma sœur a pris le train. (*descendre*)

Les verbes

The structure *après avoir / être* + past participle is used to say 'after doing something.'

Use *avoir* or *être* depending on the verb, just as you would in the perfect tense. With verbs that take *être*, make the past participle agree.

The imperative

11 Copy and complete the sentences with the correct form of the imperative.

a ___ à l'école à pied. (*aller*, *tu*-form)
b ___ gentil avec ta sœur! (*être*, *tu*-form)
c ___ calmes! (*être*, *vous*-form)
d ___ de nos problèmes avec nos amis. (*parler*, *nous*-form)
e Ne ___ pas sur le lien. (*cliquer*, *vous*-form)
f ___ du camping! (*faire*, *nous*-form)

Les verbes

To form an imperative, use the present tense of the verb and drop the subject pronoun. You also need to drop the *-s* for *-er* verbs in the *tu* form.

Remember that *être* has irregular imperative forms.

Negatives

12 Rewrite the sentences, using the French for the negative construction given in brackets. Then translate the sentences into English.

a Nous prenons l'avion. (*no longer*)
b Ma sœur mange des légumes. (*only*)
c Il a appris une nouvelle langue. (*not yet*)
d J'aime Internet et les réseaux sociaux. (*neither … nor*)

Grammaire

Remember that the **negative** expression sandwiches the verb: *Je **ne** bois **plus** de café.*

Modal verbs in the present tense

13 Copy and complete the sentences with the correct form of the modal verb given in brackets.

a Je ___ réduire mon temps sur Internet. (*devoir*)
b Mon frère ___ utiliser moins de plastique. (*pouvoir*)
c Nous ___ comment protéger la planète. (*savoir*)
d Les touristes ___ essayer le nouveau restaurant. (*vouloir*)
e Cette année, on ___ aller en vacances. (*vouloir*)
f Je ___ prendre l'avion moins souvent. (*pouvoir*)

si and *quand*

14 Copy and complete the sentences with *si* or *quand* to match the English translations.

a ___ il fait chaud, on va à la plage. (*If it is hot, we go to the beach.*)
b Je fabrique mes propres produits ___ j'ai le temps. (*I make my own products when I have time.*)
c ___ il pleut, ma sœur prend le bus. (*If it rains, my sister takes the bus.*)
d ___ ils vont à Sarlat, les touristes visitent le château. (When they go to Sarlat, tourists visit the castle.)

Grammaire

Remember that *si* will become *s'* before a word that starts with a vowel.

The conditional

15 Copy and complete the sentences with the correct form of the verb in the conditional.

a Je ___ acheter des produits locaux. (*préférer*)
b J'___ plus d'applis amusantes. (*utiliser*)
c Mon frère ___ moins de viande s'il aimait les légumes. (*manger*)
d Les générations futures ___ de mieux protéger l'environnement. (*essayer*)
e Nous ___ moins de temps sur Internet si nous en connaissions les risques. (*passer*)

Les verbes

The conditional is made up of two parts: the stem (for *-er* verbs it's the same as the infinitive) and an ending (the same as the imperfect tense endings).

Indirect object pronouns (plural)

16 Rewrite the sentences, replacing the words in brackets with the correct indirect object pronoun (*nous*, *vous*, *leur*).

a Je parle (**à vous**).
b Ils montrent la maison (**à nous**).
c J'explique le problème (**à mes copains**).
d J'ai dit (**à mes parents**) qu'il fallait faire du recyclage.
e J'envoie un e-mail (**à vous**).
f La ville offre beaucoup de possibilités (**à nous**).

Grammaire

Indirect object pronouns replace a noun that would be introduced with the preposition *à* (to). They are always placed **before** the verb.

Higher Vocabulary

Words that are highlighted in grey in this list are words that may be useful, but you won't need to know them for the exam.

Introductory vocabulary

à pied on foot
adorer to love
aider to help
aimer to like
aller to go
l' *ami(e) (m./f.)* friend
les *animaux (m. pl.)* animals
l' *appartement (m.)* flat
s' *appeler* to be called
assez quite, enough
au bord de la mer by the sea
au restaurant at, in a restaurant
l' *avion (m.)* plane
avoir le mal de mer to be sea sick
le *bain* bath
le *bateau* boat
beaucoup (de) a lot (of), lots (of)
bouger to move
le *bus* bus
la *campagne* countryside
car because
cependant however
le *centre-ville* city centre
la *chambre* bedroom
chaque each, every
chez at someone's place
le *collège* (secondary) school
la *cuisine* kitchen, cooking
dangereux/dangereuse dangerous
de plus en plus more and more
dehors outside
détester to hate
les *devoirs (m. pl.)* homework
dormir to sleep
écouter to listen (to)
l' *émission (f.)* TV program
en in, by (doing something)
en ligne online
en Suisse in Switzerland
en vacances on holiday
ennuyeux/ennuyeuse boring
et and
l' *étage (m.)* floor
être to be
faire to do, make
faire de la natation to go swimming
faire du camping to go camping
faire du shopping to go shopping
faire du vélo to go cycling
faire les courses to go grocery shopping
la *famille* family
le *fruit* fruit
grand(e) big, large
habiter to live
l' *heure (f.)* hour, time, o'clock
historique historic
l' *hôtel (m.)* hotel
ici here
il fait beau it is fine weather
il fait chaud it is hot
il fait froid it is cold
il y a there is/are
il y a du soleil it is sunny
l' *information (f.)* information
Internet (m.) internet
jamais never
le *jardin* garden
jeter to throw (away)
jouer to play
le *journal* newspaper, diary
le *jour* day
le *lac* lake
le *légume* vegetable
lire to read
le *magasin* shop
la *maison* house
manger to eat
le *marché* market
marcher to walk
mauvais pour l'environnement (m.) bad for the environment
la *mer* sea
le *message* message
moi me
moins (de) less (of), fewer (of)
les *montagnes (f. pl.)* mountains
le *musée* museum
la *musique* music
la *nature* nature
normalement normally
on we, one
l' *ordinateur (m.)* computer
parce que because
parler (de) to speak, to talk (about)
partager to share
partir to leave
passer (du temps) to spend (time)
pas cher cheap
la *photo* photo
la *pièce* room
la *plage* beach
la *planète* planet
le *plastique* plastic
pleuvoir to rain
plus (de) more (of)
la *pollution* pollution
poster to post
la *poubelle* bin
pour for, in order to
pouvoir to be able to, can
pratique practical
préférer to prefer
prendre to take
près de near
le *problème* problem
protéger to protect
quand when
la *radio* radio
rapide fast
le *réchauffement du climat* global warming
rechercher to look for, to research
le *recyclage* recycling
regarder to watch, to look
le *repas* meal
les *réseaux sociaux (m. pl.)* social media
le *restaurant* restaurant
la *rue* street
la *salle à manger* dining room
la *salle de bains* bathroom
le *salon* lounge, living room
si if
le *site* site
situer to situate, to locate
le *soir* evening
surtout especially
la *télé* TV
télécharger to download
le *temps* time, weather
tous/toutes every, all
le *train* train
le *transport public* public transport
trop de too many, much of
l' *usine (f.)* factory
utiliser to use
les *vacances (f. pl.)* holiday
le *vélo* bike
la *viande* meat
la *ville* town, city
visiter to visit
la *voiture* car
vouloir to want
voyager to travel

7.1F Les îles francophones

l' *âge (m.)* age
l' *an (m.)/année (f.)* year
apprendre to learn
aujourd'hui today
autre (adj.) other
bien good, well
bonjour good morning, afternoon
calme (adj.) calm, quiet
les *Caraïbes (f. pl.)* Caribbean
ce/cet/cette/ces this, these
chaud(e) hot, warm
cher/chère expensive
comme such as, like, since
comment how
la *Corse* Corsica
la *côte* coast
différent(e) (de) different (from)
dix ten
en hiver in winter
entre between
espérer que to hope that
être situé to be situated
l' *euro (m.)* euro
l' *expérience (f.)* experience
faire des promenades to go for walks
la *forêt* forest, wood
frais/fraîche fresh

la ***frontière*** border
le ***gateau*** cake
l' ***histoire (f.)*** history, story
l' ***hiver (m.)*** winter
il faisait froid it was cold
il faisait beau it was nice weather
il y avait there was, there were
il y avait du vent it was windy
l' ***île (f.)*** island
intéressant(e) interesting
l' ***invitation (f.)*** invitation
le/la ***jeune (n.)*** young person
jeune (adj.) young
là there
là-bas over there
le/la/l'/les the
local(e) local
long(ue) long
le ***nord*** north
nouveau/nouvelle (adj.) new
la ***Nouvelle-Calédonie*** New Caledonia
l' ***océan Atlantique (m.)*** Atlantic ocean
l' ***océan Indien (m.)*** Indian ocean
l' ***océan Pacifique (m.)*** Pacific ocean
par contre on the other hand
le ***parc naturel*** natural park
parfait(e) perfect
parfois sometimes
pendant during
plusieurs several
le ***podcast*** podcast
populaire popular
préparer to prepare
qu'est-ce que what
quel(le) what, which
raconter to tell
la ***religion*** religion
retourner to go back, to return
souvent often
traditionnel(le) traditional
très very
trouver to find
venir (de) to come (from)
vivre to live
vrai true, real
vraiment really

7.1H Mon blog de voyage

abandonner to abandon / give up
acheter to buy
l' ***agriculture (f.)*** agriculture
l' ***année sabbatique (f.)*** gap year
après after
arriver à to succeed in
l' ***Asie (f.)*** Asia
l' ***Australie (f.)*** Australia
aussi also
l' ***autre(s) (m./f.)*** other
avant (de) before
l' ***aventure (f.)*** adventure
le ***blog*** blog
le ***centre*** centre
chercher to look for
communiquer to communicate
comprendre to understand
contribuer (à) to contribute (to)
découvrir to discover, to find out
depuis since
la ***destination*** destination
le ***détail*** detail
direct(e) direct
donner to give
écrire to write
en même temps at the same time
ensemble together
les ***études (f. pl.)*** studies
évidemment evidently, obviously
l' ***examen (m.)*** exam
faire la découverte to discover
la ***ferme*** farm
le ***festival*** festival
gagner to win, earn
l' ***habitant(e)*** inhabitant
l' ***identité (f.)*** identity
important(e) important
indépendant(e) independent
insolite unusual
international(e) international
la ***langue*** language
loger to stay
leur(s) (to) them, their
le ***mois*** month
le ***monde*** world
le/la ***musicien(ne)*** musician
l' ***objectif (m.)*** objective
offrir to offer, give
organiser to organise
l' ***ouest (m.)*** west
partout everywhere
la ***passion*** passion
le ***paysage*** scenery
se ***perdre*** to lose oneself, to get lost
la/les ***personne(s)*** person / people
la ***photographie*** photography
proche near
profiter de to enjoy
le ***projet*** project
le ***quartier*** area, neighbourhood
se ***relaxer*** to relax
rencontrer to meet
rester to stay
rêver to dream
le ***sac à dos*** rucksack
le ***séjour*** stay
le ***temple*** temple
le ***Togo*** Togo
traverser to cross
l' ***université (f.)*** university
le ***Vietnam*** Vietnam
vif/vive lively
le ***village*** village
vivant(e) lively
y there

7.2F Vacances de rêve

à at, to
à bientôt see you soon
arriver to arrive
la ***Belgique*** Belgium
le ***brouillard*** fog
dernier/dernière last
en plus in addition
l' ***Espagne (f.)*** Spain
faire chaud to be hot
froid(e) cold
génial (e) great
il faisait mauvais it was bad weather
jusque until
le ***livre*** book
le ***logement*** accommodation
(le) ***lundi*** Monday
(le) ***mardi*** Tuesday
le ***matin*** morning
oublier to forget
le/les ***parent(s) (m. pl.)*** parent(s)
le ***père*** father
le ***portable*** mobile phone
propre clean, own
quitter to leave
récemment recently
sortir to go out
réserver to book
le ***rêve*** dream
sans without
le ***sud*** south
sympa nice
la ***synagogue*** synagogue
tard late
tous les jours every day
vite quick, fast, quickly

7.2H Découvrir de grandes villes

accompagner to accompany
accueil welcome
accueillant(e) welcoming
l' ***ambiance (f.)*** atmosphere
au at the / to the
beau/bel/belle beautiful
central(e) central
célébré(e) celebrated
le ***chef (de cuisine)*** chef
choisir to choose
classique classic
le ***climat*** climate
colonisé(e) colonised
le ***déjeuner*** lunch
devenir to become
donc so
l' ***empire (m.)*** empire
l' ***endroit (m.)*** place
l' ***esclavage (m.)*** slavery
être en retard to be late
l' ***Europe (f.)*** Europe
la ***fête*** party, celebration
il n'y a pas there is / are not
la ***librairie*** bookshop
le ***lieu*** place
meilleur(e) better
le/la/les ***meilleur(e)(s)*** best
même si even if
mériter de to deserve
national(e)(s)/nationaux national
offrir to offer

par by
la *partie* part
le *plat* dish
portugais(e) Portuguese
présenter to present
prochain(e) next
que that
la *réputation* reputation
scolaire (adj.) school
le *Sénégal* Senegal
sénégalais(e) Senegalese
le *siècle* century
se *situer* to be situated
le *spectacle* show
tôt early
le/la *touriste* tourist
tout(e) each
la *tradition* tradition
unique unique
le/les *vêtement(s) (m. pl.)* clothes
voir to see
le *vol* flight

8.1F Le monde avant et après Internet

l' *appli (f.)* app
content(e) happy
le *danger* danger
de plus besides, moreover
devoir to have to
du/de la/des/de l' some, of the
facile easy
la *façon* way, manner
faire des progrès to make progress
hier yesterday
le *jeu vidéo* video game
maintenant now
mais but
mondial(e) global
ne … jamais never
l' *ordinateur portable (m.)* laptop
présent(e) (adj.) present
seulement only
le *smartphone* smartphone
la *société* society
le *téléphone* phone
toujours always
tout d'abord first of all
la *vie quotidienne* daily life

8.1H Ma vie dans le monde numérique

à mon avis in my opinion
adopter to adopt
alors so, therefore
améliorer to improve
appeler to call
s' *arrêter* to stop oneself
l' *article (m.)* article
au début at the beginning
augmenter to increase
aussi … que as … as
l' *avis (m.)* opinion
cliquer to click
commencer to start
le *commentaire* comment, commentary
compliqué(e) complicated
la *connaissance* knowledge
le *contenu* content
créer to create
croire que to believe that
de temps en temps from time to time
le *dialogue* dialogue
la *discussion* discussion
discuter to discuss
divers varied
durable sustainable
l' *environnement (m.)* environment
faire de la publicité to advertise
haut high
moderne modern
ne … rien nothing
ne … personne nobody
le *nombre* number
numérique digital
l' *outil (m.)* tool
la *personne* person
plus (…) que more (…) than
le *produit* product
le *profil* profile
le *public* public
la *publicité* advertisement
puissant powerful, strong
quelle joie! what a joy!
quelques some, a few
qui who
réagir to react
recevoir to receive
régulier regular
régulièrement regularly
respecter to respect
savoir to know
la *semaine* week
suivre to follow
tchatter to chat
la *vie* life

8.2F J'utilise la technologie!

à l'avenir in the future
l' *anniversaire (m.)* birthday
changer to change
la *chanson* song
complet/complète complete
cool cool
la *dépendance* addiction
en ce moment at the moment
enregistrer to record
envoyer to send
faire attention à to be careful of, to pay attention to
impossible impossible
inaccessible inaccessible
l' *inactivité (f.)* inactivity
incomplet/incomplète incomplete
l' *indépendance (f.)* independence
indifférent(e) indifferent
injuste unfair
presque almost
réduire to reduce
la *sécurité* safety, security
la *technologie* technology

8.2H Attention aux dangers en ligne!

à qui to whom
l' *achat (m.)* purchase
l' *adresse (f.)* address
âgé(e) elderly
l' *année dernière (f.)* last year
attaquer to attack
attentif/attentive attentive
l' *attention (f.)* attention
aussi bien que as well as
bancaire (adj.) banking
connaître to know (person, place)
courant(e) ordinary, habitual
d'origine of origin
le *détail personnel* personal detail, information
le *document* document
également equally, as well, too, also
en effet indeed
en toute sécurité safely
ensuite next
essayer de to try
étrange strange
être victime de to be victim of
éviter to avoid
exister to exist
l' *expert(e) (m./f.)* expert
facilement easily
faciliter to make easier, to facilitate
faire des recherches to do research
fort(e) strong
la *fraude* fraud
il est essentiel de it is essential to
il est facile de it is easy to
il faut it's necessary to
l' *information personnelle (f.)* personal detail, information
inquiet/inquiète worried
juste fair, just, only
le *lien* link
la *main* hand
malheureusement unfortunately
le *mot de passe* password
négatif/négative negative
nombreux/nombreuses numerous
notre/nos our
perdre to lose (something)
la *personne* person
personnel(le) personal
le *pirate informatique* hacker
positif/positive positive
la *possibilité* possibility
se *protéger* to protect oneself
quelque chose something
quotidien(ne) daily
réaliser que to realise that
réponse answer, response
le *risque* risk
simplement simply
sûr safe
utliser to use
vigilant careful

le ***virus*** virus
le ***vol d'identité*** identity theft
voler to steal
votre/vos your (polite, plural)

9.1F Sauvons la planète!

animal (adj.) from, of animals
l' ***arbre (m.)*** tree
certain(e)(s) some, certain
le ***choix*** choice
la ***chose*** thing
couper to cut
la ***date*** date
la ***douche*** shower
droit right
l' ***énergie (f.)*** energy
fabriquer to make
faire une différence to make a difference
la ***génération*** generation
inquiétant(e) worrying
la ***journée*** day
se ***laver*** to wash
le ***mode de vie*** way of life
le ***moyen de vivre*** way of living
naturel(le) natural
novembre November
l' ***oxygène (m.)*** oxygen
par exemple for example
planter to plant
possible possible
le/la ***premier/première*** first
le ***produit ménager*** household product
le ***respect*** respect
la ***ressource*** resource
le ***savon*** soap
scientifique (adj.) scientific
selon according to
le ***soleil*** sun
le ***souci*** worry
la ***Terre*** Earth
végan vegan
le ***véganisme*** veganism
le ***végétarisme*** vegetarianism
le ***vent*** wind

9.1H L'environnement local

l' ***air (m.)*** air
avoir le droit to have the right
la ***banlieue*** suburbs
cela it, this, that
le ***centre de recyclage*** recycling centre
circuler to circulate
commun common
construire to build
le/les ***déchet(s) (m. pl.)*** rubbish
dommage! what a shame!
la ***durabilité*** sustainability
l' ***économie (f.)*** economy
encourager to encourage
expliquer (que) to explain (that)
faire du recyclage to do recycling
finir to finish
le ***gaz*** gas
la ***gestion*** management
loin far
le ***manque de*** lack of
ménager (adj.) household
le ***métro*** underground (train)
le ***modèle*** model
ne … ni … ni neither … nor
ne … pas encore not yet
ne … que only
le ***papier*** paper
permettre de to allow
la ***piste cyclable*** cycle path
polluer to pollute
principal(e) main
produire to produce
le ***programme*** programme
récent(e) recent
réussir à to succeed in
recycler to recycle
le ***réseau*** network
le ***reste*** rest
la ***tonne*** ton
transformer to transform
trier to sort

9.2F Un guide de ma ville

août August
avoir faim to be hungry
avoir le temps to have time
beaucoup à faire a lot to do
bien sûr of course
la ***citadelle*** citadel
confortable comfortable
la ***couleur*** colour
délicieux/délicieuse delicious
la ***Dordogne*** Dordogne
en été in summer
en général in general
environ about, thereabouts
l' ***été (m.)*** summer
faire froid to be cold
faire les magasins to go shopping
idéal(e) ideal
joli(e) pretty
juillet July
médiéval(e) medieval
penser de to think of
le ***port*** port
quatorzième fourteenth
recommander to recommend
la ***région*** region
rien à faire nothing to do
le/la ***seul(e) …*** the only …
le ***sud-ouest*** South-West
le ***théâtre*** theatre
vieux/vieil/vieille old

9.2H Ma ville idéale

à la campagne in the countryside
actuel(le) current
l' ***air frais (m.)*** fresh air
apprécier de to appreciate to
le ***bruit*** noise
la ***circulation*** traffic
dire to say, tell
donner sur to overlook/give onto
en ville in town
entendre to hear
être au soleil to be in the sun
faire du bruit to make noise
la ***gare*** train station
il n'y a jamais rien there is never anything
l' ***inconvénient (m.)*** disadvantage, inconvenience
la plupart du temps most of the time
nager to swim, to go swimming
la ***nuit*** night
pareil(le) same
pas loin de not far from
penser (que) to think (that)
peut-être maybe
plein de lots of, full of
plus tard later
plutôt rather
rapidement quickly
rester en forme to stay fit
tout(e) petit(e) very small
tranquille quiet
la ***tranquillité*** tranquillity
le ***transport*** transport

Culture

l' ***Afrique (f.)*** Africa
la ***boue*** mud
le ***bois*** wood
la ***brique*** brick, brickwork
carré(e) square
le ***chaume*** thatch
chimique chemical
le ***corail*** coral
directement directly
disponible available
écologique ecological, environmentally friendly
élevé(e) raised
l' ***extérieur (m.)*** outside
la ***fabrication*** production, building
l' ***habitation (f.)*** house, home, dwelling
les ***matériaux (m. pl.)*** materials
la ***médina*** old walled centre in a north-African city
le ***mélange*** mix
la ***mondialisation*** globalisation
le ***mur*** wall
la ***paille*** straw
la ***pierre*** stone
le ***pilotis*** stilt
polynésien(ne) Polynesian
principalement mainly
rectangulaire rectangular
rond(e) circular, round
rudimentaire rudimentary
subsaharienne sub-Saharan
le ***sud-est*** South East
tahitienne Tahitian
la ***terrasse*** terrace, balcony
le ***toit*** a roof
la ***tôle*** corrugated iron
volcanique volcanic

Test and revise: Higher Listening

1 You hear some Belgian students talking about holidays. What opinion do they give on the following aspects (1–4)?

Write **P** for a **positive** opinion
N for a **negative** opinion
P+N for a **positive** and **negative** opinion.

1 Transport **1 mark**
2 Accommodation **1 mark**
3 Weather **1 mark**
4 Holiday activities **1 mark**

Conseil !

Listen out for positive and negative opinions and adjectives. Listen also for words such as *mais*, *cependant* and *malheureusement* which can indicate a contrasting opinion.

2 You hear this podcast about uses of technology.

Complete the sentences in **English**.

1 **a** Young people use the internet to… **1 mark**
b They also like… **1 mark**
2 **a** Yesterday morning, Khalid… **1 mark**
b After that, he… **1 mark**

Conseil !

Use the sentence starters to help you locate the answers in the recording. Make sure your English answers fit within the context of the sentence.

3 You hear Roméo describing his gap year.

Choose the correct answer and write the letter.

Answer all parts of the question.

1a When Roméo was young…

A	he lived in France.
B	he liked francophone cultures.
C	he wanted to travel to another part of the world.

1 mark

1b For his gap year, he wanted…

A	a country with a culture similar to that in France.
B	a place with a good climate.
C	to speak French.

1 mark

2a He found a job…

A	in a café.
B	on a plane.
C	on his own.

1 mark

2b Roméo lived…

A	above a small café.
B	on his own.
C	off his best friend's money.

1 mark

3 In the end, Roméo…

A	stayed there for three years.
B	found the island a bit boring.
C	learnt about the culture and traditions.

1 mark

Conseil !

This type of task provides distractors as potential answer options. These will often use language from the recording, so you need to listen carefully to the details. Listen out for negatives or other words which may change an idea mentioned as a potential answer.

4 You hear these YouTubers talking about their experience.

Choose the **two** correct statements.

Write the correct letters for each section (1–3).

1

A	Everybody is a YouTuber nowadays.
B	YouTube is a good way to share ideas online.
C	There is no advice on YouTube.
D	People can react to content on YouTube.

2 marks

2

A	He used to write blogs.
B	YouTube has always been popular.
C	He used to watch videos online.
D	He wants to promote his city.

2 marks

3

A	Being a YouTuber is not time-consuming.
B	He posts new content once a month.
C	Regular content allows him to be popular.
D	He uses comments as inspiration.

2 marks

Conseil

You could treat this type of task as a true / false activity: use ticks and crosses on the first listening, then check on the second listening before making your final decision.

5 You hear this environmental activist discussing climate change.

Answer all parts of the questions in **English**.

1 a Why is pollution such a big problem in cities? Give **two** details. **2 marks**

b How does he say we can reduce pollution? Give **two** details. **2 marks**

2 Name **two** types of transport suggested as potential alternatives to using a car. **2 marks**

6 You hear this discussion on the radio.

Write **A** if only statement **A** is correct
B if only statement **B** is correct
A+B if both statements **A** and **B** are correct.

Write the correct letter(s).

Answer all parts of the question.

1a To protect young people against new technologies…

A	they should learn to use the internet in an effective way.
B	they should not spend all their time online.

1 mark

1b Spending time online…

A	is recommended.
B	can be dangerous.

1 mark

2 We can use our phones to…

A	live our lives.
B	do research and shopping.

1 mark

Dictation A

You will now hear **five** short sentences.

Listen carefully and, using your knowledge of French sounds, write down in French exactly what you hear for each sentence.

You will hear each sentence **three** times: the first time as a full sentence, the second time in short sections and the third time again as a full sentence.

Use your knowledge of French sounds and grammar to make sure that what you have written makes sense. Check carefully that your spelling is accurate.

10 marks

Dictation B

You will now hear **five** more sentences.

Write down in French exactly what you hear for each sentence.

10 marks

Test and revise: Higher Speaking

Role play

You are talking to your friend from Guadeloupe.

Your teacher will play the part of your friend and will speak first.

You should address your friend as *tu*.

When you see this – ? – you will have to ask a question.

In order to score full marks, you must include a verb in your response to each task.

1 Give **one** opinion about where you live.

2 Give **two** environmental problems in your town / city.

3 Say what you usually do at home to help the environment. (Give **two** details.)

4 Say what you will do in the future to protect the environment. (Give **two** details.)

? 5 Ask your friend what they do to protect the environment.

10 marks

Conseil

In order to complete the role play successfully, read the instructions and bullet points carefully so you know exactly what you need to say. Check which time frame you are required to answer in for each task and make sure your verb is conjugated in the right tense.

Reading aloud

When your teacher asks you, read aloud the following text **in French**.

Cet été, je vais en vacances à l'étranger avec ma famille.

Nous préférons voyager en train.

C'est moins cher et meilleur pour l'environnement que l'avion.

J'adore passer du temps à la plage avec ma sœur et mes deux frères.

Normalement, nous faisons de la natation et nous jouons dans la mer ensemble.

You will then be asked **four** questions **in French** that relate to the topic of **Travel and tourism, including places of interest**. Make sure you **answer all four questions as fully as you can**.

15 marks

Conseil

Listen to the questions and use the vocabulary from the questions to help you formulate your answers.

Photo card

- During your preparation time, look at the two photos. You may make as many notes as you wish on an Additional Answer Sheet and use these notes during the task.
- Your teacher will ask you to talk about the content of these photos. The recommended time is approximately **one and a half minutes**. You must **say at least one thing about each photo**.
- After you have spoken about the content of the photos, your teacher will then ask you questions related to **any** of the topics within the theme of **Communication and the world around us**.

25 marks

Conseil

Listen carefully to the tense used in each question before answering. Try to use a variety of structures, and include opinions and reasons.

Photo 1

Photo 2

Test and revise: Higher Reading

1 You read this email that Molly sent to her friend in France. She describes where she lives.

Answer the following questions in **English**.

Bonjour,

J'habite dans une petite ville située dans l'ouest de l'Angleterre. Notre appartement est assez grand car il y a trois chambres. J'ai ma propre chambre mais ma petite sœur et mon petit frère doivent partager. Chez moi, on aime regarder la télé ensemble dans le salon mais moi, je lis souvent des livres dans ma chambre.

Ma ville n'est pas historique parce qu'il n'y a pas de châteaux ni de vieux bâtiments. Malgré ça, les jeunes aiment la ville parce qu'ils peuvent faire du shopping au centre commercial et manger dans de bons restaurants.

Molly

a Give **two** details about Molly's flat. **2 marks**

b What does Molly's family like to do at home? **1 mark**

c Why does she describe her town as 'not historic'? Give **two** details. **2 marks**

d Why do young people like her town? Give **two** details. **2 marks**

Conseil

Don't feel overwhelmed by longer texts. Take your time and focus on what you understand. Use the questions to identify the parts of the text you need to answer them. For example, in question a, you are looking for details about Molly's flat, so the information you need is likely to follow shortly after the cognate *appartement*.

2 You see these opinions on a travel blog. What do these people (a–d) think of each means of transport?

Write **P** for a **positive** opinion
N for a **negative** opinion
P+N for a **positive** and **negative** opinion.

a  L'avion est mon moyen de transport préféré, surtout pour aller en vacances. C'est rapide et pratique et on peut dormir pendant le vol. Par contre, c'est mauvais pour l'environnement à cause de la pollution.

b  Le bus est un moyen de transport qui n'est pas rapide du tout. En plus, les bus polluent parce que beaucoup sont assez vieux. Je ne prends jamais le bus!

c  Ma sœur ne prend jamais son vélo car elle trouve cela trop ennuyeux. Mais moi, j'adore mon vélo! C'est le moyen de transport le plus rapide et le plus facile qui existe et en plus, cela me permet de rester en bonne santé.

d  J'adore prendre le train. C'est rapide et bon marché et on peut aller partout où on veut. En plus, le train est meilleur pour l'environnement que d'autres moyens de transports.

4 marks

Conseil

Look for positive or negative opinions and adjectives, as well as changeover words and phrases such as *par contre*, *mais* and *cependant*.

3 You read an online forum about how people use the internet.

Answer the following questions in **English**.

Soraya

Quand j'étais plus jeune, il y avait un ordinateur dans mon salon, alors je pouvais l'utiliser pour regarder des vidéos pour enfants. Maintenant, j'ai un ordinateur dans ma chambre, sur mon bureau, et je l'utilise tous les jours pour faire des recherches pour mes devoirs.

Yanis

Hier, j'ai téléchargé un film et ma famille et moi l'avons regardé sur notre nouvelle télé. Normalement, j'aime aller sur les réseaux sociaux mais ma sœur les déteste. Elle dit qu'ils sont trop dangereux.

Candice

Avant, je communiquais avec mes amis au téléphone mais maintenant, je trouve qu'utiliser les réseaux sociaux est plus facile, et pas cher. Alors, j'envoie souvent des messages à mes amis et nous discutons ensemble tous les soirs.

a What did Soraya do online when she was younger? **1 mark**

b Where is her computer now? Give **two** details. **2 marks**

c Give **three** details about the film that Yanis watched yesterday, **3 marks**

d Read Candice's account again. Choose the **two** correct statements. Write the correct letters. **2 marks**

A	She communicates with friends by phone.
B	Using social media is cheap.
C	She messages her family.
D	She chats online with friends every evening.

Conseil

Always give the correct number of details for each question: check the numbers in bold and the marks in brackets.

4 Translate these sentences into English.

a Dans le nord de la France, il pleut souvent.

b On me dit toujours que j'habite dans une belle ville.

c Nous voyagerons en avion mais ce n'est pas bon pour l'environnement.

d Je n'aimerais pas vivre sans réseaux sociaux.

e Il a arrêté de manger de la viande pour pouvoir aider la planète.

10 marks

5 Translate these sentences into English.

a Je travaille dans un magasin depuis six mois.

b Au collège, le recyclage est organisé par les élèves.

c J'ai commencé à lire des blogs quand j'avais 18 ans.

d Nous sommes partis le dimanche après-midi après avoir mangé.

e Il donnera des conseils pratiques pour vous permettre de découvrir le monde.

10 marks

Conseil

If there is a word or expression that you don't understand, translate the gist (general idea) of the meaning, rather than leaving it blank.

Test and revise: Higher Writing

1 Translate the following sentences into French.

a Helping our planet is important for the future.

b I will try to travel less often by car.

c My parents only like holidays in France.

d If it was hot, she would swim in the sea.

e When tourists come, they visit the castle.

10 marks

Conseil

Pay careful attention to tenses and verbs when you translate into French. Check the time markers in the English sentences to help you.

Either question 2.1 or question 2.2

2.1 You are emailing your Canadian friend about holidays.

Write approximately **90** words in **French**.

You must write something about each bullet point.

Describe:

- what sort of holidays you like
- a recent holiday
- what you will do in your summer holiday.

15 marks

Conseil

Make sure you read the bullet points carefully and write something about each one. Your verbs and time phrases need to match what each bullet point is asking you.

2.2 You are writing an article about the environment.

Write approximately **90** words in **French**.

You must write something about each bullet point.

Describe:

- the main environmental problems in your region
- what you did recently to help the environment
- a habit you will change to protect the planet.

15 marks

Either question 3.1 or question 3.2

3.1 You are writing a post for a media and new technologies forum.

Write approximately **150** words in **French**.

You must write something about both bullet points.

Describe:

- how you use the internet
- how you will use technologies responsibly in the future.

25 marks

3.2 You are writing an article about where you live and your local area. Your article is for your school website.

Write approximately **150** words in **French**.

You must write something about both bullet points.

Describe:

- where you live now
- where you would like to live in the future.

25 marks

Conseil

In this task, you will be awarded marks not only for communication and accuracy, but also for using varied and complex language. Try to use a range of tenses, verbs + infinitive, longer sentences linked with *où*, *si* and *quand*, different persons of the verb and other complex expressions such *après avoir…* and *avant de…*

Test and revise: Higher Listening

1 You hear some French teenagers talking about their family relationships. What opinion do they give of their relationship with the following family members (1–4)?

Write **P** for a **positive** opinion
N for a **negative** opinion
P+N for a **positive** and **negative** opinion.

1 Brothers
2 Cousin
3 Father
4 Aunt and uncle

4 marks

Conseil

In this type of task, a negative expression doesn't always indicate a negative opinion. Take care to understand the context of each expression.

2 You hear this podcast about the Quebec summer festival.

Choose the correct answer and write the letter.

1 The festival takes place…

A	in the city centre.
B	on the edge of the city.
C	just outside the city.

1 mark

2 The most popular concert attracted…

A	60,000 people.
B	80,000 people.
C	100,000 people.

1 mark

3 One well-known singer has said that he will never…

A	stop coming to the festival.
B	forget that festival.
C	find a better festival.

1 mark

4 According to the festival director, the city benefits most from…

A	improving its image.
B	having foreign visitors.
C	seeing talented artists.

1 mark

5 Next year's concerts may take place…

A	with different security arrangements.
B	at a different time.
C	at different locations.

1 mark

Conseil

Before you listen to the recording, look at the key English words in the sentence starters and answer options, and anticipate which French words you might expect to hear. Remember that you won't always hear a literal translation of them.

3 You hear this radio advertisement for a leisure centre.

Write **A** if only statement **A** is correct.
B if only statement **B** is correct.
A+B if both statements **A** and **B** are correct.

1 The centre is open on…
A Saturdays. B Sundays. **1 mark**

2 There are reductions for…
A retired people. B local people. **1 mark**

3 There are swimming lessons for…
A children. B adults. **1 mark**

4 At the moment, you can get to the centre by…
A train. B bike. **1 mark**

Conseil

Not everything you hear will be directly relevant to the answer, but you need to understand everything in order to know which answer option is correct.

4 You hear three Belgian people talking about environmental issues.

Choose the **two** correct statements.

Write the correct letters for each section (1–3).

1

A	The situation in Belgium is better than in some countries.
B	Public transport remains expensive.
C	Vehicle pollution affects both town and country.
D	Cycling must be encouraged.

2 marks

2

A	Even for long trips there are alternatives to flying.
B	The number of flights must be reduced.
C	My family uses the car for holidays.
D	We could take the train if we really wanted to.

2 marks

3

A	Everyone accepts that environmental protection is essential.
B	My town has traffic problems.
C	The bus service is fast but people don't use it.
D	I walk into town in all weathers.

2 marks

5 You hear this interview with a French influencer.

Answer the questions in **English**.

1 **a** How did the influencer's friend help her? **1 mark**

b What happened after one year? **1 mark**

2 How **exactly** does the influencer explain her success? Give **two** details. **2 marks**

Conseil

In this task, there are two marks for each section. Each section has either two separate questions or one two-mark question. Be aware of this before you start listening.

6 You hear three young people from Switzerland talking about their use of technology.

Complete the sentences in **English**.

1 **a** Sophie finds social media… **1 mark**

b Yesterday, Sophie… **1 mark**

2 **a** When Khalid was younger, he… **1 mark**

b Today, Khalid is… **1 mark**

3 **a** To find information, Colette prefers… **1 mark**

b Colette uses her laptop to… **1 mark**

Conseil

Use the sentence starters to help you locate the answers in the recording.

In each section (1–3), make sure you listen out for the answers to both questions.

Dictation A

You will now hear **five** short sentences.

Listen carefully and, using your knowledge of French sounds, write down in French exactly what you hear for each sentence.

You will hear each sentence **three** times: the first time as a full sentence, the second time in short sections and the third time again as a full sentence.

Use your knowledge of French sounds and grammar to make sure that what you have written makes sense. Check carefully that your spelling is accurate.

10 marks

Dictation B

You will now hear **five** more sentences.

Write down in French exactly what you hear for each sentence.

10 marks

Test and revise: Higher Speaking

Role play

You are talking to your friend from the island of La Réunion.

Your teacher will play the part of your friend and will speak first.

You should address your friend as *tu*.

When you see this – ? – you will have to ask a question.

In order to score full marks, you must include a verb in your response to each task.

1 Give **two** details about your favourite food and drink.

2 Give **one** detail about what makes a healthy lifestyle.

3 Say what you usually do to relax, and why. (Give **one** detail and **one** reason.)

4 Say what you will do in the future to be healthier. (Give **two** details.)

? 5 Ask your friend a question about their lifestyle.

10 marks

Conseil

Remember that you are allowed to take notes for all tasks in the speaking exam. You can refer to these at any point during the test. Use this to help you!

Conseil

The role play should usually last one to one and half minutes. There are two marks for each task (1–5) on the role play card. Make sure you use a conjugated verb in each response.

Read the tasks carefully to make sure you respond in the required time frame.

Note the number of details required for each response. Remember to give an opinion and ask a question where required.

Reading aloud

When your teacher asks you, read aloud the following text **in French**.

J'aime aider les gens.

Je veux donc faire un métier où je peux faire une différence.

Après le lycée, je vais étudier à l'université car je veux devenir médecin.

Je préfère aller au collège à vélo parce que ça ne pollue pas.

Je pense aussi que c'est meilleur pour la santé.

You will then be asked four questions **in French** that relate to the topic of **Education and work** with others. Make sure you **answer all four questions as fully as you can**.

15 marks

Conseil

The reading aloud task and follow-up questions should usually last three to three and half minutes in total.

When reading the text aloud, focus on your pronunciation, particularly verb and noun endings. You may lose marks if your pronunciation affects communication.

Listen closely to the follow-up questions and use vocabulary from the questions to help you formulate your answers.

Photo card

- During your preparation time, look at the two photos. You may make as many notes as you wish and use these notes during the test.
- Your teacher will ask you to talk about the content of these photos. The recommended time is approximately **one and a half minutes**. You must **say at least one thing about each photo**.
- After you have spoken about the content of the photos, your teacher will then ask you questions related to **any** of the topics within the theme of **Popular culture**.

25 marks

Conseil

Your description of the two photos should last about one and half minutes and you need to say something about both photos. The follow-up conversation should last four and half to five and half minutes.

Listen carefully to the tense of the follow-up questions before answering. If the question includes an opinion, make sure you include one in your answer.

Photo 1

Photo 2

Test and revise: Higher Reading

1 You read this online forum about lifestyle. Answer the questions that follow.

Write **M** for **Momina**
J for **Jérémie**
M+J for **Momina** and **Jérémie**.

Momina

Je suis en bonne santé parce que je mange équilibré. Par exemple, je mange des fruits et des légumes à chaque repas et je bois chaque jour beaucoup d'eau. En semaine, je me couche tôt mais le week-end, j'aime regarder des films, alors je me couche un peu plus tard. L'année prochaine, je gérerai mieux mon temps. Comme je réviserai pour mes examens, j'aurai moins de temps pour me relaxer.

Jérémie

Je fais tous les jours du sport et je vais à l'école à vélo car c'est meilleur pour la santé et aussi pour l'environnement. Par contre, j'adore les gâteaux, alors j'en mange plusieurs par jour. Mes projets pour l'année prochaine? J'essayerai de me lever plus tôt car ça m'aide à me concentrer, surtout pour mes examens au collège l'année prochaine. En plus, comme j'aime passer du temps dans la nature, j'irai marcher à la campagne avec mes amis. Ça sera amusant et je me relaxerai!

a Who has a good diet? **1 mark**

b Who will have exams next year? **1 mark**

c Who likes to spend time outside to relax? **1 mark**

d Who will manage their time better? **1 mark**

e Read Momina's text again.
Choose the **two** correct statements.
Write the correct letters.

A	She is vegetarian.
B	She eats a lot of sugary foods.
C	She drinks water regularly.
D	She goes to bed late on weekdays.
E	She likes to watch films at the weekend.

2 marks

2 You read an article in your school magazine about Awen's school in Belgium.

Answer the questions in **English**.

J'adore vraiment mon école parce qu'on peut y porter nos propres vêtements. C'est moins cher et on peut choisir des vêtements qu'on aime. Dans mon collège, les cours commencent à huit heures trente, alors je dois me lever tôt. Dans l'ensemble, j'adore mes professeurs car ils sont sympas et ils m'aident avec mon travail quand je ne comprends pas. Ma professeure de français est ma prof préférée car elle est la plus gentille. À midi, je mange à l'école. En général, mes amis et moi, nous aimons les repas car il y a beaucoup de choix. Nous préférerions avoir une récréation plus longue car nous aimerions discuter plus longtemps. À l'avenir, j'aimerais avoir une bibliothèque plus grande. Comme la matière que je préfère est le français, j'aime beaucoup lire.

a Why does Awen like wearing her own clothes? (Give **two** details.) **2 marks**

b Why does she have to get up early? **1 mark**

c Why does Awen like her French teacher best? **1 mark**

d Why do Awen and her friends like the meals at lunchtime? **1 mark**

Complete these sentences.

Write the letter for the correct option.

e Awen and her friends would prefer longer…

A	meals.
B	break times.
C	English lessons.

1 mark

f Awen would like a bigger…

A	bookshop.
B	French classroom.
C	library.

1 mark

3 You read this social media post from Christine about swimming.

Complete these sentences.

Write the letter for the correct option.

Christine

J'aime plein de sports, mais j'aime surtout être active dehors, alors je fais souvent de la natation dans la mer. J'ai de la chance car j'habite au bord de la mer! Je trouve cela amusant, mais c'est assez difficile quand il y a de grandes vagues. Comme l'eau peut parfois être froide, je rentre vite chez moi après et je prends une douche chaude. À l'avenir, je vais essayer un autre sport nautique. Je ne suis pas encore sûre du sport que j'essayerai, mais ce sera une nouvelle expérience.

1 Christine likes being active…

A	in the sea.
B	outdoors.
C	on the coast.

1 mark

2 She finds swimming in the sea…

A	fun but quite difficult.
B	neither fun nor difficult.
C	fun but very difficult.

1 mark

3 When the water is cold, she…

A	finishes her swim more quickly.
B	does not swim.
C	she has a warm shower after her swim.

1 mark

4 Christine…

A	knows which other sport she would like to try.
B	would like to try another water sport.
C	is not confident enough to try another sport.

1 mark

4 Translate these sentences into English.

a Je mène un mode de vie sain.

b Mes parents aimeraient m'acheter un uniforme moins cher.

c J'apprends à jouer au foot depuis deux ans mais je trouve ça difficile.

d L'année dernière, nous avons vu notre chanteur préféré en concert.

e Comme mon frère s'intéresse au cinéma, il regarde souvent des films pour se relaxer.

10 marks

5 Translate these sentences into English.

a Dans mon école idéale, il y aurait le terrain de sport le plus grand.

b Nous nous demandons à quelle heure ouvre le cinéma.

c Dès que j'ai vu ce sport, j'ai voulu y participer.

d Mes amis ont fait de la natation et nous les avons regardés.

e Essayons de protéger les jeunes en ligne car il y a trop de dangers.

10 marks

Test and revise: Higher Writing

1 Translate the following sentences into French.

a I love vegetables and I eat a lot of them.

b They liked the small town where they used to live.

c For my birthday he is going to give me a recycling bin!

d I had go to school by bike yesterday and it was tiring.

e My friend will buy a new mobile phone when he is older.

10 marks

Conseil

Remember that you need to convey the message in each sentence. Make sure you use the correct pronoun and verb form: check the tense required and conjugate your verb correctly. Try not to leave any gaps – if you don't know the exact word, you can use a synonym.

Either question 2.1 or question 2.2

2.1 You are emailing your French friend about holidays.

Write approximately **90** words in **French**.

You must write something about each bullet point.

Describe:

- what you usually do for the holidays
- the activities you did during a recent holiday
- your dream holiday.

15 marks

Conseil

For this task, you must write something about all the bullet points, but there is no need to cover them equally. Try to convey a lot of information clearly and use varied vocabulary and grammar. You should also make accurate references to all three time frames.

2.2 You are writing a blog about free time for your Canadian partner school.

Write approximately **90** words in **French**.

You must write something about each bullet point.

Describe:

- your favourite hobbies
- what you did recently at the weekend
- a new hobby you would like to try in future.

15 marks

Either question 3.1 or question 3.2

3.1 You are writing an article for a French environmental website. Your article is about your local area.

Write approximately **150** words in **French**.

You must write something about both bullet points.

Describe:

- the environmental problems in your local area
- how you would like to improve your local area.

25 marks

3.2 You are writing a post for a Belgian online forum. Your post is about celebrity culture.

Write approximately **150** words in **French**.

You must write something about both bullet points.

Describe:

- the negative aspects of being a celebrity
- a future meeting with your favourite celebrity.

25 marks

Conseil

Remember to write something about both bullet points and make sure what you write is relevant. There is no need to cover the bullet points equally. Aim to develop your ideas as much as possible, using complex, varied language and a range of tenses, and ensure you communicate your message clearly.

Grammar

Contents

Glossary of terms

Adjectives *les adjectifs*

Words that describe somebody or something:
petit small *timide* shy

Adverbs *les adverbes*

Words that complement (add meaning to) verbs, adjectives or other adverbs:
très very *lentement* slowly

Articles *les articles*

Short words used before nouns:
un/une a, an *des* some, any *le/la/les* the

The infinitive *l'infinitif*

The verb form given in the dictionary:
aller to go *avoir* to have

Nouns *les noms*

Words that identify a person, a place or a thing:
mère mother *maison* house

Prepositions *les prépositions*

Words used in front of nouns to give information about when, how, where, etc.:
à at *avec* with *de* of, from *en* in

Pronouns *les pronoms*

Short words used to replace nouns:
je I *tu* you *il* he *elle* she *moi* me *toi* you

Verbs *les verbes*

Words used to express an action or a state:
je parle I speak *il est* he is

1 Nouns

Masculine and feminine nouns

All French nouns are either masculine or feminine. In the singular, masculine nouns are introduced with *le*, *l'* or *un*:

le père	**the** father	*un livre*	**a** book
l'hôtel	**the** hotel		

Feminine nouns are introduced with *la*, *l'* or *une*:

la mère	**the** mother	*une table*	**a** table
l'eau	**the** water		

Some nouns have two different forms, masculine and feminine:

un écrivain	a male writer
une écrivaine	a female writer
un serveur	a male waiter
une serveuse	a female waiter
un facteur	a postman
une factrice	a postwoman
un physicien	a male physicist
une physicienne	a female physicist
un policier	a male police officer
une policière	a female police officer

Some nouns stay the same for masculine and feminine:

le prof	the male teacher
la prof	the female teacher
un enfant	a male child
une enfant	a female child

Singular and plural forms

As in English, French nouns can be either singular (one) or plural (more than one).

Most plural nouns end in *-s*. Unlike English, the added *-s* is usually not pronounced.

un chien, deux chiens	one dog, two dogs

As in English, there are some exceptions.

- With most nouns ending in *-al*, you change the ending to *-aux* in the plural:
  un animal, des animaux — an animal, animals
- With many nouns ending in *-au* or *-eu*, you add an *-x*:
  un gâteau, des gâteaux — a cake, cakes
  un jeu, des jeux — a game, games
- Words already ending in *-s*, or in *-x* or *-z*, do not change:
  le bras, les bras — arm, arms
  le prix, les prix — prize, prizes
- A few nouns change completely:
  un œil, des yeux — an eye, eyes

2 Articles

Definite articles: *le, la, les* – the

The word for 'the' depends on whether the noun it goes with is masculine (m), feminine (f), singular or plural.

m singular	f singular	m + f plural
le	*la*	*les*

***le** beau-père* the step-father
***la** belle-mère* the step-mother
***les** parents* the parents

When a singular noun starts with a vowel or a silent *h*, *le* and *la* are shortened to *l'*:

***l'**ami* the friend
***l'**histoire* the story

In French, you often need to use *le*, *la* and *les* even when we wouldn't say 'the' in English:

- when talking about likes and dislikes:
  *J'adore **le** fromage.* I love cheese.
  *Elle déteste **les** maths.* She hates maths.
- when referring to abstract things:
  ***La** musique est très importante.* Music is very important.

As in English, definite articles can be used before an adjective to form a noun:

seul only (m.) ***le** seul* **the** only
anglaise English (f.) ***l'**Anglaise* **the** English (girl / woman)

As in English, articles are omitted after certain prepositions, such as *en*:

*Je vais **en** France.* I am going **to** France.

Indefinite articles: *un, une, des, de* – a, an, some

Like the words for 'the' (*le / la / les*), the words for 'a / an' and 'some' depend on whether the noun they go with is masculine or feminine, singular or plural.

m. singular	f. singular	m. + f. plural
un	*une*	*des*

***un** vélo* a bike
***une** ville* a town
***des** voitures* (some) cars

When talking about jobs, *un* and *une* are not used in French where 'a' or 'an' is used in English.

Il est professeur. He is **a** teacher.

In negative constructions, *de* replaces *un*, *une* or *des* after *pas*:

*J'ai un frère. – Je n'ai **pas de** frère.** I don't have **any** brothers.
*Il y a une piscine. – Il n'y a **pas de** piscine.* There is **no** swimming pool.
*J'ai des sœurs. – Je n'ai **pas de** sœur.** I don't have **any** sisters.

** Note that in French you use a singular noun after a negative construction, unlike in English.*

Change *de* to *d'* in front of a vowel or a silent *h*:

*Je n'ai pas **d'**animal.* I don't have any pets.

Partitive articles: *du, de la, de l', des* – some, any

masculine	feminine	words beginning with a vowel or silent *h*	plural
de + le = du	*de + la = de la*	*de + l' = de l'*	*de + les = des*

du café (some) coffee
de la nourriture (some) food
de l'eau (some) water
des frites (some) chips

- ***du*** always replaces *de + le*
- ***des*** always replaces *de + les*

Use *du, de la, de l', des* to mean 'some' or 'any':

*Je voudrais **du** pain.* I'd like **some** bread.
*Elle prend **de la** glace.* She's having (**some**) ice cream.
*Elle boit **de l'**eau.* She's drinking (**some**) water.
*Avez-vous **des** croissants?* Do you have **any** croissants?

Also use *du, de la, de l'*, des to talk about activities someone is doing or musical instruments someone is playing:

*Je fais **du** judo.* I do judo.
*Elle joue **de la** guitare.* She is playing the guitar.
*Il fait **de l'**équitation.* He goes horse riding.
*Ils font **des** voyages.* They go on trips.

After a negative, *de* or *d'* (before a vowel) replaces these forms:

*Je ne fais pas **de** judo.* I don't do judo.

3 Adjectives

Feminine and masculine, singular and plural adjectives

In French, adjectives have different endings depending on whether they describe masculine, feminine, singular or plural nouns.

- The masculine singular form has no extra ending:
  Mon frère est petit. My brother is small.
- Add *-e* if the noun is feminine singular:
  *Ma sœur est petit**e**.* My sister is small.
- Add *-s* to the masculine singular form if the noun is masculine plural:
  *Mes frères sont petit**s**.* My brothers are small.
- Add *-s* to the feminine singular form if the noun is feminine plural:
  *Mes sœurs sont petit**es**.* My sisters are small.
- When an adjective describes a group of masculine and feminine people or things, it has to be the masculine plural form:
  *Mes parents sont grand**s**.* My parents are tall.

There are many exceptions in the feminine forms.

- With adjectives that already end in *-e*, don't add another *-e* in the feminine:
  *un vélo roug**e*** a red bike
  *une fleur roug**e*** a red flower
- But with adjectives that end in *-é*, do add another *-e* in the feminine:
  *mon film préfér**é*** my favourite film
  *ma chanson préfér**ée*** my favourite song
- With some adjectives, you double the final consonant before the *-e* in the feminine:
  Il est canadien. He is Canadian.
  *Elle est canadien**ne**.* She is Canadian.
  Un parc naturel. A natural park.
  *Une plage naturel**le**.* A natural beach.
- Adjective endings *-x* change to *-se* in the feminine:
  *un garçon paress**eux*** a lazy boy
  *une fille paress**euse*** a lazy girl
- The adjective ending *-f* changes to *-ve* in the feminine:
  *un copain sport**if*** a sporty (boy)friend
  *une copine sporti**ve*** a sporty (girl)friend
- The feminine of *gentil* is *gentille*:
  *Ma sœur est gentil**le**.* My sister is kind.

There are also some exceptions in the plural forms.

- Adjective endings *-al* and *-eau* change to *-aux* or *-eaux* in the masculine plural:
  *J'ai des poissons nouve**aux**.* I have got some new fish.
- With adjectives that end in *-s* or *-x*, don't add an *-s* in the masculine plural:
  *Mes frères sont paresseu**x**.* My brothers are lazy.
  *Les murs sont gri**s**.* The walls are grey.

The position of adjectives

Most adjectives follow the noun they describe:

*un prof **sympa*** a nice teacher
*une copine **intelligente*** an intelligent friend
*des idées **intéressantes*** interesting ideas

However, a few adjectives, such as *petit, grand, bon, mauvais, joli, beau, jeune* and *vieux,* usually come in front of the noun:

*un **petit** garçon* a small boy
*une **jolie** ville* a pretty town

A few adjectives that come in front of the noun have a special masculine form before a vowel or a silent *h*:

*un **bel** endroit* a beautiful place
*un **vieil** homme* an old man
*un **nouvel** ami* a new friend

Comparative and superlative adjectives

To make comparisons, use:

- *plus … que* more … than / …er than
  *La Loire est **plus** longue **que** la Tamise.*
  The Loire is long**er than** the Thames.
- *moins … que* less … than
  *Les vélos sont **moins** rapides **que** les trains.*
  Bicycles are **less** fast **than** trains.
- *aussi … que* as … as
  *Les fruits sont **aussi** chères **que** les légumes.*
  Fruits are **as** expensive **as** vegetables.

For superlatives (the most …), use:

- *le / la / les plus …* the most … / the …est
  *C'est la chambre **la plus** chère.*
  It is **the most** expensive room.
  *C'est **le plus** petit vélo.*
  It is **the smallest** bicycle.
- *le / la / les moins …* the least …
  *C'est le film **le moins** intéressant.*
  It is **the least** interesting film.

Demonstrative adjectives: *ce, cet, cette, ces* – *this, that, these, those*

The French for 'this' or 'that' is *ce*, *cet* or *cette* and for 'these' or 'those' is ces.

masculine	feminine	masculine and feminine plural
ce	*cette*	*ces*

***ce** magasin* — **this / that** shop
***cette** maison* — **this / that** house
***ces** bâtiments* — **these / those** buildings

But *ce* changes to *cet* when the noun after it is masculine and begins with a vowel or a silent *h*:

***cet** ami* — **this / that** friend
***cet** hôtel* — **this / that** hotel

Indefinite adjectives

The most common indefinite adjectives are:

autre(s) — other
chaque — each
même(s) — same
plusieurs — several
quelque(s) — some
tout / toute / tous / toutes — all

Chaque is always singular and *plusieurs* is always plural:

*Il y a une télévision dans **chaque chambre**.*
There is a television in **each room**.

*Il a **plusieurs voitures**.* He has **several cars**.

Possessive adjectives, one 'owner'

mon / ma / mes — my
ton / ta / tes — your
son / sa / ses — his / her / its

There are three different ways of saying 'my' in French, as it depends on whether the noun is masculine or feminine, singular or plural. It is the same for 'your' and 'his' / 'her' / 'its'.

masculine singular	feminine singular	masculine and feminine plural
mon, ton, son	*ma, ta, sa*	*mes, tes, ces*

***mon** père* — **my** father
***ma** mère* — **my** mother
ton ** père* — **your** father
ta ** mère* — **your** mother
***son** pied* — **his / her / its** foot
***sa** porte* — **his / her / its** door
***mes** parents* — **my** parents
tes ** parents* — **your** parents
***ses** fenêtres* — **his / her / its** windows

** to someone you normally say* tu *to*

French doesn't have three different words for 'his', 'her' and 'its'. The word changes according to whether the noun it is used with is masculine, feminine, singular or plural.

Possessive adjectives, several 'owners'

notre / nos — our
votre / vos — your
leur / leurs — their

masculine and feminine singular	masculine and feminine plural
notre, votre, leur	*nos, vos, leurs*

***notre** père* — **our** father
***notre** mère* — **our** mother
votre ** père* — **your** father
votre ** mère* — **your** mother
***leur** frère* — **their** brother
***leur** sœur* — **their** sister
***nos** parents* — **our** parents
vos ** copains* — **your** friends
***leurs** profs* — **their** teachers

** to several people* **or** *to someone you normally say* vous *to*

Interrogative adjectives: *quel, quelle, quels, quelles*

Quel (meaning 'which' or 'what') agrees with the noun it refers to.

m. singular	f. singular	m. plural	f. plural
quel	*quelle*	*quels*	*quelles*

*C'est **quel** cinéma?* — **Which** cinema is it?
***Quelle** heure est-il?* — **What** time is it?
***Quelles** sont tes matières préférées?*
What are your favourite subjects?

4 Adverbs

Adverbs are used with a verb, an adjective or another adverb to express how, when, where or to what extent something happens.
Many French adverbs are formed by adding *-ment* (the equivalent of '-ly' in English) to the feminine form of the adjective.

m. adjective	f. adjective	adverb
final	*finale*	*finalement* – finally
heureux	*heureuse*	*heureusement* – fortunately
probable	*probable*	*probablement* – probably

Comparative and superlative adverbs

As with adjectives, you can make comparisons using *plus*, *moins* and *aussi … que*:

*Tu parles **plus** lentement **que** moi.*
You speak **more** slowly **than** me.

*Je mange **moins** vite **que** ma sœur.*
I eat **less** quickly than **my** sister.

*Elle joue **aussi** bien **que** Paul.*
She plays **as** well **as** Paul.

You can also use adverbs as superlatives:
*Il a fini son travail **le plus vite**.*
He finished his work **the fastest**.

5 Pronouns

Subject pronouns: *je, tu, il, elle, on, nous, vous, ils, elles*

Subject pronouns usually come before the verb and express who or what performs the action.

singular	plural
je – I *tu* – you *il* – he / it *elle* – she / it *on* – we / you / they	*nous* – we *vous* – you *ils* – they (m.) *elles* – they (f.)

***Je** parle français.*	**I** speak French.
***Tu** as quel âge?*	How old are **you**?
***Il** s'appelle Théo.*	**He** is called Théo.
***Elle** s'appelle Aïcha.*	**She** is called Aïcha.
***On** se retrouve où?*	Where shall **we** meet?
***Nous** habitons en ville.*	**We** live in town.
***Vous** avez une chambre?*	Do **you** have a room?
***Ils** s'appellent Do et Mi.*	**They** are called Do and Mi.
***Elles** sont amusantes.*	**They** are fun.

There are two French words for 'you': *tu* and *vous*.

- Use *tu* when talking to someone (one person) of your own age or someone in your family.
- Use *vous* when talking to an adult not in your family (e.g. your teacher). For example:

***Vous** avez …*	**You have** …
*Que voudriez-**vous** … ?*	What would **you** like … ?

- Also use *vous* when talking to more than one person – whatever their age and whether you know them well or not.

Il and *elle* can both also mean 'it', depending on the gender of the noun they replace.

L'hôtel est bien? *Oui, **il** est très moderne.*	Is the hotel good? Yes, **it** is very modern.
*Je déteste ma chambre: **elle** est trop petite.*	I hate my bedroom: **it** is too small.

On can mean 'we', 'you' or 'they', depending on the context:

***On** s'entend bien.*	**We** get on well.
*Comment dit-**on** «pencil» en français?*	How do **you** say 'pencil' in French?
***On** parle français au Canada.*	**They** speak French in Canada.

There are two French words for 'they': *ils* and *elles*.

- Use ils when all the people / things you are talking about are male, or it is a mixed group of males and females:
  *J'ai un frère et une sœur; **ils** s'appellent Nicolas et Aurélie.*
  I have a brother and a sister; **they** are called Nicolas and Aurélie.
- Use elles when all the people / things you are talking about are female:
  *J'ai deux copines espagnoles; **elles** habitent à Madrid.*
  I have two Spanish friends; **they** live in Madrid.

Direct object pronouns: *me, te, le, la, nous, vous, les*

Direct object pronouns replace a noun that is not the subject of the verb.

singular	plural
me / m' – me *te / t'* – you *le / l'* – him / it (m.) *la / l'* – her / it (f.)	*nous* – us *vous* – you (plural or formal) *les* – them

Direct object pronouns come in front of the verb, unlike in English:

*Je **le** prends.*	I'll take **it**.
*Je peux **vous** aider?*	Can I help **you**?

Le and la are shortened to l' in front of a vowel or a silent h:

*Mon petit frère a deux ans. Je **l'**adore!*	My little brother is two. I love **him**!

Indirect object pronouns: *me, te, lui, nous, vous, leur*

Indirect object pronouns are used to replace a noun that would be introduced with the preposition *à*.

singular	plural
me / m' – (to) me *te / t'* – (to) you *lui* – (to) him / her / it	*nous* – (to) us *vous* – (to) you (plural or formal) *leur* – (to) them

Je donne du café à mon père.
Je lui donne du café. — I give him some coffee.

Je parle à ma mère.
Je lui parle. — I speak to her.

J'écris à mes grands-parents.
Je leur écris. — I write to them.

Indirect object pronouns: *en* – of it / them; *y* – there

Use *en* to avoid repeating a noun that is introduced with *du, de la, de l'* or *des*:

Tu as des chiens?	Have you got any dogs?
*Oui, j'**en** ai trois.*	Yes, I've got three (of them).
Tu manges de la viande?	Do you eat meat?
*Oui, j'**en** mange.*	Yes, I do.
Il y aura des gâteaux demain ?	Will there be cakes tomorrow?
*Oui, il y **en** aura.*	*Yes, there will be.*

Y usually means 'there'. You can use y to avoid repeating the name of a place:

*Tu vas **à** Paris?*	Are you going **to** Paris?
*Oui, j'**y** vais demain.*	Yes, I'm going **there** tomorrow.

Reflexive pronouns: *me, te, se, nous, vous, se*

Reflexive pronouns are an extra pronoun used in front of a reflexive verb:

me	*me je **me** réveille*	I wake up
te	*tu **te** lèves*	you get up
se	*il / elle **s'**appelle* *on **se** lave*	he / she is called we (have a) wash
nous	*nous **nous** amusons*	we have fun
vous	*vous **vous** couchez*	you go to bed
se	*ils / elles **s'**excusent*	they apologise

Note that *me*, *te* and se are shortened to *m'*, *t'* and *s'* in front of a vowel or a silent *h*.

Some common reflexive verbs that you will need to use reflexive pronouns with:

se changer	to get changed
se preparer	to get ready
s'appeler	to be called
se laver	to have a wash
se disputer	to argue
se lever	to get up
se coucher	to go to bed
se passer	to happen
se trouver	to be situated
se perdre	to get lost
s'excuser	to apologise
se relaxer	to relax

Order of object pronouns

When two object pronouns are used together in the same sentence, follow this sequence:

me *te* *nous* *vous*	come before	*le* *la* *l'* *les*	come before	*leur* *lui*	come before	*y* *en*

*Je **te les** donne maintenant.*	I'm giving **them** to **you** now.
*Il **nous en** a parlé.*	He has talked to **us** about **it**.

Emphatic pronouns: *moi, toi, lui, elle, nous, vous, eux, elles*

Emphatic pronouns are also called disjunctive pronouns. Use them:

- for emphasis:

Moi, *j'adore les fraises.*	**I** love strawberries.
Toi, *tu as quel âge?*	How old are **you**?

- after *c'est*:

C'est ***moi***.	It's **me.**

- after a preposition:

avec ***moi***	with **me**
avec ***nous***	with **us**
pour ***toi***	for **you**
pour ***vous***	for **you**
chez ***lui***	at **his** house
chez ***eux***	at **their** house
*à côté d'****elle***	next to **her**
*à côté d'****elles***	next to **them**

- after a comparative:

Elle est plus sympa que ***toi***.	She is nicer than **you**.

- with *à*, to express possession:

Il est ***à toi***, *ce livre?*	Does this book **belong to you**?

Relative pronouns: *qui, que, qu'*

Relative pronouns are used to link phrases together.

Use *qui* as the subject of the relative clause. It can refer to people and things, and means 'who', 'that' or 'which':

le copain ***qui*** *habite à Lyon*	the friend **who** lives in Lyon
le livre ***qui*** *est sur la chaise*	the book **that** is on the table

Use *que* (*qu'* before a vowel or a silent *h*) as the object of the relative clause. It means 'whom' or 'that':

le copain ***que*** *j'ai vu*	the friend (**that** / **whom**) I saw
le livre ***qu'****il a acheté*	the book (**that**) he bought

- Remember that *que* is not optional. Although it is often not translated in English, you cannot leave it out in French.
- If you cannot decide between *qui* and *que*, remember that qui is subject and que is object. If the relative clause already has a subject, then the pronoun you need must be *que*.

J'ai trouvé un travail ***qui*** *me va.*	I have found a job **that** suits me.

Here, the subject of *va* is *qui*.

C'est une couleur ***que*** *je déteste.*	It's a colour (**that**) I hate.

Here, the subject of *déteste* is *je*, and *que* is object.

Où and *quand* (where and when) can also be used to form relative clauses, for example:

On entend la musique ***quand*** *le festival commence.*	*We hear the music when the festival starts.*
On voit la salle ***où*** *les acteurs reçoivent leur prix.*	*We see the room where the actors receive their prizes.*

Indefinite pronouns: *personne*

The French for 'nobody' is *personne*. In a sentence, it is followed by *ne* in front a verb or n' before a vowel, and it doesn't need *pas*:

Personne *ne veut danser.*	**Nobody** wants to dance.

6 Verbs

French verbs have different endings depending on who is doing the action and whether the action takes place in the past, the present or the future. The verb tables on pages 176–180 set out the patterns of endings for several useful verbs.

When using a name or a singular noun, use the same form of the verb as for *il / elle*:

Martin ***parle*** *espagnol.*	Martin **speaks** Spanish.

When using two names or a plural noun, use the same form of the verb as for *ils / elles*:

Thomas et Lola ***jouent*** *au basket.*	Thomas and Lola **are playing** basketball.
Mes frères ***écoutent*** *de la musique.*	My brothers **are listening** to music.

The infinitive

The infinitive is the form of the verb you find in a dictionary, e.g. *jouer, finir, être*. It never changes.

- Modal verbs *vouloir*, *pouvoir* and *devoir* and the verb *savoir* are also followed by the infinitive:

Tu veux ***aller*** *au cinéma?*	Do you want **to go** to the cinema?
On peut ***faire*** *du shopping.*	You can **go** shopping.
Je dois ***faire*** *mes devoirs.*	I must **do** my homework.
Je sais ***conduire***.	I know how to **drive**.

The infinitive is used after *avant de* to mean 'before doing something':

*Je me lave les mains avant de **manger**.*	I wash my hands before **eating**.

The perfect infinitive with avoir

The perfect infinitive is the infinitive of *avoir*, plus the past participle of the verb. It is used after après to mean 'after doing something':

***Après avoir regardé** l'heure, il est parti.*	**After looking** at the time, he left.

The present tense

Use the present tense to describe:

- something that is taking place now:

***J'écoute** de la musique.*	I **am listening** to music.

- something that happens regularly:

***J'ai** maths le lundi.*	I **have** maths on Mondays.

Present tense verb endings change depending on who is doing the action:

***Je parle** à ma mère.*	I **speak** to my mother.
***Nous lavons** la voiture.*	We **wash** the car.

You can also use the present tense with adverbs of time to talk about actions in the past or future:

*Mon **ami** arrive **demain**.*	My friend **arrives tomorrow**.
*Je **joue** au foot **depuis** cinq ans.*	I **have been playing** football **for** five years.

Most verbs follow a regular pattern.

Regular *-er* verbs

To form the present tense of *-er* verbs, remove the *-er* from the infinitive to form the stem, e.g. *parl-* from *parler*. Then add the endings shown below.

parler **– to speak / to talk**	
*je parl**e***	*nous parl**ons***
*tu parl**es***	*vous parl**ez***
*il / elle / on parl**e***	*ils / elles parl**ent***

Some other regular *-er* verbs:

adorer	to love	*habiter*	to live
aimer	to like	*jouer*	to play
détester	to hate	*regarder*	to watch
écouter	to listen	*rester*	to stay

Regular *-ir* verbs

To form the present tense of *-ir* verbs, remove the *-ir* from the infinitive to form the stem, e.g. *chois-* from *choisir*. Then add the endings shown below.

choisir **– to choose**	
*je chois**is***	*nous chois**issons***
*tu chois**is***	*vous chois**issez***
*il / elle / on chois**it***	*ils / elles chois**issent***

partir **– to leave**	
je pars	*nous part**ons***
tu pars	*vous part**ez***
il / elle / on part	*ils / elles part**ent***

venir **– to come**	
*je vien**s***	*nous venons*
*tu vien**s***	*vous venez*
*il / elle / on vien**t***	*ils / elles viennent*

ouvrir **– to open**	
*j'ouvr**e***	*nous ouvr**ons***
*tu ouvr**es***	*vous ouvr**ez***
*il / elle / on ouvr**e***	*ils / elles ouvr**ent***

Other regular -ir verbs:

choisir	to choose
remplir	to fill
réussir	to succeed

Regular *-re* verbs

To form the present tense of -re verbs, remove the *-re* from the infinitive to form the stem, e.g. *attend-* from *attendre*. Then add the endings shown below.

attendre **– to wait**	
*j'attend**s***	*nous attend**ons***
*tu attend**s***	*vous attend**ez***
il / elle / on attend	*ils / elles attend**ent***

Other regular *-re* verbs:

descendre	to go down
répondre	to reply
vendre	to sell

Irregular verbs

Some verbs are irregular and do not follow these patterns. See pages 177–180 for details of the most common ones.

The perfect tense

Use the perfect tense to talk about what somebody did or has done.

*Il **a mangé** un sandwich.*

He **ate** a sandwich. / He **has eaten** a sandwich.

To make the perfect tense of most verbs, use the present tense of *avoir* + past participle:

parler **– to speak / to talk**	
j'ai parlé *tu as parlé* *il / elle / on a parlé*	*nous avons parlé* *vous avez parlé* *ils / elles ont parlé*

Some verbs use the present tense of *être* instead of *avoir*:

aller **– to go**	
je suis allé(e) *tu es allé(e)* *il est allé* *elle est allée* *on est allé(e)(s)*	*nous sommes allé(e)s* *vous êtes allé(e)(s)* *ils sont allés* *elles sont allées*

Verbs that use *être* to form the perfect tense include:

aller	to go
arriver	to arrive
descendre	to go down
entrer	to enter
monter	to go up
mourir	to die
naître	to be born
partir	to leave
rentrer	to come back
rester	to stay
retourner	to return / to go back
sortir	to go out
tomber	to fall
venir	to come

All reflexive verbs use *être* to form the perfect tense. Don't forget the extra pronoun that comes before the part of *être*:

se lever **– to get up**	
*je **me** suis levé(e)* *tu **t'**es levé(e)* *il **s'**est levé* *elle **s'**est levée* *on **s'**est levé(e)(s)*	*nous **nous** sommes levé(e)s* *vous **vous** êtes levé(e)(s)* *ils **se** sont levés* *elles **se** sont levées*

When using *être*:

- add *-e* to the past participle if the subject is female:
  *Elle est parti**e** en Écosse.* — She went off to Scotland.
- add *-s* to the past participle if the subject is masculine plural:
  *Ils sont arrivé**s** en retard.* — They arrived late.
- add *-es* to the past participle if the subject is feminine plural:
  *Elles sont arrivé**es** en retard.* — They arrived late.

When making a negative statement in the perfect tense, ne comes before *avoir / être* and *pas* comes after it:

*Je **n'**ai **pas** mangé.*	I haven't eaten.
*Elle **n'**est **pas** sortie.*	She didn't go out.

Past participles

The past participle of *-er* verbs ends in *-é*:

*aller – all**é***	gone
*donner – donn**é***	given
*parler – parl**é***	spoken

The past participle of regular *-ir* verbs ends in *-i*:

*choisir – chois**i***	chosen
*finir – fin**i***	finished

The past participle of regular *-re* verbs ends in *-u*:

*attendre – attend**u***	waited
*vendre – vend**u***	sold

Many common verbs have an irregular past participle:

*avoir – **eu***	had
*être – **été***	been
*faire – **fait***	done / made

The imperfect tense

Use the imperfect tense:

- to say what was happening at a certain time in the past:
  *Je **regardais** la télé quand il a téléphoné.*
  I **was watching** TV when he rang.
- describe something that used to happen regularly in the past:
  *Je **faisais** de la natation tous les matins.*
  I **used to swim** every morning.

To form the imperfect tense, take the nous form of the verb in the present tense, remove *-ons* to form the stem, then add the correct endings:

finir **– to finish** (present tense: *nous finissons*)
*je finiss**ais*** *tu finiss**ais*** *il / elle / on finiss**ait*** *nous finiss**ions*** *vous finiss**iez*** *ils / elles finiss**aient***

The verb *être* is the only exception. The endings are as above, but they are added to the stem *ét-*:

être **– to be**	
j'étais *tu étais* *il / elle / on était*	*nous étions* *vous étiez* *ils / elles étaient*

Perfect or imperfect?

To help you decide between the perfect and the imperfect, remember that:

- the perfect tense usually describes single events in the past:
  *Hier, je **me suis levée** à six heures.*
  Yesterday, I **got up** at six.
- the imperfect describes what used to happen:
  *Je **me levais** à huit heures.*
  I **used to get up** at eight.

The near future

Use the present tense of *aller* followed by an infinitive to say what you are going to do or what is going to happen:

*je **vais danser***	I am going to dance
*nous **allons manger***	we are going to eat
*tu **vas partir***	you are going to leave
*vous **allez boire***	you are going to drink
*elle **va chanter***	she is going to sing
*ils **vont dormir***	they are going to sleep

The future tense

The future tense expresses what will happen or will be happening in the future:

*Vous **travaillerez** dans l'informatique?*
Will you work in computing?

It is used for predictions such as weather forecasts:

*Il y **aura** du vent.*	It **will be** windy.
*Il **fera** beau*	It **will be** nice (weather)

To form the future tense, add the correct ending to the infinitive of the verb:

parler **– to speak / talk**	
*je parler**ai*** *tu parler**as*** *il / elle / on parler**a***	*nous parler**ons*** *vous parler**ez*** *ils / elles parler**ont***

The imperative

Use the imperative to give advice or instructions. Use the *tu* form with a person your own age or a person you know very well:

***Continue** tout droit.*	**Go** straight on.
***Prends** la première rue.*	**Take** the first street.
***Tourne** à gauche.*	**Turn** left.
***Fais** vos devoirs!*	**Do** your homework!
***Écris** une réponse.*	**Write** an answer.
***Choisis** une couleur.*	**Choose** a colour.
***Pars** à neuf heures.*	**Leave** at nine o'clock.
***Viens** ici.*	**Come** here.
***Ouvre** la porte.*	**Open** the door.
***Traduis** le texte.*	**Translate** the text.
***Sois** gentil!*	**Be** kind!
connais	**know**
entends	**hear**

Use the *vous* form with a person you don't know very well or to more than one person:

***Continuez** tout droit.*	**Go** straight on.
***Prenez** la première rue.*	**Take** the first street.
***Tournez** à gauche.*	**Turn** left.
Allez, Allez!	**Go, go, go**!
***Écrivez** une réponse.*	**Write** an answer.
***Choisissez** une couleur.*	**Choose** a colour.
***Partez** à neuf heures.*	**Leave at** nine o'clock.
***Venez** ici.*	**Come** here.
***Ouvrez** la porte.*	**Open** the door.
***Traduisez** le texte.*	**Translate** the text.

Soyez *calmes!*	**Be** quiet!
connaissez	**know**
entendez	**hear**

The imperative is the same as the *tu* or the *vous* form of the present tense, but without using a word for 'you' first. In the case of *-er* verbs, you miss off the *-s* of the *tu* form (unless the verb is followed by *y* or *en*):

Va *au lit!*	**Go** to bed!
Achète *des pommes.*	**Buy** some apples.
Vas*-y!*	**Go** on!
Achètes*-en un kilo.*	**Buy** a kilo (of them).

Note that all vous form imperatives end in *-ez* except for *faire*:

Faites *vos devoirs!*	**Do** your homework!

The imperative can also be used to mean 'let's ...' when conjugated in the first person plural:

Continuons *tout droit.*	Let's **go** straight on.
Tournons *à gauche.*	Let's **turn** left.
Écrivons *une réponse.*	Let's **write** an answer.
Choisissons *une couleur.*	Let's **choose** a colour.
Partons *à neuf heures.*	Let's **leave** at nine o'clock.
Venons *ici quand il fait beau!*	Let's **come** here when the weather is nice!
Ouvrons *la porte.*	Let's **open** the door.
Traduisons *le texte.*	Let's **translate** the text.
Soyez *calmes!*	Let's **be** quiet!
connaissons	Let's **know**
entendons	Let's **hear**

The conditional

The conditional is used in French where we say 'would' in English. It is useful for talking about what you would like or would do.

The conditional has the same stem as the future tense and the same endings as the imperfect:

aimer **– to like, love**	
*j'aimer**ais***	*nous aimer**ions***
*tu aimer**ais***	*vous aimer**iez***
*il / elle / on aimer**ait***	*ils / elles aimer**aient***

j'aurais	I would have
il / elle / on aurait	he / she / one would have
je ferais	I would do
il / elle / on ferait	he / she / one would do
j'irais	I would go
il / elle / on irait	he / she / one would go
je serais	I would be
il / elle / on serait	he / she / one would be

The passive

The passive is used to say what is done to someone or something. It is formed from a part of *être* and a past participle. Additional information can be added by using *par*. The past participle must agree with the noun:

active form:	*Il lave la pomme.*
	He washes the apple.
passive form:	*La pomme **est lavée** par l'homme.*
	The apple **is washed by the man.**

en + present participle

The English present participle ends in '-ing', and the French present participle ends in *-ant*. Take the nous form of the present tense, remove *-ons* and replace it with *-ant*:

arriver → *arrivons* → *arrivant*.

En + present participle can be used when two actions happen together:

*Il fait ses devoirs **en chantant**.*

He does his homework while singing.

En travaillant *le soir, je gagne de l'argent.*

By working in the evening, I earn money.

Other example of present participles:

choisir	→	*en choisissant*	while / by choosing
partir	→	*en partant*	while / by leaving
venir	→	*en venant*	while / by coming
ouvrir	→	*en ouvrant*	while / by opening
entendre	→	*en entendant*	while / by hearing
prendre	→	*en prenant*	while / by taking
traduire	→	*en traduisant*	while / by translating
connaître	→	*en connaissant*	while / by knowing
écrire	→	*en écrivant*	while / by writing
être	→	*en étant*	while / by being
avoir	→	*en ayant*	while / by having
faire	→	*en faisant*	while / by doing

Useful verbs

avoir – to have

Some useful expressions with *avoir*:

avoir chaud	to be hot
avoir faim	to be hungry
avoir froid	to be cold
avoir mal	to hurt
avoir peur	to be afraid
avoir raison	to be right
avoir soif	to be thirsty
avoir tort	to be wrong

faire – to do

This verb is also used with *il* to talk about the weather:

*Il **fait** beau.* The weather is nice.

*Il **fait** mauvais.* The weather is bad.

Modal verbs: *devoir, pouvoir, vouloir, savoir*

Modal verbs are usually followed by an infinitive.

Use *devoir* (to have to) + infinitive to say what you must / mustn't do:

*Je **dois porter** un uniforme.*

I **have to wear** a uniform.

*On **ne doit pas jeter** de papiers par terre.*

You **mustn't drop** litter on the ground.

devoir **– to have to**	
je dois *tu dois* *il / elle / on doit*	*nous devons* *vous devez* *ils / elles doivent*

perfect tense	
j'ai dû *tu as dû* *il / elle / on a dû*	*nous avons dû* *vous avez dû* *ils / elles ont dû*

Use *pouvoir* (to be able to) + infinitive to say what you can / can't do:

*On **peut faire** des promenades.*

You **can go** hiking.

*Elle **ne peut pas sortir** pendant la semaine.*

She **can't go** out during the week.

pouvoir **– to be able to**	
je peux *tu peux* *il / elle / on peut*	*nous pouvons* *vous pouvez* *ils / elles peuvent*

perfect tense	
j'ai pu *tu as pu* *il / elle / on a pu*	*nous avons pu* *vous avez pu* *ils / elles ont pu*

Use *vouloir* (to want to) + infinitive to say what you want and don't want to do. Adding *bien* changes the meaning:

*Je **veux partir**.* I **want to leave**.

*Je **veux bien partir**.* I **am happy to leave**.

vouloir **– to want**	
je veux *tu veux* *il / elle / on veut*	*nous voulons* *vous voulez* *ils / elles veulent*

perfect tense	
j'ai voulu *tu as voulu* *il / elle / on a voulu*	*nous avons voulu* *vous avez voulu* *ils / elles ont voulu*

Use *savoir* (to know (how to), can) + infinitive to say what you know how to do.

*Je **sais** parler anglais.* I **can** speak English.

*Elle **sait** jouer au foot.* She **knows how** to play football.

savoir **– to know**	
je sais *tu sais* *il / elle / on sait*	*nous savons* *vous savez* *ils / elles savent*

perfect tense	
j'ai su *tu as su* *il / elle / on a su*	*nous avons su* *vous avez su* *ils / elles ont su*

Impersonal verbs: *il pleut, il faut, il y a*

This verb is only used with *il*:

***Il** pleut.* **It**'s raining.

Il faut can be used with an infinitive to say what is is necessary or what must be done:

***Il faut** boire beaucoup d'eau.*

You must drink a lot of water.

***Il ne faut pas** fumer.*

You mustn't smoke.

Il est can be used for telling the time:

Il est huit heures. — *It is eight o'clock.*

Il y a means there is or there are:

***Il y a** une banque.* — There is a bank.

***Il y a** beaucoup de cafés.* — There are lots of cafés.

Il y avait means there was, there were or there used to be:

***Il y avait** une banque.* — There was a bank.

***Il y avait** beaucoup de cafés.* — There were lots of cafés.

Il y aura means there is going to be, there are going to be or there will be:

***Il y aura** une banque.* — There is going to be a bank.

***Il y aura** beaucoup de cafés.* — There are going to be lots of cafés.

7 Negatives

To make a sentence negative, you normally put *ne* before the verb and *pas* after it:

Je parle espagnol.. → *Je **ne** parle **pas** espagnol.* I **don't** speak Spanish.

Shorten *ne* to *n'* if the word that follows begins with *h* or a vowel:

C'est difficile.. → *Ce **n'**est **pas** difficile.* It's **not** difficult.

In negative sentences, use *de* instead of *un*, *une* or *des*:

Il y a un cinéma. → *Il **n'**y a **pas** de cinéma.* There is no cinema.

J'ai des frères. → *Je **n'**ai **pas** de frère.* I **don't** have any brothers.

Other common negative phrases:

ne … pas encore – not yet — *Je **ne** suis **pas** encore arrivé.* I **haven't** arrived **yet**.

ne … plus – no more — *Il **n'**y a **plus** de savon.* There is **no more** soap.

Aucun(e) means 'not any'. In French, it's always followed by a singular noun:

ne … aucun(e) – no, not any — *Il **n'**apprend **aucune** langue.* He **isn't** learning **any** language.

ne … jamais – never — *Je **ne** fume **jamais**.* I **never** smoke.

ne … rien, or *rien ne …* – nothing / not anything — *Il **ne** fait **rien**.* He **doesn't** do **anything**. ***Rien n'**est aussi facile qu'Internet.* **Nothing** is as easy as the internet.

ne … personne – not anybody — *Je **ne** vois personne.* I **don't** see **anybody**.

ne … que – only — *Je **n'**ai **qu'**une sœur.* I **only** have one sister.

ne … ni … ni – neither … nor — *Il **ne** parle **ni** français **ni** espagnol.* He speaks **neither** French **nor** Spanish.

Negatives in the perfect tense

In most negative phrases in the perfect tense, the phrase goes around the part of *avoir* or *être*.

*Je **n'**ai **pas** dormi.* — I **didn't** sleep.

Direct and indirect object pronouns are included within the negative phrase:

*Je ne **l'**ai pas vu.* — I didn't see **it**.

*Il ne **me** parle plus.* — He no longer speaks to **me**.

With reflexive verbs, the *ne* goes before the reflexive pronoun (*me*, *te*, etc.):

*Il **ne** s'est **pas** lavé.* — He **didn't** have a wash.

8 Questions

You can turn statements into questions by adding a question mark and making your voice go up at the end:

Tu joues au tennis. → *Tu joues au tennis?* Do you play tennis?

You can also add *est-ce que …* at the beginning of the question:

Je peux vous aider. → *Est-ce que je peux vous aider?* Can I help you?

In more formal situations, you can change the word order so that the verb comes first:

Vous pouvez m'aider. → *Pouvez-vous m'aider?* Can you help me?

In the perfect tense, the auxiliary verb comes first:

Vous avez aidé la dame. → *Avez-vous aidé la dame?* Did you help the lady?

Many questions start with *qu'est-ce que …*

***Qu'est-ce que** c'est?* — **What** is it?

***Qu'est-ce qu'**il y a à manger?* — **What** is there to eat?

***Qu'est-ce que** vous avez comme journaux?* **What** kind of newspapers do you have?

Other question words

These can also be combined with *est-ce que*:

combien (de)	how much / how many	*Tu as* ***combien de*** *chiens?* ***Combien de*** *chiens as-tu?* ***Combien de*** *chiens est-ce que tu as?* **How many** dogs do you have?
comment	how	*C'est arrivé* ***comment****?* How did that happen? ***Comment*** *vas-tu?* **How** are you? ***Comment*** *est-ce que je peux vous aider?* **How** can I help you?
où	where	*Tu habites* ***où****?* ***Où*** *habites-tu?* ***Où*** *est-ce que tu habites?* **Where** do you live?
pourquoi	why	*Tu n'aimes pas ça* ***pourquoi****?* ***Pourquoi*** *est-ce que tu n'aimes pas ça?* ***Pourquoi*** *n'aimes-tu pas ça?* **Why** don't you like it?
quand	when	*Il vient* ***quand****?* **When** is he coming? ***Quand*** *a-t-il commencé?* **When** did he start? ***Quand*** *est-ce que il arrive?* **When** is he arriving?
que / qu'	what	*Tu veux* ***quoi****?* ***Que*** *veux-tu?* ***Qu'****est-ce que tu veux?* **What** do you want?
qui	who	*C'est* ***qui****?* **Who** is it? ***Qui*** *est là?* **Who** is there? ***Qui*** *est-ce que tu vois?* **Who** do you see?
quoi	what	*Elle fait* ***quoi****?* **What** is she doing? *De* ***quoi*** *est-ce que tu parles?* **What** are you talking about?

9 Prepositions

à, au, à la, à l', aux

À can mean:

in	*J'habite* ***à*** *Nice.*	I live **in** Nice.
at	*Je me lève* ***à*** *sept heures.*	I get up **at** seven.
to	*Je vais* ***à*** *l'école.*	I go **to** school.

To say 'at the' or 'to the', you need to pay attention to the gender of the noun that follows:

masculine	feminine	nouns which start with a vowel or silent *h*	plural
au (à + le)	*à la*	*à l'*	*aux*

au *théâtre* — **at / to the** theatre
à la *piscine* — **at / to the** pool
à l'*hôtel* — **at / to the** hotel
aux *États-Unis* — **in / to the** USA

de

De is shortened to *d'* before a vowel or a silent *h*.
De can mean 'of':

la mère ***de*** *ma copine* (the mother of my friend)
my friend**'s** mother

Note that the word order can be different from English:

la maison ***de*** *mes grands-parents*
my grandparent**s'** house

en, au, aux + countries

En is used to introduce most names of countries. It means both 'to' and 'in':

Je vais ***en*** *Allemagne.* — I am going **to** Germany.
Il habite ***en*** *France.* — He lives **in** France.
Elle part ***en*** *Angleterre.* — She's going **to** England.

A few names of countries are masculine. These are introduced with *au* or *aux*:

Il va ***au*** *Portugal.* — He's going **to** Portugal.
Elle habite ***au*** *pays de Galles.* — She lives **in** Wales.
Nous partons ***aux*** *États-Unis.* — We're going **to** the USA.

More prepositions

pour	for	*C'est super* ***pour*** *les jeunes.* It's great **for** young people.
sans	without	***sans*** *mes copains* **without** my friends

Expressions of time

depuis – *for / since*

To say how long you've been doing something, use the present tense with *depuis*:

J'apprends le français ***depuis*** *quatre ans.*

I have been learning French **for** four years.

J'ai mal à la tête ***depuis*** *hier.*

I have had a headache **since** yesterday.

10 Ordinal Numbers

premier, deuxième, etc.

To write 'second', 'third', etc., simply add *-ième* to the original number:

deuxième second
troisième third

To write 'fifth', add a *u* before *-ième*:

cinquième fifth

For 'ninth', change the *f* of *neuf* to a *v*:

neuvième ninth

If the original number ends with an *-e*, drop the *-e* before adding *-ième*:

quatrième fourth
onzième eleventh

To revise how numbers are used in dates and telling the time, see the Useful language section, pages 10–11.

11 Morphology

Prefixes

You can reverse the meaning of some adjectives, adverbs and nous by adding *in-* or *im-* at the beginning of the word:

également → *inégalement*
sécurité → *insécurité*
possible → *impossible*

Suffixes

Adjectives can sometimes be created by adding *-able* or *-eable* to a verb stem:

porter → *portable*
changer → *changeable*

Similarly, adverbs can sometimes created by dropping *-ant(e)* / *-ent(e)* from an adjective and adding *-amment* / *-emment:*

courant → *couramment*
patient → *patiemment*

Nouns can sometimes be created by adding *-ion* or *-ation* to a verb stem:

progresser → *progression*
préparer → *préparation*

Agent nouns (a noun describing a person or object doing a verb) can be created by adding *-eur* or *-ateur* to a verb stem:

porter → *porteur*
consommer → *consommateur*

Verb tables

Regular *-er* verbs

infinitive	present	perfect	imperfect	future
parler	*je parle*	*j'ai parlé*	*je parlais*	*je parlerai*
to speak	*tu parles*	*tu as parlé*	*tu parlais*	*tu parleras*
	il / elle / on parle	*il / elle / on a parlé*	*il / elle / on parlait*	*il / elle / on parlera*
	nous parlons	*nous avons parlé*	*nous parlions*	*nous parlerons*
	vous parlez	*vous avez parlé*	*vous parliez*	*vous parlerez*
	ils / elles parlent	*ils / elles ont parlé*	*ils / elles parlaient*	*ils / elles parleront*

Regular *-ir* verbs

infinitive	present	perfect	imperfect	future
choisir	*je choisis*	*j'ai choisi*	*je choisissais*	*je choisirai**
to choose	*tu choisis*	*tu as choisi*	*tu choisissais*	*tu choisiras**
	il / elle / on choisit	*il / elle / on a choisi*	*il / elle / on choisissait*	*il / elle / on choisira**
	nous choisissons	*nous avons choisi*	*nous choisissions*	*nous choisirons**
	vous choisissez	*vous avez choisi*	*vous choisissiez*	*vous choisirez**
	ils / elles choisissent	*ils / elles ont choisi*	*ils / elles choisissaient*	*ils / elles choisiront**

Regular *-re* verbs

infinitive	present	perfect	imperfect	future
entendre	*j'entends*	*j'ai entendu*	*j'entendais*	*j'entendrai**
to hear	*tu entends*	*tu as entendu*	*tu entendais*	*tu entendras**
	il / elle / on entend	*il / elle / on a entendu*	*il / elle / on entendait*	*il / elle / on entendra**
	nous entendons	*nous avons entendu*	*nous entendions*	*nous entendrons**
	vous entendez	*vous avez entendu*	*vous entendiez*	*vous entendrez**
	ils / elles entendent	*ils / elles ont entendu*	*ils / elles entendaient*	*ils / elles entendront**

Reflexive verbs

infinitive	present	perfect	imperfect	future
se laver	*je me lave*	*je me suis lavé(e)*	*je me lavais*	*je me laverai*
to (have a) wash	*tu te laves* *il se lave*	*tu t'es lavé(e)* *il s'est lavé*	*tu te lavais* *il se lavait*	*tu te laveras* *il se lavera*
	elle se lave	*elle s'est lavée*	*elle se lavait*	*elle se lavera*
	on se lave	*on s'est lavé(e)(s)*	*on se lavait*	*on se lavera*
	nous nous lavons	*nous nous sommes lavé(e)s*	*nous nous lavions*	*nous nous laverons*
	vous vous lavez	*vous vous êtes lavé(e)(s)*	*vous vous laviez*	*vous vous laverez*
	ils se lavent	*ils se sont lavés*	*ils se lavaient*	*ils se laveront*
	elles se lavent	*elles se sont lavées*	*elles se lavaient*	*elles se laveront*

infinitive	present	perfect	imperfect	future
aller	*je vais*	*je suis allé(e)*	*j'allais*	*j'irai*
to go	*tu vas*	*tu es allé(e)*	*tu allais*	*tu iras*
	il va	*il est allé*	*il allait*	*il ira*
	elle va	*elle est allée*	*elle allait*	*elle ira*
	on va	*on est allé(e)(s)*	*on allait*	*on ira*
	nous allons	*nous sommes allé(e)s*	*nous allions*	*nous irons*
	vous allez	*vous êtes allé(e)(s)*	*vous alliez*	*vous irez*
	ils / elles vont	*ils /elles sont allés*	*ils / elles allaient*	*ils / elles iront*
avoir	*j'ai*	*j'ai eu*	*j'avais*	*j'aurai*
to have	*tu as*	*tu as eu*	*tu avais*	*tu auras*
	il / elle / on a	*il / elle / on a eu*	*il / elle / on avait*	*il / elle / on aura*
	nous avons	*nous avons eu*	*nous avions*	*nous aurons*
	vous avez	*vous avez eu*	*vous aviez*	*vous aurez*
	ils / elles ont	*ils / elles ont eu*	*ils / elles avaient*	*ils / elles auront*
boire	*je bois*	*j'ai bu*	*je buvais*	*je boirai**
to drink	*tu bois*	*tu as bu*	*tu buvais*	*tu boiras**
	il / elle / on boit	*il / elle / on a bu*	*il / elle / on buvait*	*il / elle / on boira**
	nous buvons	*nous avons bu*	*nous buvions*	*nous boirons**
	vous buvez	*vous avez bu*	*vous buviez*	*vous boirez**
	ils / elles boivent	*ils / elles ont bu*	*ils / elles buvaient*	*ils / elles boiront**
connaître	*je connais*	*j'ai connu*	*je connaissais*	*je connaîtrai**
to know	*tu connais*	*tu as connu*	*tu connaissais*	*tu connaîtras**
	il / elle / on connaît	*il / elle / on a connu*	*il / elle / on connaissait*	*il / elle / on connaîtra**
	nous connaissons	*nous avons connu*	*nous connaissions*	*nous connaîtrons**
	vous connaissez	*vous avez connu*	*vous connaissiez*	*vous connaîtrez**
	ils / elles connaissent	*ils / elles ont connu*	*ils / elles connaissaient*	*ils / elles connaîtront**
courir	*je cours*	*j'ai couru*	*je courais*	*je courrai**
to run	*tu cours*	*tu as couru*	*tu courais*	*tu courras**
	il / elle / on court	*il / elle / on a couru*	*il / elle / on courait*	*il / elle / on courra**
	nous courons	*nous avons couru*	*nous courions*	*nous courrons**
	vous			
	vous courez	*vous avez couru*	*vous couriez*	*vous courrez**
	ils / elles courent	*ils / elles ont couru*	*ils / elles couraient*	*ils / elles courront**
croire	*je crois*	*j'ai cru*	*je croyais*	*je croirai**
to believe	*tu crois*	*tu as cru*	*tu croyais*	*tu croiras**
	il / elle / on croit	*il / elle / on a cru*	*il / elle / on croyait*	*il / elle / on croira**
	nous croyons	*nous avons cru*	*nous croyions*	*nous croirons**
	vous croyez	*vous avez cru*	*vous croyiez*	*vous croirez**
	ils / elles croient	*ils / elles ont cru*	*ils / elles croyaient*	*ils / elles croiront**

*These verb forms are included for reference only. You won't be tested on them in your exams.

Verb tables

infinitive	present	perfect	imperfect	future
devoir to have to	*je dois* *tu dois* *il / elle / on doit* *nous devons* *vous devez* *ils / elles doivent*	*j'ai dû* *tu as dû* *il / elle / on a dû* *nous avons dû* *vous avez dû* *ils / elles ont dû*	*je devais* *tu devais* *il / elle / on devait* *nous devions* *vous deviez* *ils / elles devaient*	*je devrai** *tu devras** *il / elle / on devra** *nous devrons** *vous devrez** *ils / elles devront**
écrire to write	*j'écris* *tu écris* *il / elle / on écrit* *nous écrivons* *vous écrivez* *ils / elles écrivent*	*j'ai écrit* *tu as écrit* *il / elle / on a écrit* *nous avons écrit* *vous avez écrit* *ils / elles ont écrit*	*j'écrivais* *tu écrivais* *il / elle / on écrivait* *nous écrivions* *vous écriviez* *ils / elles écrivaient*	*j'écrirai** *tu écriras** *il / elle / on écrira** *nous écrirons** *vous écrirez** *ils / elles écriront**
être to be	*je suis* *tu es* *il / elle / on est* *nous sommes* *vous êtes* *ils / elles sont*	*j'ai été* *tu as été* *il / elle / on a été* *nous avons été* *vous avez été* *ils / elles ont été*	*j'étais* *tu étais* *il / elle / on était* *nous étions* *vous étiez* *ils / elles étaient*	*je serai* *tu seras* *il / elle / on sera* *nous serons* *vous serez* *ils / elles seront*
faire to do / to make	*je fais* *tu fais* *il / elle / on fait* *nous faisons* *vous faites* *ils / elles font*	*j'ai fait* *tu as fait* *il / elle / on a fait* *nous avons fait* *vous avez fait* *ils / elles ont fait*	*je faisais* *tu faisais* *il / elle / on faisait* *nous faisions* *vous faisiez* *ils / elles faisaient*	*je ferai* *tu feras* *il / elle / on fera* *nous ferons* *vous ferez* *ils / elles feront*
lire to read	*je lis* *tu lis* *il / elle / on lit* *nous lisons* *vous lisez* *ils / elles lisent*	*j'ai lu* *tu as lu* *il / elle / on a lu* *nous avons lu* *vous avez lu* *ils / elles ont lu*	*je lisais* *tu lisais* *il / elle / on lisait* *nous lisions* *vous lisiez* *ils / elles lisaient*	*je lirai** *tu liras** *il / elle / on lira** *nous lirons** *vous lirez** *ils / elles liront**
ouvrir to open	*j'ouvre* *tu ouvres* *il / elle / on ouvre* *nous ouvrons* *vous ouvrez* *ils / elles ouvrent*	*j'ai ouvert* *tu as ouvert* *il / elle / on a ouvert* *nous avons ouvert* *vous avez ouvert* *ils / elles ont ouvert*	*j'ouvrais* *tu ouvrais* *il / elle / on ouvrait* *nous ouvrions* *vous ouvriez* *ils / elles ouvraient*	*j'ouvrirai** *tu ouvriras** *il / elle / on ouvrira** *nous ouvrirons** *vous ouvrirez** *ils / elles ouvriront**

infinitive	present	perfect	imperfect	future
partir to leave	*je pars* *tu pars* *il part* *elle part* *on part* *nous partons* *vous partez* *ils / elles partent*	*je suis parti(e)* *tu es parti(e)* *il est parti* *elle est partie* *on est parti(e)(s)* *nous sommes parti(e)s* *vous êtes parti(e)(s)* *Ils /elles sont partis*	*je partais* *tu partais* *il partait* *elle partait* *on partait* *nous partions* *vous partiez* *ils /elles partaient*	*je partirai** *tu partiras** *il partira** *elle partira** *on partira** *nous partirons** *vous partirez** *ils /elles partiront**
pouvoir to be able to	*je peux* *tu peux* *il / elle / on peut* *nous pouvons* *vous pouvez* *ils / elles peuvent*	*j'ai pu* *tu as pu* *il / elle / on a pu* *nous avons pu* *vous avez pu* *ils / elles ont pu*	*je pouvais* *tu pouvais* *il / elle / on pouvait* *nous pouvions* *vous pouviez* *ils / elles pouvaient*	*je pourrai** *tu pourras** *il / elle / on pourra** *nous pourrons** *vous pourrez** *ils / elles pourront**
prendre to take	*je prends* *tu prends* *il / elle / on prend* *nous prenons* *vous prenez* *ils / elles prennent*	*j'ai pris* *tu as pris* *il / elle / on a pris* *nous avons pris* *vous avez pris* *ils / elles ont pris*	*je prenais* *tu prenais* *il / elle / on prenait* *nous prenions* *vous preniez* *ils / elles prenaient*	*je prendrai** *tu prendras** *il / elle / on prendra** *nous prendrons** *vous prendrez** *ils / elles prendront**
recevoir to receive	*je reçois* *tu reçois* *il / elle / on reçoit* *nous recevons* *vous recevez* *ils / elles reçoivent*	*j'ai reçu* *tu as reçu* *il / elle / on a reçu* *nous avons reçu* *vous avez reçu* *ils / elles ont reçu*	*je recevais* *tu recevais* *il / elle / on recevait* *nous recevions* *vous receviez* *ils / elles recevaient*	*je recevrai** *tu recevras** *il / elle / on recevra** *nous recevrons** *vous recevrez** *ils / elles recevront**
rire to laugh	*je ris* *tu ris* *il / elle / on rit* *nous rions* *vous riez* *ils / elles rient*	*j'ai ri* *tu as ri* *il / elle / on a ri* *nous avons ri* *vous avez ri* *ils / elles ont ri*	*je riais* *tu riais* *il / elle / on riait* *nous riions* *vous riiez* *ils / elles riaient*	*je rirai** *tu riras** *il / elle / on rira** *nous rirons** *vous rirez** *ils / elles riront**
savoir to know	*je sais* *tu sais* *il / elle / on sait* *nous savons* *vous savez* *ils / elles savent*	*j'ai su* *tu as su* *il / elle / on a su* *nous avons su* *vous avez su* *ils / elles ont su*	*je savais* *tu savais* *il / elle / on savait* *nous savions* *vous saviez* *ils / elles savaient*	*je saurai** *tu sauras** *il / elle / on saura** *nous saurons** *vous saurez** *ils / elles sauront**

*These verb forms are included for reference only. You won't be tested on them in your exams.

infinitive	present	perfect	imperfect	future
sortir to go out	*je sors* *tu sors* *il sort* *elle sort* *on sort* *nous sortons* *vous sortez* *ils /elles sortent*	*je suis sorti(e)* *tu es sorti(e)* *il est sorti* *elle est sortie* *on est sorti(e)(s)* *nous sommes sorti(e)s* *vous êtes sorti(e)(s)* *ils / elles sont sortis*	*je sortais* *tu sortais* *il sortait* *elle sortait* *on sortait* *nous sortions* *vous sortiez* *ils / elles sortaient*	*je sortirai** *tu sortiras** *il sortira** *elle sortira** *on sortira** *nous sortirons** *vous sortirez** *ils / elles sortiront**
suivre to follow	*je suis* *tu suis* *il / elle / on suit* *nous suivons* *vous suivez* *ils / elles suivent*	*j'ai suivi* *tu as suivi* *il / elle / on a suivi* *nous avons suivi* *vous avez suivi* *ils / elles ont suivi*	*je suivais* *tu suivais* *il / elle / on suivait* *nous suivions* *vous suiviez* *ils / elles suivaient*	*je suivrai** *tu suivras** *il / elle / on suivra** *nous suivrons** *vous suivrez** *ils / elles suivront**
traduire to translate	*je traduis* *tu traduis* *il / elle / on tu traduit* *nous traduisons* *vous traduisez* *ils / elles traduisent*	*j'ai traduit* *tu as traduit* *il / elle / on a traduit* *nous avons traduit* *vous avez traduit* *ils / elles ont traduit*	*je traduisais* *tu traduisais* *il / elle / on traduisait* *nous traduisions* *vous traduisiez* *ils / elles traduisaient*	*je traduirai* *tu traduiras* *il / elle / on traduira* *nous traduirons* *vous traduirez* *ils / elles traduiront*
venir to come	*je viens* *tu viens* *il vient* *elle vient* *on vient* *nous venons* *vous venez* *ils / elles viennent*	*je suis venu(e)* *tu es venu(e)* *il est venu* *elle est venue* *on est venu(e)(s)* *nous sommes venu(e)s* *vous êtes venu(e)(s)* *ils / elles sont venus*	*je venais* *tu venais* *il venait* *elle venait* *on venait* *nous venions* *vous veniez* *ils / elles venaient*	*je viendrai** *tu viendras** *il viendra** *elle viendra** *on viendra** *nous viendrons** *vous viendrez** *ils / elles viendront**
vivre to live	*je vis* *tu vis* *il / elle / on vit* *nous vivons* *vous vivez* *ils / elles vivent*	*j'ai vécu* *tu as vécu* *il / elle / on a vécu* *nous avons vécu* *vous avez vécu* *ils / elles ont vécu*	*je vivais* *tu vivais* *il / elle / on vivait* *nous vivions* *vous viviez* *ils / elles vivaient*	*je vivrai** *tu vivras** *il / elle / on vivra** *nous vivrons** *vous vivrez** *ils / elles vivront**
voir to see	*je vois* *tu vois* *il / elle / on voit* *nous voyons* *vous voyez* *ils / elles voient*	*j'ai vu* *tu as vu* *il / elle / on a vu* *nous avons vu* *vous avez vu* *ils / elles ont vu*	*je voyais* *tu voyais* *il / elle / on voyait* *nous voyions* *vous voyiez* *ils / elles voyaient*	*je verrai** *tu verras** *il / elle / on verra** *nous verrons** *vous verrez** *ils / elles verront**

infinitive	present	perfect	imperfect	future
vouloir to want	*je veux* *tu veux* *il / elle / on veut* *nous voulons* *vous voulez* *ils / elles veulent*	*j'ai voulu* *tu as voulu* *il / elle / on a voulu* *nous avons voulu* *vous avez voulu* *ils / elles ont voulu*	*je voulais* *tu voulais* *il / elle / on voulait* *nous voulions* *vous vouliez* *ils / elles voulaient*	*je voudrai** *tu voudras** *il / elle / on voudra** *nous voudrons** *vous voudrez** *ils / elles voudront**

*These verb forms are included for reference only. You won't be tested on them in your exams.

Glossary

Words that are highlighted in grey in this list are words that may be useful, but you won't need to know them for the exam.

à at, to
à bientôt see you soon
à cause de because of
à côté de near
à l'âge de at the age of
à l'avenir in the future
à l'étranger abroad
à l'heure on time
à la campagne in the countryside
à l'avenir in the future
à mon avis in my opinion
à pied on foot
à qui to whom
abandonner to abandon / give up
l' ***abbaye (f.)*** abbey
accepter to accept, authorise
l' ***accès (m.)*** access
accessible accessible
l' ***accident (m.)*** accident
accompagner to accompany
accueil welcome
accueillant(e) welcoming
l' ***achat (m.)*** purchase
acheter to buy
l' ***acteur/actrice (m./f.)*** actor, actress
actif/active active
l' ***action (f.)*** action
l' ***activité (f.)*** activity
les ***actualités (f. pl.)*** current affairs
actuel(le) current
actuellement currently
adapter to adapt
adopté(e) adopted
adopter to adopt
adorer to love
l' ***adresse (f.)*** address
adulte adult
africain(e) African
l' ***Afrique (f.)*** Africa
l' ***âge (m.)*** age
âgé(e) elderly
agréable pleasant
l' ***agriculture (f.)*** agriculture
Aïd-el-Fitr Eid al-Fitr
aider to help
aimer to like
aimer mieux to prefer
l' ***air (m.)*** air
l' ***air frais (m.)*** fresh air
l' ***alcool (m.)*** alcohol
l' ***Algérie (f.)*** Algeria
Allah Allah
l' ***allemand (n.) (m.)*** German (language)
aller to go
allumer to switch on, to light
alors so, therefore
les ***Alpes (f. pl.)*** Alps
l' ***ambiance (f.)*** atmosphere
améliorer to improve
américain(e) (adj.) American
l' ***Amérique (f.)*** America
l' ***ami(e) (m./f.)*** friend
l' ***amitié (f.)*** friendship
l' ***amour (m.)*** love
l' ***amoureux/amoureuse (m./f.)*** lover
amusant(e) amusing, fun, funny
s' ***amuser*** to have fun
l' ***an (m.)/année (f.)*** year
ancien(ne) ancient
l' ***anglais (n.) (m.)*** English (language)
anglais(e) (adj.) English
l' ***Angleterre (f.)*** England
animal (adj.) from, of animals
l' ***animal (m.)*** animal
l' ***animation (f.)*** animation
les ***animaux (m. pl.)*** animals
l' ***année (f.)*** year
l' ***année dernière (f.)*** last year
l' ***année sabbatique (f.)*** gap year
l' ***année (f.)*** year
l' ***anniversaire (m.)*** birthday
août August
l' ***appartement (m.)*** flat
s' ***appeler*** to be called
appeler to call
l' ***appli (f.)*** app
apporter to bring
apprécier to enjoy, appreciate, like
apprécier de to appreciate to
apprendre to learn, to teach
après after
l' ***après-midi (m.)*** afternoon
l' ***arbre (m.)*** tree
l' ***architecte (m.)*** architect
l' ***architecture (f.)*** architecture
l' ***argent (m.)*** money
s' ***arrêter*** to stop oneself
arrêter to stop
arriver to arrive
arriver à to succeed in
l' ***article (m.)*** article
artistique artistic
l' ***ascension (f.)*** climb
l' ***Asie (f.)*** Asia
l' ***assemblée (f.)*** assembly
assez (de) enough, quite
assis(e) sat
l'/les ***association(s) (f.)*** associations
l' ***atmosphere (f.)*** atmosphere
attaquer to attack
attendre to wait
attentif/attentive attentive
l' ***attention (f.)*** attention
au at the/to the
au bord de la mer by the sea
au chômage unemployed
au début at the beginning
au restaurant at, in a restaurant
au revoir goodbye
au sujet de about
aucun(e) no, not one
augmenter to increase
aujourd'hui today
aussi also
aussi ... que as ... as
aussi bien que as well as
l' ***Australie (f.)*** Australia
l' ***auteur/autrice (m./f.)*** author
l' ***automne (m.)*** autumn
autre (adj.) other
autre (adj.) other
autre chose anything else
l' ***autre(s) (m./f.)*** other
l' ***autrice (f.)*** author (female)
avant (de) before
l' ***avantage (m.)*** advantage
l' ***avenir (m.)*** future
l' ***aventure (f.)*** adventure
l' ***avion (m.)*** plane
l' ***avis (m.)*** opinion
l' ***avocat(e) (m./f.)*** lawyer
avoir to have
avoir besoin de to need
avoir faim to be hungry
avoir l'air to seem, look
avoir le droit to have the right
avoir le mal de mer to be sea sick
avoir le temps to have time
avoir lieu to take place
avoir mal to hurt
avoir peur to be scared
avril April
le ***bain*** bath
bancaire (adj.) banking
la ***banlieue*** suburbs
la ***banque*** bank
le ***basket*** basketball
le ***bateau*** boat
le ***bâtiment*** building
bavard(e) chatty
beau/bel/belle beautiful
beaucoup (de) a lot (of), lots (of)
beaucoup à faire a lot to do
le ***beau-père*** stepfather, father-in-law
la ***Belgique*** Belgium
la ***belle-mère*** stepmother, mother-in-law
la ***bénédiction*** blessing
bénéficier to benefit
bénévole (adj.) voluntary
le/la ***bénévole (n.)*** volunteer
la ***bibliothèque*** library
bien good, well
bien sûr of course
bien sûr of course
le ***billet*** ticket
blanc (adj.) white
se ***blesser*** to get hurt
le ***blog*** blog
boire to drink
le ***bois*** wood
la ***boisson*** drink
bon(ne) good
le ***bonheur*** happiness

bonjour good morning, afternoon
bonne chance good luck
le *bord* edge
la *bouche* mouth
la *boue* mud
bouger to move
la *bougie* candle
la *boulangerie* bakery
la *boule* ball, bubble
le *bras* arm
la *brique* brick, brickwork
britannique British
la *brochure* brochure
le *bronze* bronze
le *brouillard* fog
le *bruit* noise
brun(e) brown
le *bureau* office, desk
le *bus* bus
le *but* goal
ça it, that
ça me rend it makes me
le *cadeau* present
le *café* coffee, coffee shop
calme (adj.) calm, quiet
le *Cameroun* Cameroon
camerounais(e) Cameroonian
la *campagne* countryside
le *camping* campsite
le *Canada* Canada
canadien(ne) Canadian
la *cantine* canteen
le *canyoning* gorge walking
capable capable
la *capitale* capital city
car because
le *car* bus, coach
les *Caraïbes (f. pl.)* Caribbean
le *carnaval* carnival
carré(e) square
la *carrière* career
la *carte* card
la *catastrophe* catastrophe
catholique Catholic
ce/cet/cette/ces this
ce que which
cela it, this, that
la *célébration* celebration
célèbre famous
célébré(e) celebrated
célébrer to celebrate
la *célébrité* celebrity
célibataire single
la *centaine* about a hundred
central(e) central
le *centre* centre
le *centre commercial* shopping centre
le *centre de recyclage* recycling centre
le *centre-ville* city centre
cependant however
la *cérémonie* ceremony
certain(e)(s) some, certain
certainement certainly
la *chambre* bedroom
le *champ* field
la *chance* luck, opportunity
le *changement* change
changer to change
la *chanson* song
chanter to sing
le/la *chanteur/chanteuse* singer
le *chapeau* hat
chaque each, every
le *château* castle
chaud(e) hot, warm
le *chaume* thatch
la *chaussure* shoe
le *chef (de cuisine)* chef
cher/chère expensive
chercher to research, to look for
les *cheveux (m. pl.)* hair
le *chewing-gum* chewing-gum
chez to the place of, at the place of, at, with
chez moi at my place, at mine
chez nous at/to our place
le *chien* dog
chimique chemical
choisir to choose
le *choix* choice
le *chômage* unemployment
la *chose* thing
chrétien(ne) (adj.) Christian
la *cigarette* cigarette
le *cinéma* cinema
cinq five
la *circulation* traffic
circuler to circulate
la *citadelle* citadel
le/la *citoyen(ne)* citizen
la *classe* class, classroom
classique classic
classique (adj.) classical
la *clé* key
le *climat* climate
cliquer to click
le *club* club
le *cœur* heart
le *cola* coke
la *collecte* collection
le *collège* (secondary) school
le/la *collègue* colleague
la *colonie* colony
colonisé(e) colonised
combiner to combine
la *comédie* comedy
comme such as, like, since
commencer to start
comment how
le *commentaire* comment, commentary
commercial commercial
commun common
la *communication* communication
communiquer to communicate
la *compétence* skill
la *compétition* competition
complet/complète complete
complètement completely
compliqué(e) complicated
comprendre to understand
se *concentrer* to concentrate, focus
le *concert* concert
le *concours* competition
le *concurrent* competitor
la *confiance* trust, confidence
confirmer to confirm
le *conflit* conflict
confortable comfortable
la *connaissance* knowledge
connaître to know (person, place)
connu(e) known, famous
conscient(e) conscious
le *conseil* advice
conseiller to advise
considérer to consider
la *construction* construction
construire to build
le *conte* tale
content(e) pleased, happy
le *contenu* content
continuer to continue
contribuer (à) to contribute (to)
la *conversation* conversation
cool cool
la *coopération* cooperation
le *copain* friend, boyfriend
la *copine* friend, girlfriend
le *corail* coral
le *corps* body
la *Corse* Corsica
la *côte* coast
la *Côte d'Ivoire* Ivory Coast
la *couleur* colour
couper to cut
le *couple* couple
le *courage* courage
courant(e) current, ordinary, common
courir to run
le *cours* lesson
la *course* race
les *courses (f. pl.)* (grocery) shopping
court(e) short
le/la *cousin(e)* cousin
coûter to cost
la *couverture* rug, duvet
le/la *créateur/créatrice* creator, designer
créatif/créative creative
la *créativité* creativity
créer to create
croire (que) to believe (that)
la *cuisine* kitchen, cooking
la *culture* culture
culturel(le) cultural
le *cyber intimidation* cyber bullying
le/la *cycliste* cyclist
d'abord firstly, first of all
d'accord okay, agreed
la *dame* lady
le *danger* danger
dangereux/dangereuse dangerous
la *danse* dancing
le/la *danseur/danseuse* dancer
la *date* date
de nos jours nowadays
de plus besides, moreover
de plus en plus more and more
de saison seasonal

de temps en temps from time to time
le *débat* debate
le *début* beginning
décembre December
le / les *déchet(s) (m. pl.)* rubbish
se *décider* to make up one's mind
la *décision* decision
découvrir to discover, find out
décrire to describe
défavorisé(e) disadvantaged
le *défi* challenge
le *défilé* parade
défiler to parade
dehors outside
déjà already
le *déjeuner* lunch
délicieux / délicieuse delicious
demain tomorrow
se *demander* to wonder
demander to ask
le *demi-frère* half-brother
la *demi-soeur* half-sister
démocratique democratic
la *dépendance* addiction
dépendant dependent, addicted
dépendre de to depend on
le *dépliant* leaflet
depuis since
le / la *député(e)* deputy, MP
dernier / dernière last
dès que as soon as
descendre to go down, descend, get off
le *dessin* drawing
la *destination* destination
le *détail* detail
le *détail personnel* personal detail, information
détester to hate
deux two
deuxième second
devant in front of
développer to develop
devenir to become
devoir to have to
les *devoirs (m. pl.)* homework
le *dialogue* dialogue
différent(e) (de) different (from)
difficile difficult
(le) *dimanche* Sunday
le *dîner* dinner
dîner (v.) to have dinner
dire to say, tell
direct(e) direct
directement directly
la *discussion* discussion
discuter to discuss
disponible available
se *disputer* to argue
la *distance* distance
la *distinction* distinction
divers varied
divorcé(e) divorced
dix ten
le *document* document
le *documentaire* documentary
dommage! what a shame!
donc so
donner to give
donner sur to overlook / give onto
la *Dordogne* Dordogne
d'origine of origin
dormir to sleep
le *dos* back
double double
la *douche* shower
dramatique dramatic
la *drogue* drug
droit right
drôle funny
du / de la / des / de l' some
dur(e) hard
la *durabilité* sustainability
durable sustainable
la *dynastie* dynasty
l' *eau (m.)* water
l' *école (f.)* school
écologique ecological, environmentally friendly
l' *économie (f.)* economy
écouter to listen (to)
l' *écran (m.)* screen
écrire to write
l' *écrivain(e) (m. / f.)* writer
l' *éducation (f.)* education
l' *effort (m.)* effort
également equally, as well, too, also
l' *église (f.)* church
l' *élève (m.)* pupil
élevé(e) raised
elle-même herself
l' *e-mail (m.)* e-mail
embêtant(e) annoying
l' *émission (f.)* TV program
l' *émotion (f.)* emotion
émouvant(e) moving
l' *empire (m.)* empire
l' *employeur / employeuse (m. / f.)* employer
en in, by (doing something)
en ce moment at the moment
en effet indeed
en été in summer
en fait in fact, in reality
en général in general
en hiver in winter
en ligne online
en même temps at the same time
en plus in addition
en premier first of all, firstly
en retard late
en Suisse in Switzerland
en toute sécurité safely
en vacances on holiday
en ville in town
encore again, still
encourager to encourage
l' *endroit (m.)* place
l' *énergie (f.)* energy
l' *enfance (f.)* childhood
l' *enfant (m.)* child
enfin finally
ennuyeux / ennuyeuse boring
énorme enormous
l' *enquête (f.)* survey
enregistrer to record
ensemble together
ensuite then
entendre to hear
s' *entraîner* to train
entre between
l' *entreprise (f.)* company
entrer to enter
entrer dans to go into
environ roughly
l' *environnement (m.)* environment
envoyer to send
équilibré(e) balanced
l' *équipe (f.)* team
l' *escalade (f.)* climbing
l' *esclavage (m.)* slavery
l' *Espagne (f.)* Spain
l' *espagnol (n.) (m.)* Spanish (language)
espagnol(e) (adj.) Spanish
espérer (que) to hope (that)
l' *esprit (m.)* spirit
essayer (de) to try
essentiel(le) essential
et and
et demie half past
établir to be established
l' *établissement (m.)* establishment
l' *étage (m.)* floor
l' *étape (f.)* stage
les *États-Unis (m. pl.)* United States
l' *été* summer
l' *été (m.)* summer
étonnant astonishing
étrange strange
être to be
être au soleil to be in the sun
être en retard to be late
être en train de to be in the middle of
être situé to be situated
être victime de to be victim of
l' *étude (f.)* study
les *études (f. pl.)* studies
étudier to study
l' *euro (m.)* euro
l' *Europe (f.)* Europe
eux them
l' *événement (m.)* event
évidemment evidently, obviously
éviter (de) to avoid
l' *examen (m.)* exam
examiner to examine
excellent(e) excellent
exemplaire copy
l' *exemple (m.)* example
l' *exercice (m.)* exercise
exister to exist
l' *expérience (f.)* experience
l' *expert(e) (m. / f.)* expert
l' *explication (f.)* explanation
expliquer (que) to explain (that)
l' *expression (f.)* expression
l' *extérieur (m.)* outside

extraordinaire extraordinary
la *fabrication* production, building
fabriquer to make
facile easy
facilement easily
faciliter to make easier, to facilitate
la *façon* way
le/la *facteur/factrice* postman/postwoman
faible weak
faire to do, make
faire attention (à) to be careful (of), to pay attention (to)
faire beau to be nice (weather)
faire chaud to be hot
faire de la natation to go swimming
faire de la publicité to advertise
faire de son mieux to do your best
faire des progrès to make progress
faire des promenades to go for walks
faire des recherches to do research
faire du bruit to make noise
faire du camping to go camping
faire du jardinage to garden
faire du recyclage to do recycling
faire du shopping to go shopping
faire du vélo to go cycling
faire froid to be cold
faire la découverte to discover
faire les courses to go grocery shopping
faire les magasins to go shopping
faire mauvais to be bad (weather)
faire une différence to make a difference
familial(e) (adj.) family
la *famille* family
le *fan* fan
fantastique fantastic
fatigué(e) tired
la *femme* woman, wife
la *femme politique* politician (female)
la *ferme* farm
festif/festive festive
le *festival* festival
la *fête* party, celebration
le *feu d'artifice* firework displays
la *feuille* piece of paper, leaf
février February
fier/fière proud
la *fille* girl, daughter
le *film* film
le *fils* son
la *fin* end
finir to finish
la *fleur* flower
la *fois* time, occasion
... fois ... time, times
fonder to found
le *foot(ball)* football
le/la *footballeur/footballeuse* footballer
la *force* strength
la *forêt* forest, wood
la *forme* shape
fort(e) strong
fou/folle mad
frais/fraîche fresh
le *français (n.)* French (language)
français(e) (adj.) French
la *France* France
francophone French-language
la *fraude* fraud
le *frère* brother
le *frigo* fridge
les *frites (f. pl.)* chips
froid(e) cold
le *fromage* cheese
la *frontière* border
le *fruit* fruit
fumer to smoke
le *futur (n.)* future
futur(e) (adj.) future
le/la *gagnant(e)* winner
gagner to win, to earn
gagner du temps to save time
garder to keep
la *gare* train station
le *gâteau* cake
gauche left
le *gaz* gas
généralement generally
la *génération* generation
Genève Geneva
génial(e) great
le *genre* kind, type
les *gens (m. pl.)* people
gentil(le) kind
la *géographie* geography
gérer to organise
la *gestion* management
la *girafe* giraffe
la *glace* ice, ice cream
la *gorge* throat
le *goût* taste
le *gouvernement* government
grand(e) big, large
grandir to grow (up)
la *grand-mère* grandmother
le *grand-père* grandfather
les *grands-parents (m. pl.)* grandparents
grave serious
la *grève* strike
la *grotte* grotto, cave
le *groupe* band
la *Guadeloupe* Guadeloupe
la *guerre* war
le *gymnase* gymnasium
la *gymnastique* gymnastics
l' *habitant(e)* inhabitant
l' *habitation (f.)* house, home, dwelling
habiter to live
le *Hajj* Hajj
handicapé(e) handicapped
handicapé(e) (adj.) disabled
Hanouka Hanukkah
haut high
l' *herbe (f.)* grass
l' *heroine (f.)* (female) hero
l' *héros (m.)* (male) hero
l' *heure (f.)* hour, time, o'clock
hier yesterday
le *hip-hop* hip-hop
l' *histoire (f.)* history, story
historique historic
l' *hiver (m.)* winter
le *hockey sur glace* ice hockey
l' *homme politique (m.)* politician (male)
l' *hôpital (m.)* hospital
l' *hôtel (m.)* hotel
ici here
idéal(e) ideal
l' *idée (f.)* idea
l' *identité (f.)* identity
il est essentiel de it is essential to
il est facile de it is easy to
il faisait beau it was nice weather
il faisait froid it was cold
il faisait mauvais it was bad weather
il fait beau it is fine weather
il fait chaud it is hot
il fait froid it is cold
il faut it is necessary to, must
il n'y a jamais rien there is never anything
il n'y a pas there is/are not
il vaut la peine **it is worth** il vaut la peine de
il vaut mieux it is worth
il vaut mieux it is better to
il y a there is/are
il y a du soleil it is sunny
il y avait there was, there were
il y avait du vent it was windy
l' *île (f.)* island
l' *image (f.)* image, picture
immédiatement immediately
l' *importance (f.)* importance
important(e) important
s' *imposer* to get established
impossible impossible
inaccessible inaccessible
l' *inactivité (f.)* inactivity
incomplet/incomplète incomplete
l' *inconvénient (m.)* disadvantage, inconvenience
l' *indépendance (f.)* independence
indépendant(e) independent
indifférent(e) indifferent
l' *influence (f.)* influence
l' *influenceur/influenceuse (m./f.)* influencer
l' *information (f.)* information
l' *information personnelle (f.)* personal detail, information

l' ***informatique (m.)*** IT, computer science
injuste unfair
l' ***innovation (f.)*** innovation
inquiet / inquiète worried
inquiétant(e) worrying
insolite unusual
inspirer to inspire
s' ***installer*** to settle
l' ***instrument (m.)*** instrument
intelligent(e) intelligent
interculturel(le) intercultural
interdir to forbid, ban
interdit forbidden
intéressant(e) interesting
intéresser to interest
s' ***intéresser à*** to be interested in
l' ***intérêt (m.)*** interest
international(e) international
Internet (m.) internet
l' ***invitation (f.)*** invitation
inviter to invite
islamique Islamic
jamais never
la ***jambe*** leg
janvier January
le ***jardin*** garden
je voudrais (vouloir) I would like
jeter to throw (away)
le ***jeu*** game
le ***jeu de société*** board game
le ***jeu vidéo*** video game
(le) ***jeudi*** Thursday
jeune young
jeune (adj.) young
le / la ***jeune (n.)*** young person
la ***Joconde*** Mona Lisa
joli(e) pretty
jouer to play
le / la ***joueur / joueuse*** player
le ***jour*** day
le ***jour de l'An*** New Year's Day
le ***jour férié*** public holiday
le ***journal*** newspaper, diary
le / la ***journaliste*** journalist
la ***journée*** day
le ***judo*** judo
juger to judge
juif / juive (adj.) Jewish
juillet July
le ***jury*** jury
jusque until
juste fair, just, only
le ***kayak*** kayaking
le ***kilomètre*** kilometre
là there
la plupart du temps most of the time
là-bas over there
le ***lac*** lake
le ***lait*** milk
lancer to launch
la ***langue*** language
largement widely
se ***laver*** to wash
le / la / l' / les the
la ***leçon*** lesson
la ***lecture*** reading
le(s) ***legume(s)*** vegetable(s)
les ***les îles Caraïbes (f. pl.)*** Caribbean islands
la ***lettre*** letter
leur(s) (to) them, their
lever to raise
se ***lever*** to get up
la ***librairie*** bookshop
le ***lien*** link
le ***lieu*** place
lire to read
le ***lit*** bed
littéraire literary
la ***littérature*** literature
le ***livre*** book
local(e)(s) / locaux local
le ***logement*** accommodation
loger to stay
la ***loi*** law
loin far
long(ue) long
longtemps long time
lui (to) him, (to) her
la ***lumière*** light
(le) ***lundi*** Monday
le ***lycée*** school, sixth form
le ***magasin*** shop
mai May
la ***main*** hand
maintenant now
mais but
la ***maison*** house
la ***majorité*** majority
le ***mal*** ache
malade ill, sick
malgré despite
malheureusement unfortunately
manger to eat
le ***manque de*** lack of
manquer to miss, lack
le ***marché*** market
marcher to walk
(le) ***mardi*** Tuesday
Mardi gras Shrove Tuesday
le ***mari*** husband
le ***mariage*** marriage
se ***marier*** to marry
le ***Maroc*** Morocco
marocain(e) Moroccan
la ***marque*** brand
marquer to mark, score
mars March
le ***match*** match
les ***matériaux (m. pl.)*** materials
les ***maths (f. pl.)*** maths
la ***matière*** subject
le ***matin*** morning
mauvais bad
mauvais pour l'environnement (m.) bad for the environment
méchant(e) naughty, nasty
la ***Mecque*** Mecca
le ***médecin*** doctor
la ***médecine*** medicine
les ***médias (m. pl.)*** media
le ***médicament*** medication
médiéval(e) medieval
la ***médina*** old walled centre in a north-African city
méditerranéen Mediterranean
le / la / les ***meilleur(e)(s)*** the best
meilleur(e) better
meilleur(e) que better than
le ***mélange*** mix
même same
même si even if
ménager (adj.) household
mener to lead
mentir to lie
la ***mer*** sea
merci thank you
(le) ***mercredi*** Wednesday
la ***mère*** mother
mériter de to deserve
le ***message*** message
la ***messe*** mass
le ***métier*** job
le ***métro*** underground (train)
mettre to put (on)
se ***mettre à*** to begin to
le ***midi*** midday
mieux better
militaire (adj.) military
le ***millier*** about a thousand
le ***million*** million
le ***ministre*** minister
minuit midnight
la ***minute*** minute
la ***mission*** mission
la ***mode*** fashion
le ***mode de vie*** way of life
le ***modèle*** role model
moderne modern
moi me
moins (de) less (of), fewer (of)
moins ... que less than
le ***mois*** month
le ***moment*** moment
la ***monarchie*** monarchy
le ***monde*** people, world
mondial(e) world(wide)
la ***mondialisation*** globalisation
la ***montagne*** mountain
la ***montée*** climb
monter to go up
montrer to show
la ***mort*** death
la ***mosquée*** mosque
le ***mot de passe*** password
mourir to die
le ***moyen*** means
le ***moyen de vivre*** way of living
le ***mur*** wall
le ***musée*** museum
le / la ***musicien(enne)*** musician
le / la ***musicien(ne)*** musician
la ***musique*** music
musulman(e) (adj.) Muslim
nager to swim, to go swimming
la ***naissance*** birth
naître to be born
la ***natation*** swimming
national(e)(s) / nationaux national
la ***nationalité*** nationality
la ***nature*** nature
naturel(le) natural
ne ... jamais never

ne … ni … ni neither … nor
ne … pas encore not yet
ne … personne nobody
ne … que only
ne … rien nothing
né(e) born
nécessaire necessary
négatif / négative negative
neuf / neuve new
Noël Christmas
noir(e) (adj.) black
le ***nombre*** number
nombreux / nombreuses numerous
non no
le ***nord*** north
normal(e) normal
normalement normally
la ***Normandie*** Normandy
la ***note*** grade, result
notre / nos our
la ***nourriture*** food
nous we
nouveau / nouvelle (adj.) new
la ***nouvelle*** short story
la ***Nouvelle-Calédonie*** New Caledonia
novembre November
la ***nuit*** night
nul(le) rubbish
numérique digital
le ***numéro*** number
l' ***objectif (m.)*** objective
l' ***objet (m.)*** object, subject
obliger to obligate
obtenir to obtain
l' ***occasion (f.)*** occasion, chance, opportunity
occidental(e) western
l' ***océan Atlantique (m.)*** Atlantic ocean
l' ***océan Indien (m.)*** Indian ocean
l' ***océan Pacifique (m.)*** Pacific ocean
octobre October
officiel(le) official
l' ***offre (f.)*** offer
offrir to offer, give
olympique Olympic
on we, one
l' ***oncle (m.)*** uncle
l' ***opinion (f.)*** opinion
oral(e) oral
l' ***ordinateur (m.)*** computer
l' ***ordinateur portable (m.)*** laptop
l' ***oreille (f.)*** ear
l' ***organisation caritative (f.)*** charity
l' ***organisation (f.)*** organisation
organisé(e) organised
organiser to organise
original(e) original
l' ***origine (f.)*** origin
où where
oublier to forget
l' ***ouest (m.)*** west
oui yes
l' ***outil (m.)*** tool
ouvert(e) open
ouvrir to open
l' ***oxygène (m.)*** oxygen
le ***PACS*** civil partnership
la ***pagode*** pagoda
la ***paille*** straw
le ***pain*** bread
le ***palais*** palace
le ***pantalon*** trousers
le ***papa*** dad
le ***papier*** paper
Pâques Easter
le ***paquet*** parcel
par by
par contre on the other hand
par exemple for example
le ***parc*** park
le ***parc naturel*** natural park
parce que because
pareil(le) same
le / les ***parent(s) (m. pl.)*** parent(s)
paresseux / paresseuse lazy
parfait(e) perfect
parfois sometimes
le ***parlement*** parliament
parler (de) to speak, talk (about)
parmi among
les ***paroles (f. pl.)*** words, lyrics
partager to share
le / la ***partenaire*** partner
le / la ***participant(e)*** participant
la ***participation*** contribution
participer (à) to participate, take part (in)
la ***partie*** part, round of (game)
la ***partie (de foot)*** (football) match, game
partir to leave
partout everywhere
pas cher cheap
pas loin de not far from
le ***passé*** past
passer (du temps) to spend (time)
passer du temps to spend time
passer les examens to take exams
le ***passe-temps*** hobby, past time
la ***passion*** passion
passionnant(e) exciting
passionné(e) passionate
patient(e) (adj.) patient
pauvre poor
le ***pays*** country
le ***paysage*** scenery
le ***pêcheur*** fisherman
le / la ***peintre*** painter
le / la ***pèlerin(e)*** pilgrim
le ***pèlerinage*** pilgrimage
pendant during
penser (que) to think (that)
penser de to think of
la ***pente*** slope
se ***perdre*** to lose oneself, to get lost
perdre to lose (something)
le ***père*** father
permettre de to allow
la ***personnalité*** personality
personne nobody
la ***personne*** person
personnel personal
personnel(le) personal
les ***personnes (f. pl.)*** people
petit(e) small
le ***petit-déjeuner*** breakfast
le ***peuple*** people
peut-être maybe
la ***photo*** photo
la ***photographie*** photography
le ***piano*** piano
la ***pièce*** room
la ***pièce (de théâtre)*** play (theatre)
le ***pied*** foot
la ***pierre*** stone
le ***pilote*** pilot
le ***pilotis*** stilt
le ***pique-nique*** picnic
le ***pirate informatique*** hacker
le / la / les ***pire(s)*** the worst
pire que worse than
la ***piscine*** swimming pool
la ***piste cyclable*** cycle path
la ***place*** place, square, spot
la ***plage*** beach
le ***plaisir*** pleasure
la ***planète*** planet
planter to plant
le ***plastique*** plastic
le ***plat*** dish
plein (de) lots (of), full (of)
le ***plein air*** open air
pleuvoir to rain
la ***plupart (de)*** most (of)
plus (de) more (of)
plus (…) que more (…) than
plus tard later
plus tard later
plusieurs several, many
plutôt rather, quite
le ***podcast*** podcast
le ***poème*** poem
le / la ***poète*** poet
le ***poisson*** fish
le / la ***policier / policière*** policeman / policewoman
la ***politique*** politics
politique (adj.) political
polluer to pollute
la ***pollution*** pollution
polynésien(ne) Polynesian
populaire popular
la ***population*** population
le ***port*** port
le ***portable*** mobile phone
porter to wear
portugais(e) Portuguese
positif / positive positive
la ***position*** position
la ***possibilité*** possibility
possible possible
le ***poste*** post office
poster to post
la ***poubelle*** bin
pour for, in order to
pourquoi why
pouvoir to be able to, can
pratique practical
pratiquer to practice
préféré(e) favourite

préférer to prefer
le / la *premier / première* first
prendre to take
préparer to prepare
près (de) near, next to
présent(e) (adj.) present
présenter to present
le *président* president
presque almost
la *presse* press
la *pression* pressure
prêt(e) ready
prier to pray
la *prière* prayer
principal(e) main
principalement mainly
le *prix* prize, price
probablement probably
le *problème* problem
prochain(e) next
proche close
produire to produce
le *produit* product, produce
le *produit ménager* household product
le *professeur, prof* teacher
professionnel(le) professional
le *profil* profile
profiter de to make the most of, enjoy
le *programme* schedule
le *progrès* progress
progresser to progress
le *projet* project
la *promenade* walk
la *promesse* promise
promouvoir to promote
proposer to offer, to propose
la *proposition* proposition
propre clean, own
(se) *protéger* to protect (oneself)
le *public* public
la *publicité* advertisement
publier to publish
puis then
puissant powerful, strong
les *Pyrénées (f. pl.)* Pyrenees
la *qualité* quality
quand when
le *quartier* area, neighbourhood
quatorzième fourteenth
que that
le *Québec* Quebec
le / la *Québécois(e)* person from Quebec
quel(le) which
quelle joie! what a joy!
quelque some
quelque chose something
quelques some, a few
quelqu'un somebody, someone
qu'est-ce que what
la *question* question
la *queue* queue
qui who, which
quitter to leave
quoi what
quotidien(ne) daily
raconter to tell, to relay a story
raconteur to tell
la *radio* radio
la *raison* reason
le *rap* rap
rapide fast
rapidement quickly
rarement rarely
réagir to react
le / la *réalisateur / réalisatrice* film director
réaliser que to realise that
récemment recently
récent(e) recent
la *réception* reception
la *recette* recipe
recevoir to receive
le *réchauffement du climat* global warming
rechercher to look for, to research
recommander to recommend
la *récré(ation)* breaktime
rectangulaire rectangular
le *recyclage* recycling
recycler to recycle
réduire to reduce
le *refuge* shelter
regarder to watch, to look
la *région* region
le *règlement* regulation, rule
régulier regular
régulièrement regularly
relaxant(e) relaxing
se *relaxer* to relax
religieux / religieuse religious
la *religion* religion
remercier to thank
remplir to fill up
la *rencontre* meeting
rencontrer to meet
rendez-vous rendez-vous, meeting, appointment
rentrer to go back, to go home
le *repas* meal
répondre to answer
la *réponse* answer
reposer to rest
la *République* Republic
la *réputation* reputation
le *réseau* network
les *réseaux sociaux (m. pl.)* social media
les *réseaux sociaux (m. pl.)* social media
réservé reserved
réserver to book
la *resource* resource
le *respect* respect
respecter to respect
la *responsabilité* responsibility
ressembler to look like, to resemble
le *restaurant* restaurant
le *reste* rest
rester to stay
rester en forme to stay fit
retirer to withdraw
le *retour* return
retourner to go back, to return
la *réunion* meeting
la *Réunion* Reunion (island)
réunir to gather, to reunite
réussir (à) to succeed (in)
le *rêve* dream
revenir to come back
rêver to dream
riche rich
rien à faire nothing to do
rire to laugh
le *risqué* risk
risquer to risk
le *riz* rice
le *rôle* role
le *roman* novel
rond(e) circular, round
la *route* road
rudimentaire rudimentary
la *rue* street
le *sac* bag
le *sac à dos* rucksack
sacré(e) sacred
sain(e) healthy
sainement healthily
le *salaire* salary
la *salle* room
la *salle à manger* dining room
la *salle de bains* bathroom
la *salle informatique* IT room
le *salon* lounge, living room
salut hi, hello
(le) *samedi* Saturday
la *sandwicherie* sandwich bar
sans without
la *santé* health
sauver to rescue
savoir to know
le *savon* soap
les *sciences (f. pl.)* sciences
scientifique (adj.) scientific
scolaire (adj.) school
le / la *secrétaire* secretary
la *sécurité* security
la *Seine* River Seine
le *séjour* stay
la *sélection* selection
selon according to
la *semaine* week
le *Sénégal* Senegal
sénégalais(e) Senegalese
sensible sensitive
se *sentir* to feel
séparé(e) separated
septembre September
la *série* (TV) series
sérieux / sérieuse serious
le / la *serveur / serveuse* waiter / waitress
seul(e) alone
le / la *seul(e) …* the only …
seulement only
si if
le *siècle* century
simple simple
simplement simply
la *simplicité* simplicity
le *site* (tourist) site
le *site web* website
la *situation* situation

situé(e) situated
situer to situate, to locate
se *situer* to be situated
le *ski* ski
le *smartphone* smartphone
le *SMS* text message
social social
la *société* society
la *sœur* sister
le *soleil* sun
le *soir* evening
la *soirée* evening
soixante sixty
le *soleil* sun
son/sa/ses his, her
sortir to go out
le *souci* worry
souhaiter to wish
la *soupe* soup
sourire to smile
soutenir to support
le *soutien* support
le *souvenir* souvenir
se *souvenir de* to remember
souvent often
spécial(e) special
se *spécialiser* to specialise
la *spécialité* speciality
le *spectacle* show
spirituel(le) spiritual
le *sport* sport
sportif/sportive sporty
le *stade* stadium
le *stage (en entreprise)* work experience
la *star* star, celebrity
la *statue* statue
strict(e) strict
le *studio* studio
subsaharienne sub-Saharan
le *succès* success
le *sud* south
le *sud-est* South East
le *sud-ouest* South-West
la *Suisse* Switzerland
suivre to follow
super great
le *supermarché* supermarket
sûr(e) safe, sure, secure
le *surf* surfing
surtout especially
sympa nice
la *synagogue* synagogue

le *tabac* tobacco
tahitienne Tahitian
talentueux/talentueuse talented
la *tante* aunt
le *tapis* carpet
tard late
tchatter to chat
te/t' (to) you
la *technologie* DT
le *tee-shirt* T-shirt
la *télé(vision)* television
télécharger to download
le *téléphone* phone
tellement so
le *temple* temple
le *temps* time, weather
tenir to hold
la *terrasse* terrace, balcony
la *Terre* Earth
la *tête* head
le *texte* text
le *thé* tea
le *théâtre* theatre, drama
le *thème* theme
timide timid, shy
le *Togo* Togo
toi you
le *toit* a roof
la *tôle* corrugated iron
le *tombeau* tomb
tomber to fall
ton/ta/tes your
la *tonne* ton
tôt early
toucher to touch
toujours always
le *Tour de France* Tour de France
le/la *touriste* tourist
tous/toutes every, all
tous/toutes les deux both
tous les jours every day
tout d'abord first of all
tout le monde everyone
tout(e) each
tout(e) petit(e) very small
la *tradition* tradition
traditionnel(le) traditional
traduire to translate
le *train* train
le *traitement* treatment
tranquille quiet

la *tranquillité* tranquillity
transformer to transform
le *transport* transport
le *transport public* public transport
le *travail* work
travailler to work
travailleur/travailleuse hard-working
traverser to cross
très very
trier to sort
triste sad
trop (de) too much, many (of)
trouver to find
tuer to kill
le *type* type
l' *ultra-marathon (m.)* ultramarathon
un peu a little
un(e) a
une fois once
unique unique
l' *université (f.)* university
l' *urgence (f.)* emergency
l' *usine (f.)* factory
utiliser to use
les *vacances (f. pl.)* holidays
vapoter to vape
végan vegan
le *véganisme* veganism
le *végétarisme* vegetarianism
le *vélo* bike
vendre to sell
(le) *vendredi* Friday
venir (de) to come (from)
venir de to have just (done something)
le *vent* wind
vers towards, at about (time)
le/les *vêtement(s) (m. pl.)* clothes
la *viande* meat
la *vidéo* video
la *vie* life
la *vie quotidienne* daily life
la *vierge* virgin
le *Vietnam* Vietnam
vieux/vieil/vieille old
vif/vive lively
vigilant careful
le *village* village
la *ville* town, city

le *vin* wine
le *vin chaud* mulled wine
le *virus* virus
la *visite* visit
visiter to visit (place)
vite quick, fast, quickly
vivant(e) lively
vivre to live
voici here is
voir to see
le/la *voisin(e)* neighbour
la *voiture* car
la *voix* voice
le *vol* theft
le *vol d'identité* identity theft
volcanique volcanic
voter to vote
votre/vos your (polite, plural)
vouloir to want
vouloir dire to mean
vous you (polite, plural)
le *voyage* journey
voyager to travel
vrai(e) true, real
vraiment really
le *week-end* weekend
y there
le *yoga* yoga